MY CREATIVE SPACE

How to Design Your Home to Stimulate Ideas and Spark Innovation

Donald M. Rattner

Skyhorse Publishing

Skyhorse Publishing books may be purchased in bulk at special discounts for sales promotion, corporate gifts, fund-raising, or educational purposes. Special editions can also be created to specifications. For details, contact the Special Sales Department, Skyhorse Publishing, 307 West 36th Street, 11th Floor, New York, NY 10018 or info@skyhorsepublishing.com.

Skyhorse® and Skyhorse Publishing® are registered trademarks of Skyhorse Publishing, Inc.®, a Delaware corporation.

Visit our website at www.skyhorsepublishing.com.

10 9 8 7 6 5 4 3 2 1

Library of Congress Cataloging-in-Publication Data is available on file.

Cover design by Brian Peterson
Cover image: Study. Melbourne, Victoria, Australia. Architecture by Austin Maynard Architects. Photography by Peter Bennetts.

Print ISBN: 978-1-5107-3671-9
Ebook ISBN: 978-1-5107-3672-6

Printed in China

We shape our buildings, and afterwards our buildings shape us.

—*Winston Churchill*

CONTENTS

INTRODUCTION

Home is where one starts from.
—T. S. Eliot

THE CREATIVE HOME

Several times a year I travel around the country to deliver a talk or run a workshop based on the material in this book. Like many presenters, I like to engage with the audience at the start of the event by calling for a show of hands in response to a question. My query is simple, but comes with a twist.

How many people here live at home? I ask.

My question is often greeted with a respectable laugh as hands climb confidently into the air. Invariably, though, a few people will shoot me a puzzled look instead, or titter nervously while looking to see what others in the room are doing. For their benefit I'll repeat the question with my own hand up, until everyone understands that they can answer straightforwardly without fear of falling for a prank.

Once in a while I might be confronted with a recalcitrant holdout. On those occasions I'll ask the reluctant responder if by any chance he or she lives at the office or the gym instead. (Between you and me, I suspect some of them do.) Ultimately, most decide to be a good sport after all and join in with those who have patiently kept their hands high.

I then follow up my initial survey by asking the attendees if they would like to improve their ability to be creative. This time the response is almost always unanimous in the affirmative.

So here's the good news, I announce. Everybody here lives at home. And everybody here would like to enhance their creativity.

Then I deliver the bad news. I tell them that I can almost guarantee that every person in the room is underutilizing an enormously powerful creative asset in their possession, something so potent it can change how their mind works when they are being creative. For the better, I add reassuringly.

I pause for a moment to let that remark sink in, and perhaps build a little suspense before revealing the identity of this mysterious resource. Then I go in for the kill, the coup de grâce, the denouement.

That asset, I announce, is their home.

And so it is with you. Though we have probably never met, I feel safe in saying that by picking up this book you have signaled a desire to up your creative game. That desire might be driven by career, personal enjoyment, child-rearing, or

Floating container home. Copenhagen, Denmark. Photography by Nick Karvounis.

Living room. Calgary, Alberta, Canada. Architecture and interior design by Richard Davignon and Doris Martin for Davignon Martin Architecture + Interior Design. Photography by Ric Kokotovic.

other motivation. I also figure you live at home, in which case I remain reasonably confident that you too are sitting on (or in) a resource for achieving your goal that is going largely unused.

My goal in writing this book is to show how you can unlock the hidden power of home to boost creativity and spur innovation. That goes for just about any home you are likely to have. It doesn't matter what style it is, how many square feet it holds, how elaborately it's decorated, where it's located, or whether it's a freestanding house, apartment, recreational vehicle, houseboat, teepee, tiny house, converted shipping container, or dorm room. What's important is that you have a place that you identify as your sanctuary, your place of refuge, a safe harbor that you have carved out from the rest of the world as your own. If such a place exists, then you can benefit from the techniques I share in this book.

As far as I am aware, this is the first full-length publication to explore the domestic realm as a catalyst of creativity. That might sound like an odd boast, given that the world clearly suffers no shortage of books connecting creativity to our

Home office and shed. London, United Kingdom. Architecture by Platform 5 Architects. Photography by Alan Williams.

place of residence. The difference between them and mine lies in the nature of that connection.

Until now, books about home and creativity have fallen into one of two categories. The first category contains books that treat the home as an *object* of human inventiveness. These include style books, monographs by and about decorators, architects, and residential designers, pattern books illustrating house plans and details, books about historic homes or periods, and academic excursions into theory.

The second group explores the domicile as a *container* of creative activities. The titles in this category focus on creative pursuits typically conducted *within* the home. Cookbooks, books demonstrating how to quilt, garden, paint, build furniture, carry out home science projects, or bring up creative children belong here. Ditto for publications that offer guidance on running home-based businesses, entrepreneurship being one of many areas of human endeavor now regarded as creative undertakings in their own

Office. Sweden. Interior design by Alvhem. Photography by Cim EK.

right, alongside the traditional spheres of the arts and crafts.

Here's where *My Creative Space* diverges from the established genres. Rather than approach the home as either a hub or a subject of the imagination, I explore it as a *stimulant*, an *agent* of creativity. That is, in addition to furnishing a setting in which to pursue our creative interests, or being an expression of them, your home also can be designed to make you more creative by subliminally influencing how you think, feel, and act.

That our physical surroundings affect our psychological disposition and behavior is hardly an original observation. People have been designing buildings and spaces to evoke calculated responses in the observer for thousands of years. For the master builders of ancient Greek temples it was a feeling of awe, for medieval masons erecting soaring Gothic cathedrals a sense of reverence, for architects of palaces like Versailles the impression of power, for a carpenter erecting a teahouse in a Japanese garden a state of serenity, and for the builder of a modest Craftsman bungalow the experience of domestic comfort. Seen in this light, the notion that you can shape your home for the express purpose of improving your creativity seems perfectly feasible.

But how do you go about achieving this end? Where do you start?

To my mind, you have three possible strategies to choose from. The first is to rely on your intuition. More instinctive than analytical, your intuition tells you that if doing something feels like it will enhance your creative performance, then do it.

The intuitive approach has both strengths and weaknesses. On the plus side, it's easy to implement, it's tailored to your personality (no one-size-fits-all solutions here!), and it draws from a deeply ingrained source of human ingenuity. On the less positive side, it limits you to what can be gleaned from your past experiences and current

Fig. 1: Study. Down House, home of Charles Darwin. Downe, Kent, United Kingdom. Renovated 1845–81. Wellcome Collection.

know-how, tends to be of a hit-or-miss nature, and lacks objective validity.

A second method is to observe other creative people, and then to adapt their practices to your own efforts. Fortunately, there are plenty of case studies of home-based creatives to mine for inspiration and insight, especially among history's superlative achievers (Fig. 1). High on the list of notable figures who worked where they lived are Charles Darwin, Georgia O'Keeffe, Picasso, Einstein, Tchaikovsky, Beethoven, Frank Lloyd Wright, Edith Wharton (who authored a book about house design), Ernest Hemingway, and probably just about every other fiction writer over the past several hundred years. Not coincidentally, thousands of successful businesses were first hatched in a domestic setting as well, including such billion-dollar enterprises as Hewlett-Packard, Apple, Amazon, Disney, Mattel, Harley-Davidson, eBay, Etsy, and YouTube, adding further material to our knowledge base.

I'll be citing creative exemplars throughout the book, since they lend authority to my argument and shed light on the topics discussed. Still, the case-study method has drawbacks, too, if relied on exclusively. Finding precedents relevant to your particular circumstances can be difficult. Research is time-consuming. And, as we're constantly reminded in the fine print of advertisements for financial services, past performance is no guarantee of future results.

Which brings me to the third possible strategy: turn to science.

I'm going to delve into the story about how science came to put creativity under the microscope later in the introduction. Suffice to say for the moment that researchers have uncovered some remarkable ways in which perception and action sway the mind.

For instance, we now have evidence that exposure to the color blue makes us better problem solvers (#2). So do views of natural foliage (#13 and 14). We enjoy a similar mental spike after we glimpse a bare light bulb (#20), or when working under high ceilings (#3). That old saw about coming up with some of our best ideas in the shower (#28)? It's true, and even more interestingly, psychologists, neuroscientists, and creativity experts have come up with some intriguing opinions as to why.

Science not only verifies conventional wisdom where credit is due, as in the case of the shower, but it also prevents us from dismissing valid techniques out of hand, no matter how ridiculous they seem. Really, would you ever imagine that the sight of a bare light bulb could escalate idea generation? The very thought sounds far-fetched. Yet that's precisely what a research team out of Tufts University discovered after it tested the premise by conducting a series of lab experiments. And once you learn about their findings and understand the historical context in which this curious association evolved, it doesn't seem so off the wall after all.

More and more, information put out by the scientific community is finding its way into the design of actual buildings and spaces. Innovation-driven businesses, most notably Google, are spearheading the movement to embrace design psychology as a tool for achieving success in the marketplace. Schools are also proving to be fertile ground for applying the lessons of creativity research to shaping physical plant. Even savvy retailers are leveraging our newfound insights in the field by shaping stores to encourage open-mindedness among customers browsing their merchandise.

Yet the one place that's largely been overlooked in the quest to optimize creativity through informed design is the home—the place we spend more time in than anywhere else.

Why home hasn't received the attention it deserves as an idea farm is unclear. Perhaps it's because most residential environments are ultimately the handiwork of the people who live in them, rather than design professionals, educators, psychologists, academics, and other interested parties familiar with research into creative environments. Or that there's no profit motive or mission statement to stimulate action. Or that the kinds of creativity practiced at home are looked on as pleasant pastimes to be enjoyed at our leisure, rather than an imperative for success or survival.

Except that was then, and this is now. Home has evolved. Among other things, the once-firm boundary between work and domicile has greatly eroded. A growing segment of the labor force in developed countries now does business either part- or full-time in the place where they live, whether employed by outside companies and organizations or as freelancers. Many of these workers are involved in creative industries, including art and design, finance, marketing, education, publishing, technology, product development, health care, philanthropy, science, writing, and other knowledge-based fields that thrive on skillful problem-solving, information management, and innovative thinking. If the home was once indifferent to, and even deliberately inoculated from the call of career, it certainly can't afford to be these days. Too much is at stake to work in an environment that isn't engineered for peak creative performance.

This is true even if you spend most of your workday in a traditional office outside the boundaries of domestic space. Because, let's face it—the contemporary workplace can be at best indifferent and at worst downright hostile to creative productivity. Whether it's noise wafting through the open floor plan, frequent interruptions, inadequate resources, management indifference, politics, or the interminable meetings that drain a person of the will to live, much conspires in the contemporary workplace to keep those good ideas inside us from ever seeing the light of day.

That's not a matter of my opinion, or the grumblings of a few disgruntled employees. Surveys show that the office ranks toward the bottom of the list of places where people gain creative insights. Instead, according to the data, it's far more likely you'll be at home or doing something associated with residential life during moments of illumination. The more you can condition your home and habits to exploit this circumstance, the more you stand to benefit, regardless of where you punch a time clock.

None of this takes away from home's time-honored role as a favored place to enjoy creativity for its own sake. Indeed, if science has taught us anything in the last fifty years, it's that the pleasures of everyday creativity are vital to maintaining our mental and physical well-being. Happily, the creative mind works essentially the same whether you're concocting a Halloween costume out of found materials, launching the next category-busting start-up, inventing a better mousetrap, writing a screenplay, brainstorming a new ad campaign, finger painting, preparing a lesson plan, coding, or coming up with a fresh color scheme for your

Artist's studio. London, United Kingdom. Building design and construction by Black Oak Builders Ltd. Photography by Chris Snook.

living room. I say *happily* because it means you stand to gain from *Your Creative Haven* whatever your motivation in picking it up in the first place—personal, professional, or both.

CREATIVITY DEFINED

How should creativity be defined? Is it a type of genetically determined talent that only a lucky few possess? A mental process that flows from the right side of our brains? Artistic flair?

Or is creativity ultimately a mysterious process that renders a clear-cut definition impossible?

Let me begin to address the last question first. No, creativity is not mysterious, and it is not indefinable. In fact, a sizable population of scholars has been toiling diligently over the past half-century or so to develop a viable framework for explaining it, one that has achieved widespread consensus among those who spend most of their waking time thinking about the subject.

My version of their definition goes like this:

Creativity is the act of developing novel and useful ideas for products, services, and systems.

By *product* I refer to things both tangible (e.g., a physical object) and intangible (a scientific formula). To provide a *service* is to do work for a person (offering legal advice), while a *system* is an organized method for producing a desired outcome (a democratic system of government). The term *novel* denotes an idea that's new, fresh, original, inventive, surprising, or unique—all the standard synonyms of the word—whereas to say something is *useful* is to assert that it has utility or value, either pragmatic (a tool, appliance, or building) or qualitative (an emotionally moving or intellectually provocative work of art).

Now, you'll notice my definition stipulates that a newly invented product, service, or system must be both new *and* useful to qualify as creative.

That both criteria must be satisfied is essential. I can conjure up totally new nonsense words all day long, but if no one can appreciate my gibberish—including me—then my inventions fail to be useful and are therefore uncreative. Nor is it creative to publish verbatim a successful book written by another author under my own name, even though strictly speaking the resulting object remains perfectly useful to readers.

Stipulating that a creative idea be both novel and useful raises an important question, however: novel and useful *to whom*? On this issue creativity experts do not entirely agree. Some argue that a truly creative idea has to be original and provide value to a large community or field; to their minds, Grandma's cherished recipe for upside-down cake that you and your family have been gobbling down for generations doesn't quite cut it. Others take a more liberal view, arguing that a novel and useful idea has creative merit regardless of the size of its audience or its impact on the world.

One way to resolve these competing stances is to understand creativity as a graduated phenomenon, rather than as an all-or-nothing proposition. In other words, creativity comes in various sizes and shapes, from the personal to the professional, from the local to the global. In the latter categories fall the world-moving achievements of a Dylan, Gandhi, Curie, or Gates; in the former, the humble scribbling of the child artist, the simple recipes of an aspiring cook, the first stab at a new business by a budding entrepreneur. In between lie a great many other acts of human invention, including, let us say, this book, the latest refinements to our favorite app, and the smaller, everyday moments of creativity we perform for ourselves that enable us to both physically survive and reap pleasure.

Most creative acts are chiefly ends in themselves; that is, they produce little or no discernible change in the course of human invention or existence, nor are they adopted by others as a new direction for

Potting area and mudroom. Minneapolis, Minnesota. Architecture and interior design by Meriwether Felt, AIA. Photography by Susan Gilmore.

their own creativity. They simply express creative ideas that are already in circulation, however deftly and distinctively this is accomplished.

Every now and then, however, a novel idea comes along that does find an audience well beyond that of its originator and does impact the actions of others. We have a special umbrella term for these persistent and influential acts of creativity. We call it *innovation*.

Innovation and creativity are often used inter-changeably, but it's a mistake to conflate them. To understand the difference, compare my work as an architect with that of an innovator like Frank Lloyd Wright (this is probably be the first and last time I'll ever be mentioned in the same sentence as the American master, but such are the perks of authorship). I'd like to think that buildings of my design are creative insofar as they are both novel and useful—novel in the sense of them being unique and imaginative solutions to a problem (the client's brief), and useful to the degree that they satisfy the clients' requirements as well as public expectations. However, it's safe to say that on the whole, few if any elements from my design portfolio are going to be deemed sufficiently seminal as to be picked up by other architects and incorporated into their own work, let alone constitute a new school or artistic direction.

Mr. Wright, on the other hand, introduced novel ideas into the architectural marketplace with astonishing frequency. Whether it was slab-on-grade construction, modern radiant floor heating, open floor planning, or the Prairie Style itself, time and again we find him breaking ground, so to speak, on new ways to envision, build, and adorn space (Fig. 2).

Fig. 2: Robie House. Chicago, Illinois. Architecture and interior design by Frank Lloyd Wright. 1911. Historic American Buildings Survey, Library of Congress.

Which is not to say that everything he did eventually burrowed into common practice either. Some of his initiatives were rejected at their inception. Others have proven to be failures—his buildings exhibit an alarming propensity to leak water on their inhabitants, among other complaints. But failure is frequently the cost of invention—if the term deserves to be connected with creativity at all, that is. As Thomas Edison once remarked, "I have not failed once. I've just found 10,000 ways that didn't work." (Just tell that to the poor souls wielding mops and buckets inside their Frank Lloyd Wright homes.)

Another distinction between creativity and innovation concerns the issue of individuality. Most people associate creativity with the solitary figure, the stand-alone genius battling to bring his or her brilliance to bear on a recalcitrant world. Very often that image is promoted by the creative person in question, whether it's Wright, Steve Jobs, or Alfred Hitchcock—all certifiable egotists who want us to believe that they alone are responsible for the inventive achievements with which they're most closely identified. Occasionally, the image of the Lone Creator is replaced by the Dynamic Duo, as embodied by such creative couples as the Curies, Laurel and Hardy, and Lennon and McCartney (the last in their early collaborations,

at least). But for the most part, the generation of novel and useful ideas is generally deemed the province of the individual.

Is this an accurate picture of creativity? Up to a point. The fact is that no one truly operates in a historical or cultural vacuum. No less a personage than Sir Isaac Newton, who was a jerk of the first order when it came to discrediting his rivals, voiced the idea of our shared debt to our predecessors by writing that "if I have seen further, it is because I have stood on the shoulders of giants." Nor can creatives function in isolation when it comes time to get the work out. Even writers, who toil in one of the most solitary of professions, must eventually interact with a publishing entity or platform if they want readers to see their output. A similar need to interact with an external network applies to nearly every field.

Still, the historical record demonstrates that collective creativity rarely yields success when it comes to giving coherent form to incipient ideas. Like a good soup, ideas are liable to suffer with too many cooks in the kitchen. Witness the old adage that a camel is a horse designed by committee.

Innovation, on the other hand, is unquestionably dependent on a group dynamic. Some creativity experts even define innovation as contingent on the presence of an organization, whether in the guise of a business, institution, social movement, industry, or field. Take Google as an example. While Larry Page and Sergey Brin were certainly the insightful masterminds behind the development of its proprietary algorithm, without the human and physical resources of a corporate entity behind them, as well as the support of venture capitalists, it's inconceivable that their innovative search engine would have achieved the level of success it currently enjoys in the marketplace.

Does this mean that home can harbor creativity but not innovation, since the residential domain tends to be intensely personal and private by

Artist's studio. Mill Valley, California. Architecture by Feldman Architects. Photography by Joe Fletcher.

nature? Not at all. Time and again home has given literal and figural shelter to innovative ideas on the cusp of finding wider application, proving that it can be an incubator of innovation after all. Where did Steve Jobs and Steve Wozniak build the first version of a computer that would eventually spawn the world's most valuable company? In a bedroom and garage of a modest suburban house in Los Altos, California. Where did Jeff Bezos run his fledgling online bookstore after relocating from New York to Seattle with a burning idea to transform a nascent Internet into an engine of commerce? Another garage. Where did the author Marcel Proust write his groundbreaking modern masterpiece *Remembrance of Things Past*? In bed in his Paris apartment.

I can't promise that the material contained in this book will turn you into the next home-grown Frank Lloyd Wright or Jeff Bezos or Marcel Proust—if that's your goal at all. But I would suggest that it can help you optimize your potential as a creative individual. To explain why, I need to tell you more about how science got into the business of creativity.

THE SCIENCE OF CREATIVITY

Rarely is it possible to pinpoint the time and place when the collective consciousness of an entire scientific discipline was irrevocably altered. But that's essentially what happened at Pennsylvania State College beginning at 8:15 p.m. on September 5, 1950, when a psychologist named J. P. Guilford stood up to deliver the keynote address at the annual meeting of the American Psychological Association.

Guilford's subject was creativity. Today we wouldn't bat an eyelash at his choice of topic, but back then it left plenty of people in the room puzzled, since almost no one in the field was paying any attention to it.

Which was precisely Guilford's point. "The neglect of creativity is appalling," he bluntly announced at the start of the speech. And he had the stats to prove it. Of the 121,000 abstracts indexed in psychology journals in the previous twenty-three years, he told the audience, only a minuscule 186 were related to creativity. Dedicated chapters in general psychology textbooks were equally scarce, he added.

Guilford didn't use the podium solely to wag his finger, however. He spent most of his time that night expounding on the misconceptions about creativity that he felt had led to his colleagues' indifference, and why it more than deserved to be studied in its own right.

His excoriations clearly struck a nerve. Creativity research positively exploded in the conference's aftermath, with more papers and books on the topic published every year since then than in the previous twenty-three years combined. That's a pretty amazing reaction, considering the man didn't even use PowerPoint.

THE CREATIVE PROCESS

Besides igniting a wholly fresh approach to the study of creativity, Guilford also introduced some important concepts that have proven to be of enduring value to those interested in understanding how creativity unfolds and, by extension, how to maximize creative performance in others. Of these, perhaps the most relevant to this book is his proposition that creativity results from the interplay of two opposing styles of mental processing. In his speech he refers to these cognitive styles as *analytic* and *synthetic*; he later rechristened them *divergent* and *convergent*. You probably know them by their more popular names: right- and left-brain thinking (although, as I'll explain later in the book, this particular terminology has led to some misunderstandings about creativity and is therefore best left unused).

DIVERGENT	CONVERGENT
Intuition / Imagination	Reason / Logic
Zigzag / Circuitous	Linear / Sequential
Abstract / Generalized	Concrete / Detailed
Broad / Big-picture / Global	Narrow / Focused / Local
Figural / Metaphorical	Literal
Internally Directed	Externally Directed
Multiple Solutions	Single Solution
Synthetic	Analytic
What Could Be / Exploration	What Is / Exploitation

Table 1: Properties of divergent and convergent thinking. After J. P. Guilford (1967).

Table 1 summarizes the properties of the two modalities. As is evident, they are nearly polar opposites of each other. Where divergent thinking is freewheeling, nonjudgmental, and unselfconscious, convergent thinking is sequential, selective, and deliberate. Divergency looks inward to intuition, judgment, and imagination to find creative solutions to problems; convergency applies reason, logic, and other outside knowledge systems to arrive at definitive answers. Divergency is by nature abstract and takes a holistic, big-picture perspective of the world,

Treehouse. Philadelphia, Pennsylvania. Architecture by Verner Architects. Photography by Todd Mason for Halkin Mason Photography.

So how do the two cognitive styles relate to the creative process? In essence, they *are* the process, or at least, the psychological meat of it. Two other components need to be added to the mix, however, to fully flesh out of Guilford's model of creative thinking. The first is a problem that wants to be solved. The second is its solution.

What do we mean by a problem? By definition, a problem is a goal with one or more obstacles that must be overcome to realize it. Not all problems lend themselves to creative solutions, however. To find the sum of two plus two, for example, requires no creativity because the answer is obvious and objectively determined. The problem as posed also contains a single correct answer, whereas creative problems generally hold open the possibility of arriving at multiple solutions.

A handy litmus test for determining if a problem warrants a creative solution is to frame it as a question, prefaced with the words "How might we" (or "How might I," if you're flying solo), and then judge whether it might be easily answered, mechanically computed, or logically constrained in the number of possible responses. If not, then you could well have yourself a creative problem in your grasp, as in "How might I . . ."

while convergency narrowly focuses attention on concrete details and particulars. Divergency contends with things as they could be, convergency with things as they are.

A similar contrast between the two modes of thought applies to the harvesting of ideas. Divergent thinking opens our mental floodgates to let loose as many potential solutions to a creative problem in a given period of time as possible, no matter how unworkable or bizarre they might initially seem. Convergent thinking aims for a single, viable answer. Divergency favors quantity of ideas, convergency quality.

Raise more money for my favorite charity this
   year?
Decorate my client's study?
Promote my company's website?
Find a cure for the common cold?
Compose a still-life from the objects placed on
   a table?
Make filing tax returns easier?
Invent an app for checking grammar?
Renovate my kitchen for greater efficiency?
Sharpen my tennis serve?
Write a book on creativity people will want to read?
Improve our system of governance?
Retire at age ___?

Master bath suite. Newport Beach, California. Architecture by Frank Stolz for South Coast Architects. Photography by Mark Davidson.

As should be evident from this list, creative problems can stem from personal goals as well as from external sources, be it a client, employer, social group, market need, or the world at large. It should also be apparent that creative problems embrace a wide range of human interests, from business to hobbies, technology to governance, design to sports, making clear that the days of associating creativity solely with the arts and crafts are over.

Putting all this together, we can now describe creativity as a multistep process (Fig. 3):

Step One: Define the problem you wish to solve.

Step Two: Exercise divergent thinking in order to generate as many choices for solving the problem as can be mustered in the time allowed. This stage is sometimes called the *ideation* or *generative* phase,

since the focus is on harvesting ideas without regard for viability or practicalities. Brainstorming sessions are a managed form of Step Two creativity.

Step Three: Shift to convergent thinking in order to eliminate, modify, or combine the ideas gathered in the divergent phase and zero in on a solution that can be tested and eventually confirmed. Some refer to this phase as the *verification* or

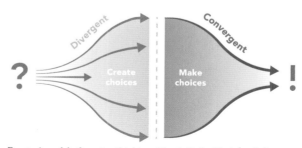

Fig. 3: A model of creative thinking. After J. P. Guilford (1967).

validation stage, underscoring the fact that the answer to a creative problem ultimately must be proved feasible to constitute a true solution. Prototyping, test marketing, trial runs, mockups, and red-marking are techniques commonly used during the convergent phase.

Step Four: Finalize a solution and ready it for implementation.

While the divergent-convergent model of creative thinking is a useful tool for understanding how the mind operates as creative ideas are born and developed, it's important to remember that it's an abstraction rather than a faithful representation of real-world problem solving. For instance, in real life the creative process rarely travels in a steady and uninterrupted straight-line trajectory from problem to solution. I know this from experience; as an architect, I frequently find myself retracing steps or jumping back and forth among stages as a project progresses. It's not that I'm incompetent (at least, I'd like to think I'm not); it's that creativity is by nature iterative. What you want to ensure as a creative is that the swings between divergent and convergent thinking are kept manageable so as not to have a debilitating effect on your forward motion. Later in the book I'll share techniques for controlling your environment to keep your mind on track.

Another difference between diagram and reality is that while some creative projects might be expressed as a single, unifying problem, they

Home office. Photography by IdeaPaint.

are in fact made up of multiple subproblems. Designing a house, for instance, is not one but hundreds and even thousands of design tasks and technical puzzles all rolled up into one. No unified model of creative problem solving such as the one proposed by Guilford could possibly capture the complexity of the endeavor by itself. To do so requires multiplying the diagram many times over, arranging some units like links in a chain, others in parallel, still others as offshoots from the main threads.

Finally, there's nothing in our model to help us judge the *quality* of the ideas produced in the course of the creative process. How do we know if a solution that pops out at the end of the process is good, and therefore whether the person who produced it is creative or not? Don't we have to be able to rank or grade creative performance to ascertain this? In fact, isn't the whole premise of this book—that you can sharpen your creative acumen by knowingly manipulating your physical surroundings—dependent on the notion that creative output can be measured? Otherwise, how would anyone know that one's creativity has improved?

All good questions. The answers boil down to something you're probably very familiar with. It's called testing.

MEASURING CREATIVITY

If you ever took a creativity assessment test to get yourself or a child into a gifted and talented school program, or land a job, or undergo an employment review, then you can thank (or blame) J. P. Guilford for the experience.

No, Guilford didn't invent these tests entirely by himself. But he did change the face of creativity testing by arguing in his landmark 1950 speech that divergent thinking wasn't merely a function of general intelligence, as was generally thought back then. Instead of lumping it in with IQ scores and other broad measures of smarts, he proposed to invent a whole new type of test tailored specifically to measuring a person's ability to generate fresh ideas for solutions to creative problems.

To achieve this goal, Guilford recommended replacing the multiple-choice and fill-in-the-blank questions typical of standardized exams with open-ended problems that required test-takers to draw as well as write out or verbalize their responses. Since answers could no longer be determined to be right or wrong according to a grading sheet, he also established four new criteria by which to score the results:

1. **Originality**: how unique was each response
2. **Fluency**: how many responses were produced for a given problem
3. **Flexibility**: how varied were the responses
4. **Complexity, or elaboration**: how much detail or information was contained in a response

Guilford might have laid the groundwork for the development of creativity testing, but the person who really brought it into our daily lives was the well-known psychologist E. P. Torrance, namesake of the widely used Torrance Tests of Creativity (TTCT). Torrance began formulating his eponymous tests in the 1960s, starting with a suite of four exercises, which has since grown substantially. He and his followers also greatly expanded Guilford's original set of evaluative criteria, and more recently adapted them to the computer age.

The TTCT and other testing formats that sprang from Guilford's initiative haven't been without controversy, however. Academics, psychologists, and educators continue to debate what exactly these tests measure, how closely they reflect real-world creativity, whether subjective bias plays into scoring, how predictive they are, and whether creativity can be quantified at all. Still, it's hard to argue with tangible success. If nothing else, the huge volume of testing that goes on every day, the mountains of academic research built on accrued results, and their sheer longevity, make a pretty compelling case for their continued usefulness and acceptance.

And thank goodness for that, because without the ability to objectively assess creative task performance I would never have written this book. I'm too much of a rationalist to be content with the kind of homespun conjecture that characterizes a lot of self-help advice these days. Instead, I and the researchers whose work I draw from use logical inference to translate empirical observation and laboratory-generated data into guidelines for best practices.

Consider the example of sound (#17). A few years ago a research trio led by a professor at the University of British Columbia ran an experiment in which three different groups of subjects took a battery of creativity assessment exercises while listening to a soundtrack through headphones. The first group heard it played at low volume, the second at medium volume, and the third had it cranked up. When the results were tallied, it was discovered that the second group had scored noticeably higher on their tests than the others. You don't have to be a Nobel Laureate to deduce that the deviation in performance was owed to the variation in volume, since the audio level was the only inconsistent environmental factor among the three groups.

I mentioned that this experiment is of relatively recent vintage. So is most of the research that serves as the foundation for the techniques you'll

Kitchen. Kennebunk, Maine. Interior design by Deborah Farrand for Dressing Rooms. Photography by Eric Roth.

be learning about in this book. That's because the notion of deploying creativity metrics to establish optimal environments for conceiving ideas is comparatively new. Guilford didn't bring it up in his famous address. There's no reference to it in Torrance's efforts to develop the TTCT either.

The omission isn't surprising. The notion that our surroundings can significantly alter our mental state had yet to emerge as its own special topic within the field of creativity studies at the time the two psychologists were bringing testing into the mainstream. But a few things were going on in other disciplines that anticipated its eventual appearance. One came out of particularly unlikely quarters: a dingy basement lab in Pittsburgh, Pennsylvania, where a young scientist was working nearly around the clock to find a cure for a deadly disease. How this man came to be a leading evangelist for the power of space to catalyze creative thinking is the next part of our story.

THE PSYCHOLOGY OF SPACE

Jonas Salk was at the start of his career when he was lured to the University of Pittsburgh Medical School in 1947 with the promise of his own laboratory. It was only when he arrived for work that he discovered his so-called laboratory was actually a cramped, dark room in the basement of a local municipal hospital. Undeterred by his depressing surroundings, Salk plunged into his work, anxious to find a vaccine that would eradicate the polio scourge devastating young people around the world.

Success proved elusive. Roadblock after roadblock impeded progress. Salk became physically and mentally exhausted. After several years of hard labor, it was painfully evident he needed a break to clear his mind. Traveling to the charming Italian hill town of Assisi, the scientist took up residence in a thirteenth-century Franciscan monastery for a period of reflection and relaxation (Fig. 4).

Architecturally, the hilltop monastery complex was worlds away from the scruffy subterranean lair he'd left behind in Pittsburgh. In place of narrow hospital corridors lit by harsh fluorescent bulbs, he now found himself ambling about expansive courtyards encircled by columned arcades. Inside the monastery church he would gaze at walls decorated with beautiful frescoes, their colorful surfaces illuminated by natural light streaming in from the tall windows running down the building's flanks.

Transported to an idyllic environment, Salk's mind began to unlock as he pondered the problem of the vaccine once again. In time he was able to break through the mental blocks that had stymied him back home. As Salk himself later wrote:

The spirituality of the architecture there was so inspiring that I was able to do intuitive thinking far beyond any I had done in the past. Under the influence of that historic place I intuitively designed the research that I felt would result in a vaccine for polio. I returned to my laboratory in Pittsburgh to validate my concepts and found that they were correct.

Forever convinced of the positive interplay of mind, creativity, and environment, Salk went on to commission one of the great architects of his era, Louis I. Kahn, to design a building to house an institute for science and the humanities he was founding in La Jolla, California. Salk spoke fondly of his time in Italy in his conversations with the architect, and asked him to incorporate elements he'd seen at Assisi in the new complex. He also insisted that the interiors be column-free, convinced that minimizing physical encumbrances would facilitate collaboration among the scholars working at the facility.

The building was finally completed in 1965, and today is ranked among the seminal works of modern architecture and landscape design. Groundbreaking research continues in the complex as well (Fig. 5).

Salk's story of his travels to Assisi and their aftermath is enthralling. But did things actually happen as he described them? That is, was there really a cause-and-effect relationship between the beauty of the setting and his creative break-through? Could the sight and experience of his surroundings have penetrated so deeply into his psyche that it affected his brain functions? Or is the story of Salk's Italian sojourn little more than a charming anecdote that confuses coincidence for causation, feeling for fact?

As it turned out, just as his institute was getting under way in its new facility, a small cadre of fellow scientists was beginning to explore the very questions Salk's experience appeared to raise. By the end of the decade their discoveries had coalesced into a new area of scientific investigation. That field was environmental psychology, the science of person-to-place interaction.

Simply put, environmental psychology studies the influence of the built and natural environments on how we think, feel, and act. Among its goals are to replace intuitive inferences with scientifically verified deductions, and to raise the quality of life by solving real-world problems.

Many fascinating insights emerged from its ranks over the ensuing years. But it was in 1984 that a paper on environmental psychology was published that would have a profound effect on the design fields, and in some respects lay the groundwork for books like this.

The paper was written by a professor at the University of Delaware named Roger S. Ulrich.

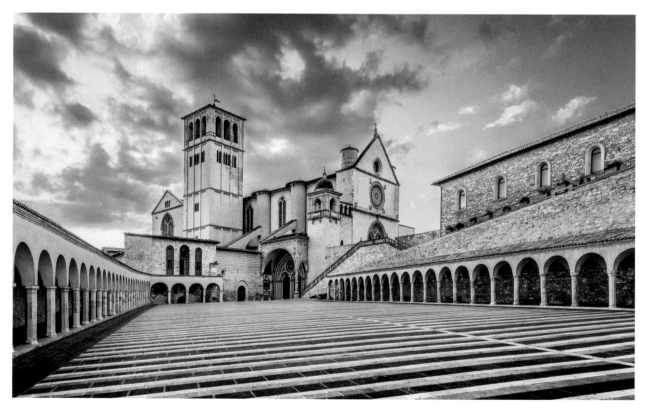

Fig. 4: Papal Basilica of St. Francis of Assisi. Assisi, Italy.
Thirteenth through fifteenth centuries.

Trained as a medical biologist, Ulrich had a personal and long-held interest in the relationship between environment and human health because of his experience as a teenager, when a kidney ailment kept him bedridden at his house for long stretches. Hours were spent with little to do other than look out the window, where a tall pine tree stood. In time the young Ulrich began to intuit that the sight of the tree was ameliorating the stress of his condition, aiding his eventual recovery.

Years later, he had the opportunity to test his hunch by conducting a study in a hospital in Paoli, Pennsylvania. He chose for his subjects a group of patients with a similar profile. All had been at the hospital for a particular type of gallbladder surgery within the same nine-year period. All were between twenty and sixty-nine years old, all were free of past psychological disorders, and all had undergone the procedure between the months of May and October. Most importantly for our purposes, all had stayed in rooms identical in appearance. Identical, that is, except for one significant detail: the view out the window. One segment of the study group saw foliage on trees planted in an outside courtyard. The other looked across to a blank brick wall.

The question Ulrich sought to answer was this: did the difference in view have any impact on the health of his subjects?

Ulrich scrutinized the patient records to find out. What he discovered was striking. Patients who could see treetops from their hospital beds required less medication during their stay, experienced fewer complications during convalescence, and were released more quickly after the operation was performed than those exposed to the masonry wall.

Fig. 5: Courtyard, Salk Institute. La Jolla, California. Architecture, interior, and landscape design by Louis I. Kahn. 1959–1965. Salk Institute for Biological Studies.

Like many breakthrough discoveries, Ulrich's findings raised as many new questions as it answered. First and foremost, how and why was the mere sight of a leafy canopy powerful enough to alter human physiology, whereas the bricks were not?

There are a lot of theories out there attempting to explain the why, so I'll reserve that discussion until the main section of the book, where I can give it the space it deserves. As for the mechanism causing the change, the short answer is something called brain priming.

What is brain priming? In his book *Universal Principles of Design,* author and industrial designer William Lidwell defines the concept as:

The activation of specific concepts in memory for the purposes of influencing subsequent behaviors.

Whenever stimuli are received by the senses—sights, sounds, smells, touches, tastes—concepts are automatically activated in memory. Once concepts are activated, they stay activated for a period of time, capable of influencing subsequent thoughts, reactions, emotions, and behaviors.

In simplified terms, brain priming occurs when an external stimulus enters a person's consciousness through one of the five senses and then triggers a response related to the nature of

Home office. Montvale, New Jersey. Architecture by Jordan Rosenberg Architects. Interior design by Jennifer Pacca Interiors. Photography by Peter Rymwid.

the input. In Ulrich's study the prime was the view of trees, the response an improvement in patient well-being.

Keep in mind, though, that in Ulrich's case the stimulus didn't come about randomly or by accident. The fact that the trees were placed where they were, and that the hospital wing where the patients were housed was planned in such a way as to provide a view either of greenery or masonry, resulted from conscious decisions made by the architects, landscape designers, and administrators responsible for planning the facility. The visual cue impacting the patients, in other words, was specifically a *design* trigger, a consequence of choices made by the individuals in the course of configuring building and landscape, and which presumably would have been different had they been aware of Ulrich's findings at the time.

The paper raises another, even broader line of inquiry: if Ulrich was able to uncover a correlation between patient welfare and exterior views, what about all the other attributes that make up the character of a space? Could scientists utilize a similar methodology to investigate whether such design components as materials and finishes, lighting, furnishings, artwork, sound, temperature, and room shape might lead to equally positive outcomes? After all, if the principal objective of health-care design is patient wellness, then shouldn't every effort be made to maximize the designer's tool kit for achieving this end?

The answer to these questions, of course, is yes. And that's just what happened in the decades since Ulrich's paper came out. In fact, so busy did the field become, that the practice of applying scientific research to shaping buildings and spaces eventually morphed into a professionally recognized approach called evidence-based design (EBD). EBD is most prevalent in the health-care sector, as my brief history suggests, but it's since made inroads in the workplace, residential, and educational spheres as well. Its fundamental premise is that data-backed science can and should inform design decisions in tandem with the traditional determinants of aesthetics, personal preferences, client demands, fashion and history, technical and symbolic requirements, context, and so forth.

All of which invites one final question: if a physical setting can be deliberately configured to promote the healing process by priming occupants with stimuli scientifically linked to a particular outcome, then could it be configured to elicit other types of mental reactions as well? Like, say, improved creativity?

The fact is, for many years now researchers, environmental psychologists, architects, and designers have learned a great deal about how the elements of physical space influence divergent and convergent thinking, to the point where we now have at our disposal a remarkable storehouse of techniques for boosting creative productivity through the manipulation of mass and space. It's out of this data trove that I've drawn many of the creativity tactics presented in the pages that follow. To my knowledge this is the first book to aggregate this information in a single source.

So Jonas Salk was right. Place does matter. It mattered to him when he was trying to break through the creative impasse that had halted his progress toward squelching a dangerous scourge. It mattered to the patients in a Pennsylvania hospital as they struggled to recover from an invasive procedure. And it should matter to you.

BRAINS AND BODIES

So far, I've mainly framed my commentary as if creativity were principally cerebral in nature. Brain primes, idea conception, divergent thinking—all of these points of discussion would seem to suggest that a knack for unearthing novel and useful ideas is something that starts and ends in our heads. Yet a wide circle of psychologists, linguists, neuroscientists, and philosophers is putting a serious strain on that assumption by arguing that creativity is, in truth, a two-way street. Inspiration for creative insight can flow as much from the body to the brain as the other way around, they claim.

There's evidence to back them up. Time and again researchers find that engaging the body in the process of solving a problem can spur creative thinking. In one experiment, subjects who were encouraged to perform the two-arm gesture we commonly use to express the phrase "on one hand . . . on the other hand" were able to verbalize more and better solutions to a creative challenge than a comparison group confined in their use of their limbs. Another study by the same team measured the effects of different styles of walking on idea formulation. A third of the subjects walked around in a fixed rectangular path, a third roamed freely, and the last third didn't walk at all. Guess who came out on top after everyone took the same divergent thinking test? Those who wandered aimlessly.

And in my favorite demonstration, a group of subjects enacted the classic descriptor of creativity as "thinking outside the box" by literally sitting alongside a cardboard carton while completing an exercise designed to measure their ability to find connections among seemingly unrelated concepts, a key dimension of creative aptitude. Other participants sat inside the carton, and still others attempted to solve the same problems without any carton in sight. Once again, it was the people who gave physical form to the idea of unconstrained and uninhibited thought who performed the best—by a margin of 20 percent, no less.

Now, you'll notice that each study involved a metaphor, by which I mean the representation of one thing by another. In the first example it was the gesture of opposing hands to symbolize the ability to see things from different perspectives,

in the second free versus proscribed movement to stand in for divergent versus convergent thinking, and in the third a box to connote the presence or absence of mental constraint. All the metaphors were evoked by physical movement or positioning. All resonate with the theme of creativity.

To the extent that enacting these metaphors stimulated a change in behavior among the subjects—i.e., they became more creative than their non-metaphorically activated peers—it's fair to say that their enactments functioned like primes. Unlike the cases of brain priming I described in the previous section, however, the stimuli didn't issue from where the enactors were, but from what they were doing.

Primes derived from metaphor are one type of behavior-based technique for enhancing creative performance that researchers have identified. Another type involves generic activities that on the surface appear to have nothing directly to do with creativity. These include exercising, lying down, performing mundane chores, napping, sleeping, playing, and taking a shower. The fact that these are all common household behaviors is among the reasons that home is a hotbed of creativity. I'll discuss each one of them, and others, in the main section of the book.

Are we ready, then, to nudge the brain off its traditional pedestal as the principal nexus of idea origination? Certainly not. On the contrary, the creative brain is getting more attention these days than ever, thanks largely to a nifty technology called *brain imaging*. Brain scanning, as it's also termed, is an umbrella term for a variety of techniques used to map neurological activity. Functional magnetic resonance imaging (fMRI), positron emission tomography (PET), and computed axial tomography (CAT) are among the techniques garnering a lot of press in popular media as well as in scientific journals.

It's easy to see why. There's some pretty intriguing stuff coming out of the field. In one experiment, brain scans revealed that high-performing creatives have many more neural connections between their left and right-brain than average performers. So much for the long-held belief that creativity stems from right brain dominance, or that our two hemispheres operate as practically independent organisms depending on the activity.

Other studies building on neuroimaging technology indicate that musicians who improvise a lot during performance—think freestyle rappers and jazz musicians—experience lower than normal activity in the front part of our brain believed to manage planning and self-censorship functions, and higher activity in the section thought to regulate thought and action. The reverse was true when they switched to musical pieces they knew by heart. The relationship of creative style to brain function neatly parallels the polarities of divergent and convergent thinking.

Lately, though, there's been something of a backlash against exaggerating what can be gleaned from these tantalizing peeks into the gray matter contained within our craniums. Part of the problem is that the brain is simply too complex for us to fully distill the information that's coming to us at this stage of our investigations, no matter how many brightly colored snapshots of blood oozing through it we ogle. Another is that many regions of the brain appear to have multiple functions, which makes it tough to be conclusive as to which part is performing which function when a person is being creative. That said, there's much to be gained from the emerging technologies, and I'll be citing neuroscientific research in the text where

Gym and party space. Piedmont, California. Architecture by Studio Bergtraun Architects. Photography by Treve Johnson.

it helps corroborate or shed light on the creativity tactic under discussion.

Here's the thought I want to leave you with: a creative idea is not a disembodied thought bubble born and bred in our brains, but the result of an intricate interplay of mind, body, and place. Among my goals in writing this book is to show how these three factors intersect, and what you can do to exploit their interrelationships to your advantage.

CREATIVITY TACTICS

A creativity tactic is an actionable technique that has been demonstrated through scientific research or historical best practices to improve idea flow. You'll find forty-eight of them in the pages that follow.

I present each tactic independently and in a consistent format. I begin with a succinct description of the action to be taken. I then cite the principal research finding or premise underlying the tactic, followed by a lengthier explanation as to how and why it's believed to boost creative performance. This lays the theoretical groundwork for the final section, which conveys practical design tips for implementing the tactic in residential environments.

Many of the tactics interrelate insofar as they involve a particular set of design elements, entail similar activities, are applicable to the same areas of home, or have common psychological underpinnings. This presented me with a writing challenge: how do I enable readers to choose between going through the book from front to back, or jumping around among techniques in whatever order they prefer? If I only accommodated the first group, then I was undermining my intent to structure the book like a practical manual; if I catered purely to the second, then I would have to constantly repeat myself to ensure that every tactic was fully explained.

I decided to balance the two approaches by adding a list of related tactics at the end of each entry. This list includes any tactics that were referenced in the preceding text, as well as those with overlapping characteristics of the sort I list above. In addition, I've inserted a few sidebar discussions among the tactics, called "explainers." These mostly have to do with overarching theories and scientific concepts applicable to more than one tactic. I've cross-referenced pertinent explainers at the end of pertinent tactics and relevant tactics in the explainers.

Having said all this, I encourage you to read the book sequentially as a first pass, because I believe you'll get the most out of its contents if you do. Once that's done, you can treat it like a reference book, dipping into it as the need presents itself.

Four dozen techniques are a lot to wrap one's mind around. To make it easier to find material, and to enhance the book's narrative flow, I've sorted the tactics into three groups.

Creativity Tactics Group 1: Appearance and Appurtenance includes tactics having to do with design elements you can see, whether embedded in a home's material construction, or the objects residing within or around it.

Creativity Tactics Group 2: Ambience consists of tactics associated with the diffuse and intangible characteristics of a space, such as lighting, sound, and smell.

Creativity Tactics Group 3: Action comprises creativity enhancers linked to activities people typically perform at home (and in a few special cases, outside of it).

Each tactic is accompanied by photographs of well-designed interiors. The pictures show how architects, interior, landscape, and product designers, and other creatives have incorporated the tactics into the physical setting of home. While I've aimed to maintain a consistent level of quality in my choice of images, I also tried to avoid letting any particular style or vocabulary dominate the portfolio. I did this to demonstrate that the tactics are style agnostic, meaning they can be applied to or practiced in almost any environment, regardless of aesthetics. The same goes for size, type, or location of home. Whether you see your home reflected among the images is therefore less important than whether you can draw ideas for adapting the tactics they embody to your own context, objectives, and resources.

Another point to keep in mind is that you're not obliged to implement every single tactic to enhance creative performance (whew!). Sometimes the slightest adjustment in environment or behavior is enough to alter our disposition. Recall Ulrich's 1984 study; all it took was a glimpse of trees through a window to make a palpable difference in the life of the patient.

Not that I would discourage you from adopting multiple tactics either, especially since they could produce a cumulative effect, and many incur little or no cost. Besides, if your goal is to optimize home for peak creative performance, why limit yourself? Creativity is a twenty-four-hour occupation (see #25, Sleep), and an idea can strike you almost anywhere and at any time. You want to be prepared to capitalize on moments of illumination when they arrive, and you want to have as many moments as possible. The tactics you'll find here can help you realize both ends.

Even if you don't consider every tactic relevant to your personal situation, I recommend that you still try to read through as many as you can. You'll learn a lot about creativity as a whole by familiarizing yourself with the rich assortment of ideas and insights that lie behind their explication. As many experts will tell you, the more you understand what creativity is and how it works, the better you're likely to be at it.

Now come the disclaimers. Putting these tactics into practice isn't going to magically transform you into a creative superhero by itself. You've got to do your part to leverage your innate talents. That means investing the time to practice your craft. Remaining committed, persistent, and motivated. Staying open to innovative ideas and opportunities. Being unafraid to be criticized or misunderstood, even rejected.

These are difficult things to do, especially outside the home. In the workplace we're pressured to conform to company standards and other people's expectations. At school we're rewarded for coming up with a single right answer, rather than many good answers. In neither environment are we free to shape our surroundings to reflect our vision of what the world should be. In neither place are we regularly permitted to act outside the norm, to take risks, to fail without automatic censure.

Home is different. Home is your creative haven. Take advantage of the freedom and safety it affords by incorporating some or all of the suggested enhancers into your surroundings and routines. Stick with those you find valuable and discard the rest. And don't be afraid of experimenting or adjusting my prescriptions to suit your means, personality, or work habits. We're people, not robots. All the science in the world can't predict how you, as an individual, will react to the creativity catalysts described in these pages. The best scientific research can do is establish the probability that a design trigger or action will bolster creative performance among a broad population. The rest is up to you.

CREATIVITY TACTICS
GROUP ONE:
APPEARANCE AND APPURTENANCE

TACTIC #1
DESIGNATE A CREATIVE SPACE

WHAT TO DO
Establish a consistent place at home for pursuing your creative interests.

WHY DO IT?
A well-defined idea space can actuate divergent thinking, increase motivation, reinforce routine, and jump-start productivity.

WHY DOES IT WORK?
Remember Pavlov's famous experiment with dogs? The one where the Russian scientist repeatedly rang a bell right before serving food to his canine subjects, until the dogs merely had to hear the clang to start salivating at the prospect of their daily repast?

In one respect, at least, we're like those dogs: expose us to a stimulus in proximity to an event often enough and we'll be conditioned just like them to automatically associate the one with the other. Scientists call this *classical conditioning*.

Now imagine setting aside a space in your home for your creative endeavors. Maybe it's a comfortable corner where you write. A home office from which you run your creative business. A woodshop in your garage where you assemble furniture.

Studio. Ashgrove, Queensland, Australia. Architecture by Marc & Co. Interior design by Vanessa Cribb for IndigoJungle Interior Styling. Landscape design by Stephen Clegg Design. Photography by Alicia Taylor.

Do this routinely, and your brain begins to subconsciously associate these surroundings with the activities routinely performed in them, to the point where you have only to step into the space for it to automatically trigger a creative mind-set.

Sounds a lot like brain priming, doesn't it? It should, since both actions involve linking a sensory input to a change in behavior or mental state. But there's a difference. The Pavlovian experiment showed that a connection can be forged between almost any sensory stimulus and an outcome if you repeat the stimulus enough. A buzzer or a piece of music or a pat on the head—none of which connotes food—would have conditioned the dogs as effectively as the bell. Brain priming, by contrast, appears to play off existing associations stored in our brains, some of which are absorbed through cultural influences and some of which are hardwired in, but all of which have a thematic connection to the response.

Another benefit of a defined locus of creative activity applicable to at-home creative professionals is that it establishes clear boundaries between work and domestic life. That's hugely important in the era of constant communication and information access. Without a line of demarcation between the personal and the professional, we're prone to blend the two. The danger in doing so is that our brains aren't engineered to jump back and forth between distinctly different tasks and activities, or to labor around the clock. Fall prey to either temptation, and you could find yourself vulnerable to mental exhaustion, reduced attention spans, lower productivity, heightened stress, and diminished happiness.

Finally, a regular time and place for your creative work means you won't have to expend precious mental energy deciding every day where and when you should get down to business. You can invest that energy into solving the creative problems on your plate instead. Incidentally, you can apply this productivity hack to almost any recurring daily activity, from getting dressed (Steve Jobs's uniform of turtleneck and jeans) to taking meals (writer Patricia Highsmith's habit of eating eggs and bacon every day for breakfast).

Does all this mean your imagination shuts down the instant you exit your creative workstation? Not in the least. The machinery of your imagination simply shifts into the background, where it operates no less powerfully. In fact, it's because the wheels are still turning in our heads when we're not consciously trying to be creative that we get some of our best insights while outside the precincts of our regular idea space, a paradox I'll explain in subsequent tactics.

HOW TO DO IT

Scan your home environment to decide the optimal location of your creative space, if you haven't already settled on one. Here are four types of environments that lend themselves to the purpose:

1. **Detached spaces.** Spaces inside an enclosed structure separate from the main residence, though still located on property. Examples include accessory

Kitchen. Kennebunk, Maine. Architecture by Caleb Johnson Studio. Photography by Trent Bell.

Studio. San Francisco, California. Architecture by Charles Irby for ICOSA Design and Peter Suen for FifthArch. Photography by Brian Flaherty.

structures placed in the landscape, on the roof of an apartment building, or connected to the principal residence by a covered walk.

2. **Enclosed spaces.** Rooms inside the home that can be fully closed off from adjacent areas, such as libraries, studies, offices, music rooms, sewing rooms, and playrooms. Avoid bedrooms, if possible; their function as sleeping quarters can conflict with idea formation (#25).

3. **Subordinate spaces.** Areas fully dedicated to creative activities but which open to a larger adjoining space. These include alcoves, dormer recesses, the hollow under staircases, and loft mezzanines.

4. **Hybrid and flex spaces.** Spaces that mingle creative activities with other domestic functions. Think kitchens, a piano floating in a living area, or a spot at the dining table.

DAILY WORK ROUTINES OF FAMOUS CREATIVES

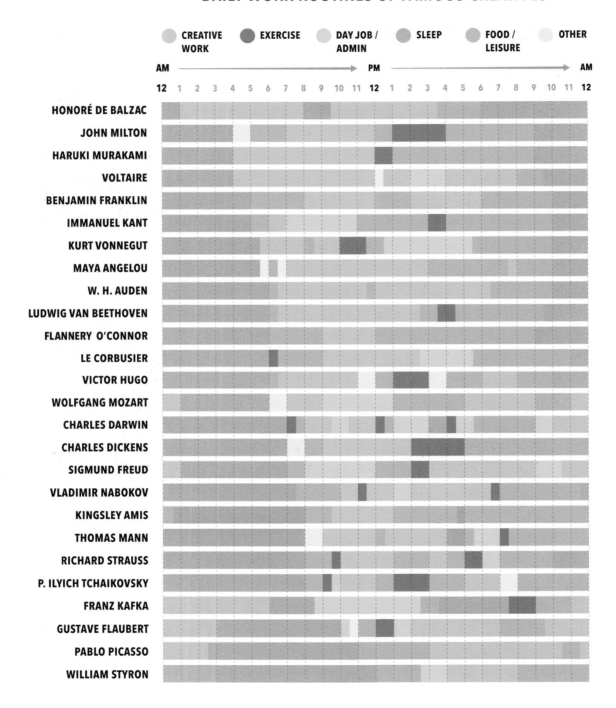

Fig. 6: Daily routines of famous creatives from past and present. Infographic adapted by
Podio from Daily Rituals: How Artists Work by Mason Currey (2013).

Establishing the location of a generative micro-environment is just the first step in the process of turning it into a powerful tool for outputting ideas. Consider these pointers as you begin to give it shape:

Use it religiously. As most creativity coaches will tell you—and as the habits of history's greatest geniuses attest—a regular routine combined with a consistent locus of activity are key to creative productivity (Fig. 6). Witness Beethoven, who went straight to the same worktable in his home on waking every day—after first counting out exactly sixty beans for his coffee. Or the architect Le Corbusier, who kicked off his morning work sessions at home with forty-five minutes of exercise, then stormed into his Paris studio precisely at 2:00 p.m. to terrorize his employees with the fruits of his brilliance. Or George Bernard Shaw, who built a small writer's hut a short walk from his house in the country, where he could escape unwanted callers by having his wife tell them he'd gone to London.

Reveal its purpose. An idea room should look like a place where creativity happens. Find ways to display your work product, whether in the form of sketches, mockups, storyboards, a copy of your best-selling book, awards, pictures, musical scores, or anything else that inspires you, to boost self-motivation and confidence. Keep the materials and tools you use in your work close at hand.

Furnish to your needs. Whenever possible, select furnishings and equipment, construct built-ins, and install features specifically designed to satisfy your requirements. Besides providing practical advantages, these appurtenances concretize your commitment to a creative life.

Zone work areas according to activity. Maximize productivity by subdividing your space to suit varying task requirements, both physical and cognitive. Author and artist Austin Kleon's garage home office contains a digital desk, an analog desk, and a separate reading area.

Segregate the personal from the professional in your digital environment. Just as creativity can suffer when the line of demarcation between home and work is eroded in physical space, so too can it be squelched when the line is blurred in digital space.

Avoid the problem by setting up separate user accounts on your computers or for your online services. Place all your files pertaining to your

Living area. Nashville, Tennessee. Building and interior design by David Latimer for New Frontier Tiny Homes. Photography by StudiObuell.

Office. Garrison, New York. Architecture and interior design by Annie Mennes for Garrison Foundry. Photography by Beatrice Pediconi.

Home office. Scarborough, Maine. Architecture by Caleb Johnson Studio. Photography by Trent Bell.

Dining room. Yonkers, New York. Architecture by Gary Brewer for Robert A.M. Stern Architects. Photography by Francis Dzikowski / Otto.

Fig. 7: Charles Dickens in his study at Gad's Hill Place, Rochester, United Kingdom. Engraving by Samuel Hollyer. c. 1875. Library of Congress.

Hall. Palo Alto, California. Architecture by YAMAMAR Design. Interior design by Alison Damonte for Alison Damonte Design. Photography by Bruce Damonte.

creative self under one login, and everything else under another. This will make it slightly more burdensome to bounce back and forth between them. An alternative option for both Mac and Windows users is to maintain multiple desktops, restricting those applications or documents opened for creative work to a single window.

Don't let limitations of space or place hinder you. Not enough room at home for a permanent setup? Try using props to transform everyday into imaginal space. For instance, rather than merely plunking your laptop onto the dining table and immediately whaling away at the keyboard, slip a pad or place mat that you don't use for meals underneath the machine at the start of each working session. Place a bud vase, a statuette of an inspiring figure, or other totems of creativity alongside. Tuck everything away when you're done. Or simply do your knitting in the same easy chair every day. Like Pavlov's bell, the recurring association of consistent visual cues with creative behavior will signal your brain that you've entered idea mode.

You road warriors can avail yourselves of similar techniques. Take along one or more easily transported items from your creative space on your travels, then pull them out in your hotel room, remote office, or wherever you've set up camp to reconnect psychologically to your regular creative environment. Charles Dickens did this assiduously while on book tour, sometimes rearranging the furniture in his temporary digs to more closely emulate his study at home (Fig. 7).

Treat the entire home as an idea lab. Assigning a specific place to imaginative work is an important step in the process of building a creative home, but keep in mind that idea origination is a whole-house phenomenon. Apply the techniques presented in this book to other areas of your home besides the one you've committed to the purpose.

LOOK AT SOMETHING BLUE

WHAT TO DO

Design your creative space to provide consistent exposure to the color blue.

WHY DO IT?

A 2009 experiment by researchers at the University of British Columbia found that subjects primed with the color blue scored higher on tests measuring divergent thinking than subjects primed with the color red. Subjects exposed to red, on the other hand, outperformed their peers on exercises requiring convergent thinking skills.

WHY DOES IT WORK?

Ever wonder why people get pumped up by the prospect of an enjoyable experience (e.g., going on vacation, receiving a gift, opening a bottle of fine wine), but are disinclined to embrace life's less appealing activities (e.g., visiting the dentist, emptying the garbage, sitting in traffic or on a crowded train)?

Simple: Nature has wired us to maximize pleasure and minimize pain, a pattern of behavior psychologists call *approach-avoidance motivation*. According to this theory, we feel compelled to advance toward potential sources of delight and steer clear of anything that might hurt us. Our frame of mind changes depending on which course of action we're prompted to pursue. Show us a path to gratification, and we'll assume an open-minded and uninhibited outlook that encourages

Bath. Nashville, Tennessee. Building and interior design by David Latimer for New Frontier Tiny Homes. Photography by StudiObuell.

us to realize the opportunity. Raise the specter of danger, and we'll turn calculating, attentive, and risk-averse to better escape it.

What has approach-avoidance motivation to do with creativity, you might ask? Apparently, a lot. Organizational psychologist Ron Friedman explains:

> Our motivational mind-set is particularly critical when we're engaged in creative activities. Research shows that when we're energized by the possibility of gain, we adopt a flexible cognitive style that allows us to easily switch between mental categories. We take a broader view, seeing the forest instead of the trees, while exploring a wider array of possibilities. In sum, when we're energized by approach motivation, we instinctively use the very mental techniques that make us more creative.
>
> It's a different story when avoidance motivation enters the picture.
>
> The moment evading a negative outcome becomes the focus, our attention narrows and our thinking becomes more rigid. We have a hard time seeing the big picture and resist the mental exploration necessary for finding a solution. All of a sudden, insights become a lot more elusive.

If Friedman's connection of motivation and cognition is correct, then it stands to reason that blue must have triggered an approach frame of mind among the subjects of the 2009 study, while red cued an avoidance mentality. But why?

Kitchen. Dartmoor, Victoria, Australia. Architecture by van Ellen + Sheryn Architects. Photography by James French.

One possible answer is that our reactions to color flow from the properties we associate with them. When we see red, for instance, we become more alert and focused because we mentally equate the color with hazard, discomfort, and failure—think spilled blood, red ink, fire, and Ferraris—all things that portend trouble and consequently to be avoided (except maybe the Ferrari). The sight of blue, on the other hand, inclines us to be less restrained in our actions because our subconscious links the color to positive and comforting conditions, like sunny skies and placid waters, both of which people almost universally find attractive and welcoming.

A fascinating experiment conducted by architect Shashi Caan in 2006 appears to corroborate this interpretation (Fig. 8). The experiment took place at the Architectural Digest Show in New York, an annual trade fair catering to home design professionals. The physical setting was a series of event tents Caan and her team constructed inside the cavernous shed where the exhibition was held. Two of the tents were designed to immerse occupants in either red or blue light. So as not to dilute the purity of effect, everything else inside the space was deliberately made white or transparent, from the hazmat suits worn by the show attendees who entered

Fig. 8: Photographs from Spatial Color: Experiencing Color in the Third Dimension. Research project by Shashi Caan for SC Collective. 2006. Photography by SC Collective.

of numbers—a hallmark of high-achieving creatives throughout history.

Participants bathed in red light did nearly the opposite. Instead of gamely exploring the periphery, they converged on the psychologically safest part of the room—the middle, their backs literally turned to the unknown world outside the walls. Instead of dogged individualism, they exhibited signs of groupthink. Instead of taking risks by delving into the unknown, they became neophobic, content to draw from the knowledge of others close by.

It was as if the guests had read Friedman's description of the two faces of approach-avoidance

voluntarily, to the free food and beverages that enticed them to remain long enough for their behavior to be observed at length by Caan and her team.

Among the many interesting observations recorded over the course of the fair, one in particular leapt out at me: visitors to the blue tent tended to scatter along the perimeter walls singly or in pairs, as if an unseen centrifugal force had propelled them there, whereas guests in the red environment were more likely to cluster in social groups at the center.

Translating this behavior within the framework of creativity, I would suggest that the guests primed by the color blue were drawn to survey the limits of their physical space just as neophiles test the boundaries of conventional thinking. That they did so independently or with a partner suggests a willingness to largely go it alone, to rely on one's own resourcefulness rather than cling to the security

Fig. 9: Mona Lisa (La Gioconda) *by Leonardo da Vinci. c. 1503–1506. Digital reconstruction after copy of da Vinci's original painted by Francesco Melzi (?).*

Foyer details. Jupiter, Florida. Interior design by JMA Interior Design. Photography by Brantley Photography.

motivation, and literally acted them out in their respective tents.

Caan's study is valuable for using scientific methods to document how color affects the way people think, feel, and act in a more or less real-world environment. But is approach-avoidance motivation the only possible basis for understanding what happened in the Digest tents or in the 2009 experiment? Could there be others?

As is often the case when it comes to ascertaining the whys of human behavior, the answer is yes. My own pet theory, for instance, is that the Digest subjects acted as they did in reaction to color's influence on our assessment of distance.

To explain, I refer you to the *Mona Lisa* (Fig. 9). Begin by looking at the landscape visible behind the figure in the upper third of the canvas. Notice how it's rendered in a distinctly bluish cast. It wasn't that Leonardo believed rocks were actually blue, and I'm pretty sure he wasn't colorblind. Rather, he was exploiting the property of cool colors to make objects appear as if they're receding from the eye so as to reinforce the illusion of physical distance.

Now examine the figure of Mona Lisa herself, and in particular, the deep saturated reds that Leonardo used to paint the sleeves of her dress. Here the artist's intention was the reverse: to move the figure nearer to the picture plane, which he accomplished by leveraging the optical effects of warm colors to advance toward the viewer.

Applying these same optics to the Digest study, we could surmise that the people in the blue tent became open-minded and explorative because they subconsciously intuited that the perimeter walls and ceiling plane were expanding outwardly, giving them plenty of room in which to roam both physically and mentally. Persons gathered in the red room, on the other hand, sensed subliminally that their environment was contracting, and so felt compelled to limit their peregrinations to the well-trafficked middle.

From these deductions can be derived a general principle of creative space design:

Our mental space (i.e., idea space) expands and contracts in direct proportion to our perception of physical space, both real and imagined.

In other words, the more expansive you feel your surroundings to be, the broader your outlook; the more compressed the setting, the more focused your thinking. These relationships hold true whether your perceptions are triggered by literal representations of physical distance, such as ceiling height (#3) or exterior views (#4), or by indirect and metaphorical cues, like color and artwork (#5).

While J. P. Guilford is no longer here to judge my theory, I'd like to think that he would have at least acknowledged its merits. After all, his diagram of divergent-convergent thinking captures the parallels between cognitive style, color, and mental space perfectly (Fig. 3).

That's not to say that everyone is in universal agreement with my conclusions or the findings published in the 2009 study. Several scientists followed up the work done by the University of British Columbia researchers with studies of their own, with mixed results. On the positive side, red by and large cemented its reputation as the color least hospitable to inducing the kinds of physical behavior and states of mind linked to creative

Study. Melbourne, Victoria, Australia. Architecture by Austin Maynard Architects. Photography by Peter Bennetts.

thinking. The story with blue, on the other hand, was a bit more muddled. An attempt to replicate one of the tests from the 2009 paper failed to yield the same results. A few researchers questioned whether blue's power to affect our actions and mental state had been proven definitively.

This is perfectly normal. Scientists debate each other all the time, often without reaching consensus. The inability to reproduce experimental data doesn't mean the original findings were wrong either; a few years back somebody tried to replicate a hundred well-known experiments in the field of psychology, only to end up with a two thirds failure rate. What are we to do then? Dump every paper based on unreplicated research or that fell short of 100 percent buy-in from the scientific community into the trash bin? The net result would be some very empty bookshelves and legions of academics and students with little to go on.

So here's my pitch for keeping blue in your creative space design tool kit: there are too many pieces of supporting evidence out there in addition to the 2009 study that lead to the same conclusions, some of which you'll be reading about in the tactics that follow.

I'd also point out that blue is the best-liked color in the world. Only two other colors—red and green—resonate as universally. Why do people from every corner of the globe cite blue as their favorite? According to the survey data, because it makes us happy. And happiness, as you'll hear from me again and again, is the emotional handmaiden of the creative mind.

HOW TO DO IT

Choose a monochromatic palette. Taken to its logical conclusion, this tactic would have you color every visible surface in your space blue.

Rest assured, however, that you don't have to go to quite that extreme to obtain the desired outcome (although it's been done). Consider instead using a monotone palette built around blue, and then applying the chosen color to assorted features within the space in various shades, tints, and tones. Use neutrals (whites, grays, blacks) or natural finishes for remaining surfaces and pieces to provide visual relief.

Take care to avoid very dark or very light blues on walls and enclosing elements. Extremely dark tones make a space feel smaller regardless of hue. Overly pale tints could be imperceptible and lack effect.

Should your activity area be small, or your line of sight generally oriented in a particular direction, you could conceivably limit your colorizing efforts to only those features that lay consistently in your field of vision, such as an accent or window wall.

Color your digital devices blue. The researchers who administered the 2009 study deployed a clever technique to deliver the designated primes: they inset the computerized test materials on their subjects' monitors, and then colored the leftover margins either blue or red. Take a page from their playbook by setting the backgrounds on your screens and monitors to be a solid blue during periods of creative activity.

RELATED TACTICS AND EXPLAINERS
#3. Work under a lofty ceiling.
#4. Take in a view.
#5. Display art.
#14. Bring nature in.
#19. Let in natural light.
#20. Be smart with your lighting.
Explainer I: Space, Time, and Creativity

TACTIC #3

WORK UNDER
A LOFTY CEILING

WHAT TO DO

Do creative work in spaces with ceilings ten feet or higher, or visually manipulate your surroundings to exaggerate apparent height.

WHY DO IT?

Researchers found that subjects occupying a room with ten-foot ceilings scored higher on creativity assessment tests than subjects who performed the same exercises under eight-foot ceilings.

WHY DOES IT WORK?

I described in the previous tactic how our perception of mental space moves in parallel with our perception of physical space. The greater our sense of spatial depth and expansiveness, the more open our minds will be to unorthodox ideas and fresh perspectives.

But space doesn't exist in strictly lateral directions, which is to say, in front of and behind us, or from side to side. It also exists in the third, vertical dimension. It therefore stands to reason that if our thinking becomes freer and more open when we perceive space to be expanding horizontally, it will do the same if we intuit that space is opening up above us as well.

This assumption was borne out in a 2007 study that explored the influence of ceiling height on cognition. Cognitive scientists discovered that subjects were more adept at coming up with out-of-the-box solutions to creative problems when placed in a room ten feet high than subjects who took the same tests in the same room, but with a hung ceiling installed at eight feet. On the flip side, they also found that people who worked under the dropped ceiling did better than their peers on exercises that measured analytic and logical thinking.

A later experiment utilizing fMRI brain scans found a neurological correlation with the laboratory results: the part of the brain involved in the visual exploration of space was activated when subjects were shown pictures of rooms with high ceilings, but not when they saw images of low-ceiling spaces. In other words, spaces with high ceilings instill a willingness in people to explore, to "boldly go where no one has gone before," whereas a less lofty ceiling plane induces a more focused, detail-oriented, and concrete point of view. The first characteristics are consistent with divergency, the second with convergency.

William Lidwell, the design writer quoted in the Introduction, dubbed this phenomenon the Cathedral Effect. His choice of words is apt. The central nave of many of the great cathedrals of the world, especially those built in Europe in the Middle Ages, are extraordinarily tall—as high as 156 feet in one case. Now refer back to Table I: among the properties of divergency is to think abstractly—and what is more abstract than contemplating the divine? It's safe to say that the people who conceived and built these structures understood the effects of extreme vertical space implicitly, and designed accordingly.

Dining area. Philip Island, Victoria, Australia. Architecture by Andrew Simpson, Charles Anderson, and Emma Parkinson for Andrew Simpson Architects. Photography by Peter Bennetts.

HOW TO DO IT

Those of you who already have an idea space with ceilings ten feet or higher are in luck. But what about everyone else? What do you do? Give up? Move? Demolish your domicile and build another?

Nothing so radical. Fortunately, in matters of the human psyche, what you *perceive* to be true is far more potent in eliciting a psychological response than what is actually true. You can take advantage of this by drawing on techniques that will make your ceiling appear taller than it really is. Some of these techniques are cosmetic in nature, a few involve light renovation. All are designed to emphasize the vertical axis by encouraging the eye to move in an upward direction, and thereby simulate the Cathedral Effect.

Apply vertical elements and patterns to walls. Wall coverings and paint treatments embellished with stripes and other vertically oriented motifs, architectural paneling, and trim or structural elements running in an upright direction will visually lift a room.

Exploit furnishings and decor. Tall bookcases, full-length drapes, artwork in portrait-oriented frames, decorative accessories mounted on walls in vertical arrangements, tall mirrors resting on the floor and angled upward, and standing lamps are among the various interior components you can leverage to amplify visual height.

Lighten up. I've read a lot of opinions about how the color of floors, walls, and ceilings affects our estimate of height. Some of it's right, some of it's wrong. To set the record straight on maybe the most prevalent misconception, the *contrast* between the color of your ceiling and the color of your walls and floors has *no impact* on height perception. What does matter is how light your walls and ceiling are independent of each other. In a nutshell, the lighter they are, the taller your

Living area. Tel Aviv—Yafo, Israel. Architecture by Pitsou Kedem Architects. Photography by Amit Geron.

space will seem. According to the research, floors don't factor at all.

Continue the wall color or material into the ceiling. Another technique involving finishes is to extend the wall color up into the ceiling as a border. This tricks the eye into reading the wall as continuing past the vertical plane. To strengthen the illusion, curve the top of the wall where it meets the ceiling and do away with any intervening horizontal trim, like cornices and picture moldings. Ready for the Full Monty? Do this, then apply the same color to both walls *and* ceiling (or construct them entirely out of a single material, as in the example of the exposed stone vaulting). Your eye will have nowhere to stop as it travels up from the floor.

Raise door and window heads. The relationship between the tops of your door and window openings and the ceiling is a crucial determinant of height perception. All things being equal, the higher up the openings, the more elevated you'll judge the space.

Living room. Palo Alto, California. Architecture by YAMAMAR Design. Interior design by Alison Damonte for Alison Damonte Design. Photography by Bruce Damonte.

Top off your space. The researchers who uncovered the Cathedral Effect took pains to point out that subjects had to be made aware of room height, if only momentarily, for the prime to function. They hung Chinese lanterns from the ceiling to draw their subjects' attention upward; you can do the same with light fixtures, skylights, ceiling fans, beams and coffers, textured finishes, decorative appliqué, and other features commonly found in residential ceilings.

Musts to avoid. Just as some design elements accentuate height, others have the contrary effect of diminishing it. Avoid chair rails, oblong wall paneling, deep friezes, picture molds, heavy cornices, wallcoverings and drapery with longitudinal patterns, openings wider than they are tall, oversized furniture and furniture with long horizontal profiles (e.g., straight-back sofas) in creative environments with ceilings lower than ten feet.

RELATED TACTICS AND EXPLAINERS
#2. Look at something blue.
#4. Take in a view.
Explainer I: Space, Time, and Creativity

TACTIC #4

TAKE IN A

WHAT TO DO

Configure your creative space to afford views to the outside.

WHY DO IT?

Windowed environments can facilitate creative task performance by restoring cognitive capacity, reducing stress, mental fatigue, and perceived risk, and promoting a sense of freedom and openness.

WHY DOES IT WORK?

Quite a few studies have been done on the effects that windows generally, and views in particular, bring to occupants in workplace, health-care, and learning environments. The near universal consensus among those who've conducted or reviewed the research is that windows and views are good for us, and that windowless settings are bad for us.

Why is this? The prevalent explanation is that we are by nature creatures of the outdoors, since that's where human life began. According to this view, much of our biology was engineered by Mother Nature eons ago to facilitate our survival in the wild. Deprive us of conditions associated with the natural environment and we're bound to suffer the consequences. A study undertaken in 2014, for example, showed that people who worked in a windowless environment on average experienced forty-six minutes less sleep per night than colleagues seated in windowed areas. Another tied the poor recovery of hospital patients to the absence of openings in their rooms.

Finding
views could
since an inr
undoubtedly
kit too—othe
humans coul
of prehistor
is evidence th
afford an infl
natural scene
both wellness

A somewha
ancestral selve   views on
creativity sten   vanced by Jay
Appleton know   e. This theory holds
that people i   x when they can see
a broad swath o   front of them, while
simultaneously fe   ected from the rear and
overhead (Fig. 1   an imagine how useful
this impulse woul   early humans; better they
should be motiva   scan the horizon from
an enclosed perch   on a hill where a hungry
animal or unfrien   neighbor couldn't sneak up
on them than be ca ght flat-footed in the open
African plains below. Rather than wither away in
the ensuing millennia, however, this instinct has
remained with us. It's why brain scans and lab
studies reveal that people still prefer to sit with
their backs to the wall in exposed spatial settings
like restaurants—especially if they're gangsters, in
which case they've probably also made sure to have
an unimpeded view of the door.

How does prospect-refuge relate to creativity?
Generally speaking, any circumstance that raises

Fig. 10: Tu̶ ̶b̶ *Espen Folgerø and students at Bergen School of Architecture. Photography by Gunnar Sørås.*

stress levels redu͏
stress naturally in͏
attention to detail, ͏
erties of analytic, cor͏
fear fosters focus. C͏
mind tends to magnif͏
we feel more secure and͏
take the kind of emotiona͏
risks that nonconformist͏
a prospect-refuge standp͏
a view to the outside pr͏
of psychologically safe s͏
exploration of maveric͏

Academic research ͏
place to find flights of p͏
help notice the comme͏
paper on the present s͏
symbolizes freedom, a re͏

͏hat's because
͏ical thinking,
͏ other prop-
͏Plainly put,
͏xed state of
͏tudes, since
͏re willing to
͏l, and social
͏nands. From
͏ indoors with
͏isely the kind
͏ncourages the

͏not usually the
͏y, but I couldn't
͏he author of one
that "the window
͏owever brief, from

the immediate world to a different, more expansive world." This brought to mind another theory that might explain the link between creativity and vistas, one I've already drawn from in my discussion of color (#2) and ceiling height (#3), namely, that our brain space—that is, our receptiveness to novel perspectives—is directly related to our awareness of distance. As I figure it, if the mere perception of expanding space triggered by exposure to cool colors or higher-than-average ceilings could escalate unconventional thinking, then the effect of seeing beyond the confines of an interior altogether would surely bring the same results.

HOW TO DO IT

Gain visual and physical access to the outside.
A standard means of accessing views to the outside is through windows or glazed exterior doors.

Rear patio. La Quinta, California. Architecture by Frank Stolz for South Coast Architects. Photography by Eric Figge.

Folding or disappearing walls are an option for inhabitants of hospitable climates. Balconies, decks, porches, rooftop gardens, and other outdoor areas naturally offer views as well.

Orient yourself in the direction of the view. To exploit the asset, arrange your furnishings and equipment to allow for a visual connection to the view. Placing a work surface under or facing an exterior window is a common method for achieving this connection; however, as I'll explain further in another tactic (#10), this is not necessarily advisable from the psycho-spatial perspective of prospect-refuge. Consider instead orientating your workstation perpendicular to the opening so that the view still lies within your cone of vision, but without exposing your back directly to the space behind.

Living area and deck. Berkeley, California. Architecture by YAMAMAR Design. Photography by Bruce Damonte.

Living area. Nashville, Tennessee. Building and interior design by David Latimer for New Frontier Tiny Homes. Photography by StudiObuell.

Implement other tactics to compensate for lack of prospect. Some spaces, such as a work surface built into a blind alcove or under a stair, will inevitably lack a direct line of sight to the outside. In those cases, consider employing alternative tactics such as color (#2), plants and natural materials (#14), and artwork (#5) within the recess in order to ameliorate the negative effects of a solid backdrop. You'll also help yourself by allowing as much natural light as possible to enter the environs through openings in the adjacent space (#19) or using a swivel chair to facilitate periodic views through any openings that might be visible behind you.

Control the scene. It's often difficult to control the extent and quality of the vista, especially when dealing with existing conditions. Where available, opt for the longest possible vista and views of natural scenery. As Ulrich's 1984 study and many others show, these qualities are optimal for fostering both wellness and creative thinking.

Configure openings for ideal view content by manipulating design elements such as size, shape, operation, sill height, sight lines, glazing,

Workspace. McClean, Virginia. Architecture and interior design by Jim Rill, AIA, and David Benton for Rill Architects. Photography by Angie Seckinger.

Bedroom and bath. Tel Aviv–Yafo, Israel. Architecture by Pitsou Kedem Architect. Photography by Amit Geron.

materials and details, blinds, and drapery. Keep obstructions to a minimum.

Got a view, but not a particularly pleasant one? Hang plants, install sheer curtains, or apply translucent window films embellished with floral motifs or other landscape themes to retain the semblance of an outside view and filter incoming light while sparing yourself the downsides.

RELATED TACTICS AND EXPLAINERS

#2. Look at something blue.
#5. Display art.
#10. Face your space.
#14. Bring nature in.
#19. Let in natural light.
Explainer I: Space, Time, and Creativity
Explainer II: We Are Who We Have Always Been

TACTIC #5
DISPLAY ART

Minds are like parachutes—they only function when open.
—Thomas Dewar

WHAT TO DO
Embellish a room with works of visual art, graphic design, and handicrafts.

WHY DO IT?
Viewing works of art and craft can stimulate creativity by encouraging openness to new experiences and learning; promoting risk-taking; increasing pleasure, advancing health and reducing stress; facilitating mind-wandering; inducing saccadic eye movement, which strengthens neural connections between the brain hemispheres; and triggering priming effects.

WHY DOES IT WORK?
The scientific evidence for appreciating artistic output not only as a product of human creativity, but as its catalyst, is mounting.

Neuroimaging is proving to be an especially powerful mechanism for gaining insights into how the brain reacts to art. In one meta-study (meaning a study that compiles data from multiple previous studies), researchers discovered evidence that viewing art stimulates us to learn new things. That's a key finding, because experts rank the desire for novel experience as the number one predictor of creative achievement and a core trait of the creative personality. It's also consistent with another study that found that seeing art sends blood to sectors of the brain associated with risk-taking, a willingness to venture into unchartered

territory being a necessary precondition for people in perpetual pursuit of original ideas.

Then there's the empirical evidence that art can give us pleasure and elevate happiness. But it goes deeper than that—approach-avoidance motivation (see #2) and the data that back it up indicate that pleasure and happiness bolster creative performance by improving cognitive flexibility, making us receptive to new information, and helping us become more adroit problem solvers. On the flip side, art can help some people reduce feelings of anger and stress and improve health, all of which similarly facilitate our powers of invention.

Most forms of visual art are reflective, requiring us only to look and think. Thing is, our minds have a tendency to meander off in random directions when we're left alone with our thoughts or are unencumbered by physically demanding activities. Psychologists call this sort of unfocused attention *mind-wandering*. I go into mind-wandering at greater length in the context of showering (#35), where it happens often. For now, suffice to say that researchers have linked this form of reverie to higher levels of divergent thinking and—here it comes again—the compulsion to explore the unfamiliar.

Even the seemingly passive act of looking plays into art's creative potency. The reason is that while our body is largely at rest, our eye is busy scanning a work of visual art by moving back and forth across its surface. Scientists have long linked eye movement and mental processing; more

Photography studio of Nicholas Yarsley. Gloucestershire, United Kingdom. Architecture, interior design, and photography by Nicholas Yarsley.

recently, they've discovered correlations between rapid shifts of the eye and improved creative task performance. More on this in my explanation of biophilia (Explainer II).

HOW TO DO IT

Coordinate art with decor. Purists will gasp in horror, but it really is okay to deliberately select pieces to harmonize aesthetically with other elements in a space. (You can also build a space around already acquired works of art.)

Pay attention to scale. A large piece in a small space might be overwhelming; a small piece alone in a big or busy setting might go unnoticed.

Follow industry wisdom in determining placement. Heed the advice of design professionals. For instance, group smaller items together to maintain scale and increase visual impact. Hang framed artwork so that the center stands between fifty-eight and sixty inches above the floor; this will avoid the impression of its having floated up the wall or sunk downward. Explore background colors other than white to bring out appealing qualities in a piece. Live with your art for a time before finalizing installation or acquisition, if possible. Be willing to break the rules when it makes sense to do so.

Select and install art strategically. Take context and objectives into account in picking and arranging pieces. Minimal exposure to the outside? Try opening up the space by showing photographs or prints that evoke or depict the outdoors. Less than optimal ceiling height for peak idea formation? Find objects with strongly vertical proportions, or stack a series of pieces on walls or shelves to direct the eye upward. Find things that inspire your creative passions—vintage movie posters if you write screenplays, a bust of Albert Einstein if physics is your beat, an inspirational quote from a figure you admire, perhaps a Campbell's soup can silkscreen by Warhol should you consider yourself a foodie or pop-culture aficionado. And of course, show your own stuff if you're a visual artist or hobbyist. Few things beget art like art.

Rotate your display periodically. Creative thinking eschews fixity of mind. Consider mixing up your pieces—and your thoughts—by occasionally swapping them out, acquiring electronic frames or monitors to project assorted images or video, using easily changed mounting systems, such as magnetics, or simply moving items around. You might be surprised how differently you'll look at a work of art depending on its freshness, location, and adjacency to other pieces.

Strive for positive affect. Mood arousal is a powerful engine of creativity. Be sure you derive happiness from what you collect. Work that raises stress levels or causes emotional distress could

Library. Yonkers, New York. Architecture by Gary Brewer for Robert A.M. Stern Architects. Photography by Francis Dzikowski/Otto.

have an unintentionally negative effect on out-of-the-box thinking.

Curate your art for its priming effects. Whether it's a tabletop sculpture carved from driftwood (#14), an old photograph (#6), or a signature blue canvas by the artist Yves Klein (#2), art can spur creative insight by triggering the primes contained in this book. Keep in mind that many primes can be realized through indirect and metaphorical representation as well as by literal means. Landscape paintings and images of outdoor scenes, for example, have been found to induce in the observer the same big-picture view of the world as an actual vista glimpsed through an exterior opening (# 4, 14).

Don't overdo it. Leave some empty space around the art you present. Sensory overload resulting from a dearth of visual relief in your presentation can undermine the generative value of artistic experience.

RELATED TACTICS AND EXPLAINERS

#2. Look at something blue.

#3. Work under a lofty ceiling.

#4. Take in a view.

#6. Think back.

#7. Embrace detail and complexity.

#12. Choose curved over straight.

#14. Bring nature in.

#18. Make music.

#29. Make a fire. Or look at a picture of one.

Explainer I: Space, Time, and Creativity

Dining area. Greenwich, Connecticut. Architecture by Peter Ogden Kinnear. Interior design by Gaby and Donald M. Rattner. Artwork by Donald M. Rattner. Photography by Gordon Beall.

TACTIC #6
THINK BACK

WHAT TO DO
Surround yourself with mementos reminiscent of experiences, events, places, and people in your life or that hold historical interest for you.

WHY DO IT?
Objects that spark a sentimental yearning or wistful affection for the past can ignite insight thinking.

Tackle shack. Holmes Beach, Florida. Interior design by Eric Brown for Epoch Solutions. Photography by Jimmy White Photography.

WHY DOES IT WORK?

As a quipster once quipped, nostalgia ain't what it used to be. Which is a good thing, because longing for what used to be was once regarded as a misguided retreat from reality. At its low point, experts even labeled nostalgia a psychiatric disorder. Now, thanks to science, it's making a comeback.

Researchers at the University of Southampton in the United Kingdom, for instance, discovered that subjects who were first asked to recall elements of their past proceeded to show greater aptitude and linguistic fluency in creative writing exercises compared to those who performed the same task without the prime.

Why would recalling times of old goose our creativity? The scientists who ran the experiment theorized that, like art (#5), nostalgic reverie broadens our mind and amplifies our desire for novel experience, both of which foster creativity. They and others also pointed to the happy feelings valued mementos impart to us; contrary to the myth of the debauched, destitute, and depressed *artiste* toiling in a wretched attic, our creativity tends to flourish when we're upbeat and contented, and suffer when we're in the dumps.

Another interpretation of the test results has to do with the distancing effects I describe in connection with the factors of color (#2), ceiling height (#3), views (#4), and artwork (#5). Distancing effects come into play when you sense things are far away or that the space around you is expansive. Sometimes your perception is triggered by material conditions, e.g., ceiling height (#3), and views (#4); in other instances, it's brought on by the pictorial representation of deep space (e.g., landscape imagery [#14]), or by inference, such as the optical illusion that blue surfaces recede from the eye (#2). In each case the end result is that your

Memento wall. Austin, Texas. Architecture and interior design by Tim Cuppett Architects. Photography by Alec Hemer.

brain shifts into the kind of abstract, big-picture style of mental processing from which novel ideas emerge. Nostalgia brings about a similar change in outlook, except that it does so by activating your sense of time rather than space.

Bottom line: think back to think ahead.

HOW TO DO IT

Cast a wide net. It's pretty much an open field when it comes to choosing props to serve a mnemonic function. Almost anything that engenders distant recall or that resurfaces pleasurable connotations of the past can elicit the desired cognitive effect. Trip souvenirs, bric-a-brac, ancestral portraits, heirlooms, scrapbooks, trinkets from treasured moments, costumes, ephemera, and objects related to historical eras of interest to you are all grist for the nostalgia mill.

Feel free to get personal, even to the point of peculiarity. According to one account, the author Roald Dahl kept all sorts of strange memorabilia on a desk alongside his writing chair. These included a piece of bone removed from his own hip and a gigantic ball of silver paper that he'd been collecting from bars of chocolate since he was a young man.

While objects of recollection can be worked into almost any style of decor, they harmonize quite well with shabby chic, steampunk, folk- and vintage-themed environments dominated by patinated finishes and preindustrial craftsmanship.

Take a casual approach to display. Mementos are often less formal than fine art, so you can be relaxed in your selections and presentation if the object warrants it. Not up to putting the baseball from your child's first home run on a pedestal or under glass? Just plunk it on a desk, table, or shelf where you can see it.

Or take a formal approach to display. On the other hand, try going the opposite route by converting the everyday into an aesthetically pleasing display that contributes to the decor.

Home office. Austin, Texas. Architecture and interior design by Tim Cuppett Architects. Photography by Alec Hemer.

A hundred colorful travel postcards arrayed in a geometric pattern on a wall or inside a frame can be eye catching. So can a shadow box housing artifacts culled from a particular time or place, recycled maps cut up in attractive shapes, vintage cubbies holding assorted knickknacks, and glass jars filled with different colored sand scooped up from beaches you've visited. As always, exercise moderation to avoid visual clutter.

BONUS FUN FACT

The etymology of the term *nostalgia*, from the Greek *nostos*, meaning to return home, and *algos*, Greek for sickness, is rooted in the concept of home both etymologically and historically. According to Israeli academic Avishai Margalit, the word first appears in 1688, when a Swiss doctor named Johannes Hofer used it in a paper he submitted to Basel University. Hofer coined the word to describe a depressed mood arising from a longing for home. The doctor had apparently observed the condition among Swiss mercenary soldiers pining for their native country while stationed in less mountainous regions of Europe.

RELATED TACTICS AND EXPLAINERS

#2. Look at something blue.
#3. Work under a lofty ceiling.
#4. Take in a view.
#5. Display art.
#14. Bring nature in.
#36. Dress nicely.
Explainer I: Space, Time, and Creativity

EXPLAINER I:

Space, Time, and Creativity

RELATED TACTICS

#2. Look at something blue.
#3. Work under a lofty ceiling.
#4. Take in a view.
#5. Display art.
#6. Think back.
#36. Dress nicely.

Have you ever been in an airplane flying over long stretches of flat farmland in the warm months, looked down, and noticed how much the scene below resembled an abstract painting, the land having been transformed into a patchwork of color, light and shade, and geometric patterning (Fig. 11)?

Now picture yourself down on the ground at the exact same spot. What do you see? Most likely, an assortment of perfectly recognizable objects—crop fields, a tractor resting idly nearby, a line of trees along the horizon.

In other words, the very same features you observed from far away look quite different when examined up close. Obviously, the objects themselves haven't changed. It's our mental impression of those objects that's shifted.

But it goes deeper than that. There's evidence that differences in vantage point not only influence how you see; they also influence how you think.

That's the underlying premise of Construal Level Theory (CLT), a somewhat awkwardly named hypothesis advanced by a trio of researchers in 2007. The basic idea behind CLT is that the distance from which you construe (i.e., interpret or analyze) an object or concept influences your

cognitive style. Gaze at an abstract arrangement of color and form spread across hundreds of acres from a mile away, the thinking goes, and your thoughts will soon turn abstract too. Scrutinize something you hold between your fingers, on the other hand, and both your vision and your mental outlook become more narrowly focused and concrete.

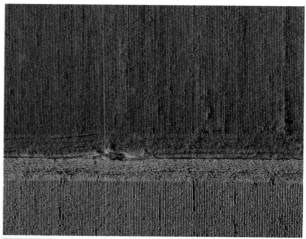

Fig. 11: Distant and proximate views of the same terrain.

Fig. 12: Travel poster for Scottish Motor Traction bus company (SMT). Artist unknown. c. 1930s.

Wave House. Malibu, California. Architecture and interior design by Mark Dziewulski Architect. Photography by Nico Marques.

Why is CLT relevant to creativity? Because abstract, big-picture thinking is a property of the same cognitive style that gives rise to novel ideas (Table 1). Stimuli that move you to assume this mind-set could therefore also stimulate your problem-solving acumen. This would explain why subjects primed by the color blue (#2), tall ceilings (#3), views (#4), and certain genres of artwork (#5) excelled on their creativity assessment tests, while those whose sense of dimensional space was constrained outperformed on analytic thinking exercises.

Proponents of CLT have identified several other metrics besides physical distance as sparking shifts in cognitive style. One is time. As I allude to in Tactic #6, objects and events that harken back to the past make us sensitive to the temporal gap that exists between then and now, engendering a feeling of apartness similar to what we experience when observing things far away physically. It's only logical that our mental state would respond similarly to either input. In that case, we can add CLT as one more possible explanation for the bump in creativity observed among subjects induced to think back in time (Fig. 12).

One other dimension linked to CLT is relevant to our area of interest. However, this particular metric has to do with neither architectural space nor time. Instead, it's based on the perception of *social* distance. You'll learn about it in Tactic #36.

TACTIC #7
EMBRACE DETAIL AND COMPLEXITY

God is in the detail.
—*Unknown, commonly attributed to Ludwig Mies van der Rohe*

The devil is in the details.
—*Unknown*

WHAT TO DO
Develop an idea space rich in visual content and distinct in shape.

WHY DO IT?
User surveys and clinical studies indicate that interiors with high levels of spatial and ornamental complexity can accelerate idea formation among occupants.

WHY DOES IT WORK?
Perhaps you've heard the famous credo attributed to Mies van der Rohe, the modernist architect known to pronounce that in matters of design, "less is more"? If so, ignore it—at least, when it comes to building out your creative space.

So advises a number of researchers who've studied the impact of visual complexity on creative output. Their general conclusion is that simpler isn't necessarily better. Environments that deviate from conventional cubic volumes, have visually arresting structural and architectural features, are stuffed with books, artwork, lamps, and other furnishings, afford views to the outside or adjacent spaces, employ naturally sourced or naturally inspired materials with animated surface patterns, and are infused with well-modulated detail, are consistently rated by users as having a greater potential to inspire innovative thinking than the pared-down, boxy spaces for which Mies and other practitioners of like-minded minimalism were and remain famous (or notorious, depending on your taste).

Living room cornice detail. Seaside, Florida. Architecture by Gary Brewer for Robert A.M. Stern Architects. Photography by Peter Aaron / Otto.

Why this is the case is a matter of speculation. One conjecture put forth by the authors of a 2002 study is that intricate environments "offer a promise of more information if explored," and are therefore "high in challenge."

This last term is significant. Challenge and creativity are often said to go hand in hand. Academics who study creative personalities frequently include a love of challenge in their list of persistent character traits. Teresa Amabile, a professor at the Harvard Business School, argues that challenging tasks—and an organization equipped to carry them out—are essential for workplace innovation and job satisfaction. Eminent psychologist and creativity scholar Mihaly Csikszentmihalyi concurs, noting that a creative problem must be formidable enough to motivate people to want to solve it, but not so daunting as to turn them off from trying. Even the keyword *problem* hints at impending mental adversity in the form of a hurdle to be overcome.

A visually intricate setting elicits other reactions in the observer linked to heightened creativity. In particular, it invites us to look around. As I point out in the case of artwork (#5), indoor greenery (#14), and in Explainer II, scientists have found that rapid side-to-side eye movement activates the opposing hemispheres in our brain, strengthening the neural connections between them, and making us more consummate creative thinkers.

Finally, richly appointed interiors energize our minds by stimulating our consciousness with a steady stream of sensory inputs. A room deprived of aesthetic interest, on the other hand, leads to boredom, which lessens our motivation to confront the creative challenges we set for ourselves.

Residence. Warsaw, Poland. Architecture and interior design by Jakub Szczęsny. Photography by Bartek Warzecha. Polish Modern Art Foundation and the National Centre for Culture. At an average width of four feet, this house is said to be the narrowest in the world.

Kitchen. Greenwich, Connecticut. Architecture by Vernon D. Swaback and Michael D. Wetzel for Swaback Architects + Planners. Interior design by Studio V Interiors. Photography by Olson Photographic.

HOW TO DO IT

Occupy spatially distinct surroundings. Inhabit spaces characterized by idiosyncratic proportions, complex floor plans, uniquely shaped ceilings, exposed structural members, openness to adjacent areas, and other distinctive features not ordinarily present in the quotidian white cube.

Invest in detail. Details come in many forms. Some varieties are three-dimensional and permanently fixed, such as moldings, trim, paneling and surfacing, built-ins and cabinetry, floor patterns and materials, and articulated structure. Others are decorative and either applied or independent of construction, including wall coverings and finishes, furnishings, equipment, fabrics and upholstery, lighting, hardware, artwork, and accessories.

Temper complexity with unity. More is sometimes too much. Chaotic, overstimulating surroundings can be every bit as neurologically debilitating as a monotonous setting. Avoid the increased stress levels, higher blood pressure, and risk of medical complications that can result from visual overload by composing your space with an eye toward aesthetic unity. Not sure what that means? Imagine you're leading a large orchestra. You could let everyone play whatever they wanted, and get noise. Or you could have them play in unison from the same score, and get music.

That's unity.

RELATED TACTICS AND EXPLAINERS

#5. Display art.
#12. Choose curved over straight.
#14. Bring nature in.
Explainer II: We Are Who We Have Always Been

TACTIC #8
PUT YOUR WALLS TO WORK

WHAT TO DO
Convert walls into surfaces for drawing, display, inspiration, idea development, and equipment storage.

WHY DO IT?
Working walls help you visualize your ideas, assume a big-picture perspective, stimulate creative exploration, encourage collaboration, facilitate feedback, and realize production.

WHY DOES IT WORK?
Where do you flesh out your creative ideas? On your computer? In a notebook? On a scattering of Post-its stuck to your desk? On a stack of index cards you tie together with a rubber band and carry around in a backpack? On the kitchen counter?

All of these are perfectly viable methods for coaxing incipient thoughts out of your head and into a form that you and others can work with. But if you really want to effectively collect, develop, organize, and implement your ideas, consider turning one or more of your walls at home into a giant drawing tablet, pinboard, or storage device.

Bringing your walls into the creative process offers several advantages. For starters, walls tend to be large relative to other types of work surfaces, which allows you to load them up with a lot of information simultaneously. This is especially helpful when you're dealing with complex undertakings, like storyboarding a feature-length video, or putting together an inspiration board for a sizable interior design project where you'd like to explore how the design elements relate to each other holistically rather than in fragments.

Having the means to amass so much content in one place, however, goes beyond mere convenience—it's a cognitive necessity. According to psychologists, the average human brain can only retain five to nine bits of information in short-term memory at one time. Once the limit is exceeded, something has to be pushed out to make room for fresh material. In some cases, the item to be replaced can be shifted to long-term memory, but it often simply evaporates. Externalizing your ideas and project data by offloading them to the equivalent of a surrogate brain preserves this precious content while freeing up your short-term memory for a continual inflow of new inputs.

The scale of most walls also makes them an excellent medium for achieving the kind of big-picture viewpoint that defines the creative mind-set (Table 1). For instance, instead of stacking your index cards so that only the one on top is visible at a given moment, you could tack them up on a wall in a grid, then step back to take them all in at a glance. The same applies to sketching and doodling—to think big, you want to draw big.

Another benefit of scale is that friends, family members, and coworkers can stand side by side with you as you develop your creative ideas. You'll be surprised how much more fluid co-creation can be when collaborators can occupy the same space and wield the same tools.

Drawing room. Photography by IdeaPaint.

But wait, there's more: working walls work on your behalf even when you're not working on them. How? By keeping your ideas and sources of inspiration on continuous display, others can come across them in the course of their day, and offer you valuable feedback in response. Sequester them in your head, in a notebook, a computer, or a drawer, and you could be depriving yourself of invaluable perspective.

Maybe best of all, working walls encourage you to think visually. This is a boon for everyone who traffics in fields dominated by pictorial content or who naturally think in images. The reason is that our brains can process pictures faster and with less mental energy than information delivered via word or number (unsurprisingly, given that our evolutionary ancestors could see long before they could communicate in written form). This goes equally for people in fields presumed to be analytic by nature, such as the sciences. Einstein was a case in point. "I very rarely think in words at all," he once told a psychologist. "A thought comes, and I may try to express it in words afterwards." (It's comforting to think that he and I have at least something in common.)

Still, nothing's perfect. A notable shortcoming of working walls is their general lack of portability—they are, after all, walls. One solution is to get yourself a whiteboard on wheels; however, even that piece of equipment is too cumbersome to take into bed or out of the home. That's where the notebook—or its modern-day-electronic equivalent—comes in. More on that in Tactic #40.

HOW TO DO IT

Apply whiteboard or chalkboard paint. A good way to enable displayed thinking in your creative space is to coat one or more walls with paints

Home office. London, United Kingdom. Interior design by Katy Orme for Apartment Apothecary. Photography by Katharine Peachey.

specially formulated for either a whiteboard or chalkboard finish. Both are commercially available, come in a multitude of colors, and can be laid down by anyone who can hold a brush. Achieving the desired sheen and smoothness, however, requires a bit more care and effort than standard paints, so be prepared to invest the time if you go DIY. Otherwise, hire a professional or wrangle a favor from a more brush-adept friend, family member, or colleague.

Do the same to other flat surfaces. Who says you have to confine yourself to doodling on your walls? The same paints can turn tabletops, appliance panels, cabinetry, and flush doors into writable surfaces as well.

Use whiteboard or chalkboard adhesive panels. If painting isn't in the cards, or if the wall you're looking to cover is modestly sized, consider self-adhesive whiteboard or chalkboard products in place of paint. They're sold in panel or roll form, and are a snap to install. Most of the products are designed to be removed without damaging the finish underneath, making them especially suitable for renters.

Line your walls with cork, Homasote, or magnetic products. Cork is a sustainable material that comes in rolls and tiles. It adds a beautifully variegated texture to the decor in addition to fulfilling its traditional pinup function.

Homasote is the trademarked name of a green commercial product made of recycled newsprint and wood fiber. It can be painted or covered in fabric should its dull gray factory finish strike you as, well, dull. Alternatively, you could spring for the company's cork-faced version to get the best of both worlds.

A third option is to mount your materials magnetically. Use tiles, boards, rolls, sheet metal, or special paint to make things stick. Be aware, however, that the holding power of some of these products is too weak to support objects much weightier than a sheet of paper.

Utilize Post-it notes, tape, mounting squares, binder clips, clipboards, picture hooks, pegboard, and other everyday hanging and fastener products. Use common adhesives and hardware to show your stuff, be it your creative output or the tools you use to realize it. The sight of them can be motivational.

Or explore nontraditional methods. Strand board, wood cladding soft enough to receive a pushpin, open wire mesh, string lights, and picture ledges are among the less traveled approaches to creating working walls I've come across.

RELATED TACTICS
#5. Display art.
#40. Pick up a pencil.
#41. Make stuff.

TACTIC #9
BE FLEXIBLE

Nothing is more dangerous than an idea when it is the only one you have.
—Émile Chartier

WHAT TO DO
Maintain a high level of flexibility in the design of your creative space.

WHY DO IT?
A creative mind is a flexible mind. A flexible space is a creative space.

WHY DOES IT WORK?
Tina Seelig has impeccable credentials in the field of creativity. She holds a PhD in neuroscience, teaches the subject at Stanford University, and at last count is the author of seventeen books, including *inGenius: A Crash Course on Creativity.* By the time you finish this paragraph she could well have written another.

She's also an energetic proselytizer for the idea of space as a creative tool.

Seelig came to this realization accidentally. She was teaching a class in creativity one day, and had split her students into two camps. Each camp received a different jigsaw puzzle to solve. The two camps were divided again to make four competitive teams in total. Seelig structured the game so that there was a hidden incentive for the two teams in each camp to work in concert in order to gain the greatest number of points.

As it happened, Seelig assigned one camp to an area of the room containing only chairs, the other to an area having just tables. The division was purely fortuitous; the furnishings had simply been left that way. Yet her unwitting decision to introduce furniture as a design variable in the exercise turned out to profoundly affect the outcome. Recalls Seelig:

> Remarkably, the students . . . on the side of the room with the chairs (but no tables) almost instantly started to collaborate with one another. Within minutes, the chairs were rearranged into one large circle or pushed aside altogether, as they worked on the puzzles on the floor. They figured out that by working together, they earned the maximum number of points for the game. On the other hand, the teams on the side of the room with tables (but no chairs) all anchored themselves to their respective tables. They did not collaborate at all and thus ended up limiting the number of points each team earned.

What happened was clear: the teams with the chairs came up with a creative solution to the problem by treating their furniture as a cognitive asset, to be commandeered or dispensed with as the situation dictated. The students gathered at the tables, on the other hand, blindly accepted the status quo, blinding them to the fact that their tables were

Studio apartment. New York, New York. Interior design by Andreas Messis, Stuart Reisch and Rozalia Kiss for transFORM. Photography by Ken Stabile.

on casters, and could have been moved around as well. Perhaps it was because tables don't speak of mobility as explicitly as chairs that led the losing teams to miss the opportunity to have the furniture work for them, rather than against them.

Why is fluidity of mind and space so important to creative problem solving? Because without it we're prone to slide into a rigid and inelastic mind-set, fall into creative ruts, resort to the tried-and-true, or stubbornly stick with a line of thought long after it's proven a dead end. More positively, mental and spatial versatility allows us to adapt to change, see both sides of the coin, and discover connections between concepts that had previously gone unnoticed.

Reconfigurable kitchen, with wheeled island, cabinetry, and stair platform. Philip Island, Victoria, Australia. Architecture by Andrew Simpson, Charles Anderson, and Emma Parkinson for Andrew Simpson Architects. Photography by Peter Bennetts.

"A foolish consistency is the hobgoblin of little minds," Ralph Waldo Emerson famously wrote about those who resist change, forever giving hobgoblins—and small-bore thinkers—a bad name.

HOW TO DO IT

Let it roll. Our tendency these days to take a set-it-and-forget-it approach to furniture placement can hinder the quality of adaptability that creative space thrives on. Overcome the inertia of laissez-faire decorating by attaching wheels to the undersides of your furnishings, then shift pieces around as needs or whims dictate.

Lighten up. Another strategy for turning static space into flex space is to utilize lightweight furniture that can be comfortably rearranged without hiring a mover or asking your burly neighbor for a hand. Seating is particularly rich in this category, unsurprisingly in light of how closely it's aligned with the body. Plenty of options exist for movable office chairs, but for living areas and secondary seating, consider outliers like foam-filled ottoman cubes, beanbag chairs, inflatable sofas, and soft seating systems that sit directly on the floor rather than on feet.

Make mine modular. My favorite type of mutable furnishing utilizes a standardized unit that can be combined and recombined in an infinite variety of permutations. Modular sofas are the best known example of reconfigurable design, but the range of household goods that fall in this

Game table. Designed and fabricated by David Roentgen. German. c. 1780–83. Metropolitan Museum of Art, New York.

category has greatly expanded over recent years. Among them are lighting, seating, shelving and storage, tableware, cookware, artwork, decorative accessories, games and toys, and even clothing.

Get things that multitask. We're well past the days where one's only piece of convertible furniture was likely to be a sleep sofa. How about a couch that turns into a pool table instead? An ironing board that doubles as a mirror? Or a work surface that folds into a whiteboard by day, a Ping-Pong table by night? All of these ideas for functional mash-ups have come off the boards of real designers. I can understand why there's so much interest in this type of design—transformable furniture adds tremendous value by saving space and expanding the usefulness of rooms beyond the single purpose to which we too often confine them.

Layer purpose on purpose. Speaking of mono-functional spaces, you could have much more home than you think you have by doubling, tripling, and quadrupling up on the roles a space plays. Sometimes the bonus function is yours for the taking; a folding table in a laundry room, for instance, is a perfect spot for kids to make art between loads. In other cases a strategic investment in infrastructure and some moveable furniture can pay off big-time. Picture a room fitted out with a sleekly updated version of a Murphy bed and a wall of built-ins serving simultaneously as a sleeping area, dressing room, sitting area, and study.

Paper softblock partitioning system by molo. Product designed by Stephanie Forsythe + Todd MacAllen. Vancouver, Canada. 2003. Photography by molo.

Use soft partitioning. Conventional fixed-in-place walls are a commitment to rigidly segmented space. Walls on wheels, movable partitions, curtaining, and adjustable screens give you greater freedom to compartmentalize your surroundings to best suit the task at hand.

Control the ambience. Flexibility needn't be limited to material elements. You can also manipulate intangible environmental conditions such as sound, lighting, and temperature by means of audio controls (#18), programmable lights (#20), dimmer switches (#21), and thermostats (#23).

RELATED TACTICS

#8. Put your walls to work.

#18. Make music.

#20. Be smart with your lighting.

#21. Dim the lights.

#23. Adjust the thermostat.

TACTIC #10
FACE YOUR SPACE

WHAT TO DO

Arrange your furnishings and equipment so that you face into your creative space and have a wall or opaque screening element behind you.

WHY DO IT?

Scientists theorize that humans are happiest and most secure in their environment when they have a clear field of vision while feeling protected from behind and above.

WHY DOES IT WORK?

Imagine you're a notorious gangster. Sure, you've got enemies, but you never let that stop you from having a good time. So three nights a week you go to your favorite restaurant for dinner.

Everyone at the restaurant knows the drill. The maître d' escorts you to your customary table at the far end of the room, bowing deeply at the waist nearly the entire distance. You sit down on a tufted leather banquette angled into a corner. A pair of wall sconces hung a few feet over your head bounce a diffuse light off the ceiling above.

From this perch you can observe every person in the restaurant. It also affords an unobstructed line of sight to the door. All looks clear. You let out a breath, then order your usual repast with an expression hovering somewhere between a smile and a snarl.

Now jump back 50,000 years in time. You're no longer a well-dressed criminal; instead, you're a primitive inhabitant of the sprawling East African savanna. Walking along flat ground one day, you spy a pack of predatory animals racing toward you in the distance. They appear intent on converting a zebra herd grazing nearby into lunch. Something inside your capacious cranium says that getting caught flat-footed in the middle of the impending carnage might be injurious to your health, so

you instinctively search for a safe harbor. Fortunately, there's a rise in the terrain on your flank. It's dotted with shrubbery and a few scattered trees with spreading saucer-shaped canopies. Your heart racing, you make haste to haul yourself onto the rise and squat down alongside some brush, where you can survey the action below without revealing yourself.

The carnage over, you take a moment to examine your hiding spot. You soon realize you've stumbled on a real find—a place that affords both prospect and refuge, surveillance and safety.

You rush off to grunt the good news to your fellow tribesmen, who later return with you to begin erecting a new habitat.

Get the connection? Both the gangster and the African plainsman found themselves in situations where they were vulnerable to physical harm. Both responded by locating positions within their environments that protected their blind spots—behind and above—while simultaneously extending visual control over the scene before them. By doing so, they not only survived, but were able to derive pleasure from the experience—the gangster got his meal unharmed, the plainsman a secure settlement. Needless to say, both were happy and inwardly relieved at the turn of events.

The suggestion of an intrinsic connection between vantage point, survival, and emotional well-being has led some academics to theorize that humans are instinctually drawn to locations that provide a balance between seeing and sanctuary. British geographer Jay Appleton was the first to propose the theory of prospect-refuge in his 1975 book *The Experience of Landscape*. Appleton frames his discussion largely in terms of the human response to views of nature, both actual and artistic, but his ideas have direct application to how we orient ourselves

Living and dining room. Toronto, Ontario, Canada. Architecture and interior design by Gloria Apostolou for Post Architecture. Photography by Arnaud Marthouret for Revelateur Studio.

in interior space as well. Grant Hildebrand, for instance, wrote an entire book proposing prospect-refuge theory as a driver of the work of Frank Lloyd Wright. Adherents of feng shui evoke similar themes in describing a desk with a view of a door as occupying a "commanding position."

I suppose some of you are wondering why you should bother adhering to the precepts of prospect-refuge in your creative space when you're neither a member of organized crime nor fifty thousand years old. My answer is this: the need to feel happy and secure in your environment is encoded into your DNA, regardless of whether you have literal cause for concern or not. Once that need is subverted, however subliminally, we're programmed to become more alert and attuned to the potential for harm—a state of mind directly contrary to the relaxed, risk-tolerant, explorative,

and flexible outlook necessary for the free flow of ideas.

HOW TO DO IT

Find an edge. Situate yourself along the edge of your space and orient your furnishings so that you look into the room and have a wall or solid element behind you.

Avoid backing up against a wall that contains a passage into the room, however; this conflicts with the psychological need for feeling protected from unseen threats. Ideally, interior openings will be opposite or perpendicular from where you're generally located during creative periods.

Compensate where necessary. Situations inevitably arise where you're compelled to face a wall or expose your back to an entryway. This commonly occurs where desks are placed in blind

*Study. Battleground, Oregon. Building design by
Blondino Design. Interior design by Garrison Hullinger.
Photography by Blackstone Edge Studios.*

*Home office. Pawleys Island, South Carolina. Building
design by Wall Building & Design. Interior design by Lance
Griffith for CHD Interiors. Photography by Matt Silk.*

alcoves, a space is too small or narrow to have freestanding furniture or equipment, or a view is so alluring that it seems criminal not to plunk yourself right smack in front of a window.

You can take steps to mitigate the downsides. For workspaces set into an alcove, consider adorning the back wall with artwork, wall coverings, paint colors, and materials that prime concepts of distance or nature to ameliorate the shallowness of the space. Another option is to hang a mirror that will give you a view back into the room, and allow you to spot people coming into the space. A mirror could work equally well for desks and upright pianos butted up against a wall.

Should you succumb to the lure of a great view, you can still assume a defensive position by placing a piece of furniture behind you to serve as a psychological barrier against your rear flank. Besides subtly improving peace of mind, the piece could also add welcome functionality and, for extra measure, fill an awkward void in the furniture plan.

Another option: rotate your work surface so that it's perpendicular to the window. You'll maintain your access to the view, enjoy the light, and be a tad less tempted to gorge yourself on the vista when you should be working.

RELATED TACTICS AND EXPLAINERS

#2. Look at something blue.

#4. Take in a view.

#6. Think back.

#8. Put your walls to work.

#14. Bring nature in.

Explainer II: We Are Who We Have Always Been

TACTIC #11
GATHER IN A CIRCLE

WHAT TO DO
Gather 'round a circular table, or in a radial seating arrangement, or in a centrally planned space while socializing or brainstorming with others.

WHY DO IT?
Research shows that people behave more collaboratively when arranged in radial patterns and in centralized spaces than when placed in rows and in non-centric environments.

WHY DOES IT WORK?
Legendary computer animator and head of Pixar Animation Studios Ed Catmull tells a revealing story about a meeting room table in his book *Creativity, Inc.: Overcoming the Unseen Forces That Stand in the Way of True Inspiration*. I present it here, lightly edited for length:

> For thirteen years we had a table in the large conference room at Pixar. Though it was beautiful, I grew to hate this table. It was long and skinny, like one of those things you'd see in a comedy sketch about an old wealthy couple that sits down for dinner— one person at either end, a candelabra in the middle—and has to shout to make conversation. The table had been chosen by a designer Steve Jobs liked, and it was elegant, all right—but it impeded our work.

Conversation pit. Richmond, Victoria, Australia. Architecture by alsoCAN Architects. Interior design by Garth Euvrard and Jane McDougall of alsoCAN Architects. Photography by Urban Angles.

Darn those designers for trying to bring beauty into the world! But I digress. Back to you, Ed:

> We'd hold regular meetings about our movies around that table—thirty of us facing off in two long lines, often with more people seated along the walls—and everyone was so spread out that it was difficult to communicate. For those unlucky enough to be seated at the far ends, ideas didn't flow because it was nearly impossible to make eye contact without craning your neck.
>
> It wasn't until we happened to have a meeting in a smaller room with a square table that [the Chief Creative Officer] and I realized what was wrong. Sitting around that table, the interplay was better, the exchange of ideas more free-flowing, the eye contact automatic. Every person there, no matter their job title, felt free to speak up. This was not only what we wanted, it was a fundamental Pixar belief: Unhindered communication was key, no matter what your position. At our long, skinny table, comfortable in our middle seats, we had utterly failed to recognize that we were behaving contrary to that basic tenet.
>
> Emboldened by this new insight, I went to our facilities department. "Please," I said, "I don't care how you do it, but get that table out of there."

Dining room and library. Albemarle County, Virginia. Architecture and interior design by Dagliesh Gilpin Paxton Architects. Photography by Gordon Beall.

And out it went.

Now, I doubt you have thirty people gathered around your living room to brainstorm creative ideas terribly often. Probably never, in fact. But you almost certainly have other people in your household either on a regular basis or from time to time, be they family members, relatives, room-mates, friends, guests, coworkers, caregivers, or assorted hangers-on who've wandered into your good graces. Whatever reason they have for being there, these individuals can be as valuable a source of creative insights as your own self, whether through normal social interaction or by intentionally pursuing opportunities for cooperative idea streaming. Indeed, as innovation expert David Burkus argues in his book *The Myths of Creativity*, the image of the creative figure as a loner operating outside of a social or intellectual milieu is exactly that—an essay in mythology. The truth is, we need others to drive our imagination. What more fitting place to engage with people for that purpose than in the creative cauldron that is home?

Your goal, then, should be to harness this potential wellspring of inspiration by fostering the free exchange of ideas among those within your household. As Ed Catmull and his fellow Pixalytes discovered, furniture can make or break that initiative. Too bad they had to learn the lesson the hard way—especially since they could have avoided the whole sorry episode had Steve Jobs's designer of choice heard of a British psychiatrist named Humphry Osmond before specifying that table of tears.

Osmond's biography is colorful and accomplished. Back in the 1950s he conducted extensive research on the effects of LSD on alcoholics and schizophrenics, convinced that hallucinogenic drugs could ease their conditions. His investigations purportedly brought him into contact with the CIA and MI6, who were probably salivating at the thought of a truth drug capable of prying open the minds and mouths of insufficiently talkative enemy agents. Among pop culturalists he's remembered for having coined the term "psychedelic" and for supplying Aldous Huxley with the mescaline hit that led to the book *The Doors of Perception* (and the name of a legendary sixties rock band).

A lesser known side of the man was his interest in the social dimension of architectural design. Osmond was drawn to the subject after seeing firsthand how poorly the architects and designers of his day appreciated the emotional needs of mental patients when building facilities for their care. Out of this experience came a conviction that the environment has the power to segregate people or bring them together, depending on how it's planned and furnished.

Osmond undoubtedly would have pointed to the first incarnation of the Pixar meeting room as a perfect example of space that elevates the individual over the collective. And he would have been right. The problem obviously wasn't the staff, who were undoubtedly talented; it was that they were oriented in a grid pattern relative to each other owing to the shape of the table and room (Figs. 13–14). Seating grids are good for maintaining top-down hierarchies (think rows of school desks facing the teacher at the front), but they tend to quell interactions within a group, all attention being focused on a single authority figure (think rows of school desks facing the teacher at

Fig. 13: Classroom seating in the Industrial Age. Oregon. Early twentieth century. Gifford Photographic Collection, OSU Special Collections & Archives Research Center.

Fig. 14: Workplace seating in the Industrial Age. Shop floor at the Atwater Kent Radio Factory, Philadelphia. 1925. Everett Historical Collection.

the front). They're particularly anathematic to creative organizations. The last thing you want in an innovation-driven enterprise is for employees to turn into human bobbleheads every time the high-ranking individual seated at the head of the table (CEO, department manager, team leader) throws out an idea, which invariably receives approbation for obvious political reasons, while those relegated to spatial Siberia struggle to have their voices heard. Ideas need to be evaluated democratically and on the merits if the best are to see the light.

Osmond would have used the same reasoning to explain why the second meeting room at Pixar succeeded where the first had failed. The grid was gone. People now sat in a concentric pattern around a piece of furniture with equal sides, which in turn focused attention toward the center of the table rather than on the kingmakers seated on its periphery. In effect, the table became a gigantic idea basket into which ideas could be tossed and hashed over cooperatively. People felt like they belonged. Everyone saw themselves as equal. Creativity thrived.

Osmond called these two types of space *sociofugal* and *sociopetal* (he clearly had a knack for the nifty neologism). The first term reflects the tendency of grid patterns to channel energy outward, i.e., centrifugally; the second to direct focus inwardly toward a center, i.e., centripetally (Fig. 15).

Now, perhaps you're wondering, if oblong tables are so detrimental to idea origination in intergroup situations, why do the vast majority of corporate boardrooms, conference rooms, and even innovation rooms still have them? The short answer is, old habits die hard. The longer answer is that they're a legacy of another era, when top-down management practices prevailed and there was a strict division between the people expected to come up with ideas and those assigned to carry out the manual labor needed to realize them.

One final detail in Catmull's story is worth noting. He mentions that the second room was smaller than the first. It's conceivable that this space was concentric in plan, or close to it, since that would be an impetus for installing a square table over a rectangular one. If so, it would underscore the point that the psychosocial potency of non-gridded planning permeates beyond the geography of furniture. Rooms, buildings, and even cities designed on its principles can promote interpersonal harmony as well.

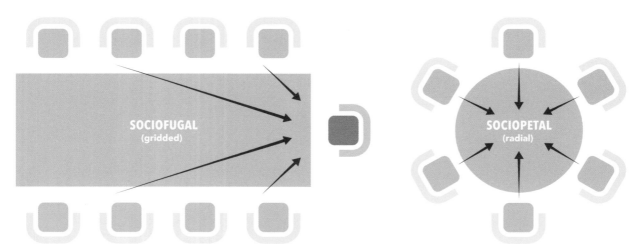

Fig. 15: Sociofugal (gridded) versus sociopetal (radial) seating arrangements. After Humphry Osmond (1957).

Outdoor lounge. Scottsdale, Arizona. Architecture by Tate Studio Architects. Landscape design by Desert Foothills Landscape. Photography by Thompson Photographic.

HOW TO DO IT

Don't go straight. Opt for circular tables in work areas, dining rooms, and living spaces—anywhere people gather in groups. (Catmull's square table could work too, but circular tends to be more flexible in the number of people that can gather around it comfortably.) Consider the same for sofas, banquettes, and outdoor seating.

Get off the grid. Resist the temptation to arrange the furniture in your seating cluster exclusively at right angles to each other. Inject a curved element or skew pieces in the grouping to relax its rectilinear quality and more closely approximate a concentric condition.

Find pushy furniture. Rather than have people come to the furniture, have the furniture come to the people. Locate pieces you can move into a radial arrangement when appropriate to encourage social engagement and cross-promote idea exchange.

Centralize your space. Rooms shaped according to concentric geometries amplify the collaborative influence of circular tables and radial seating. If you don't have one, get one. If you can't get one, try manipulating the existing decor to focus attention toward a common center point. Appropriately designed ceiling ornaments, floor coverings, and lighting fixtures can contribute to the desired effect.

RELATED TACTICS
#9. Be flexible.
#12. Choose curved over straight.
#13. Stand up for yourself.

TACTIC #12
CHOOSE CURVED OVER STRAIGHT

In life, as in art, the beautiful moves in curves.
—*Edward Robert Bullwer-Lytton*

WHAT TO DO
Pursue creative activities in settings dominated by rounded shapes.

WHY DO IT?
Curved objects and spaces make us happy and less fearful; being happy and less fearful makes us more creative.

WHY DOES IT WORK?
If you want to know what makes people happy, just ask them.

In 2012 a pair of researchers ran an experiment in which over a hundred subjects looked at four computer-generated perspectives of the sort of furniture grouping you might have had in your living room growing up. Each ensemble consisted of a sofa, one or two lounge chairs, a couple of side tables, a lamp, a coffee table, and an area rug. Two of the renderings contained furnishings that were predominantly curved in contour and detail. The other two showed pieces characterized by straight lines and squared-off shapes (Fig. 16).

The researchers took steps to keep anything unrelated to the form factor out of the picture. The renderings were printed in grayscale to make color choices a nonissue. Artwork was absent from the walls, while the furnishings lacked decorative embellishments. From a style standpoint

Fig. 16: Psychological effects of straight versus curved furniture. After Sibel S. Dazkir and Marilyn A. Read (2012).

everything visible could be charitably categorized as Comfortably Generic Modern.

Administrators then asked subjects to rate the images according to how pleasing they found their contents, how much time they'd want to spend in the pictured environment, and how sociable the simulated setting made them feel.

The results came in: rounded beat rectilinear by every measure.

Intriguing. But how does our innate preference for the sinuous over the straight enhance our creativity?

Maybe I can answer this best by asking you a question: have you ever cut yourself with a spoon?

I didn't think so.

How about with a knife?

I figured as much.

So what do you think happens to your unconscious mind when you pick up a big cutting knife to slice the turkey for Thanksgiving? I'll tell you

Atrium, living, and dining areas. Pine Lake, Village of Chenequa, Wisconsin. Architecture by Robert Harvey Oshatz. Photography by Cameron R. Neilson.

what: it enters into an elevated state of alert. Not exactly overt panic, but enough to prompt you to play closer attention to how you handle the implement than when you're ladling Cheerios into your mouth for breakfast.

Now, partly that reaction is the result of learned experience. But partly it's the result of human beings being innately conditioned to feel more comfortable and relaxed at the sight of curved things than at straight things, regardless of whether they're a literal threat to our well-being. Why did Mother Nature endow us with this response mechanism? Probably to ensure our survival back in our caveman days, when straight-edged and pointy stuff (jagged rock outlines, animal teeth) really did constitute a clear and present danger,

while rounded shapes (a newborn baby, foliage) generally signaled safety. These impulses affect us to this very day, to where we're psychologically at greater ease with curved objects than with hard-edged things.

Several brain imaging studies confirm these preferences. One investigation discovered that our *amygdala*—the region of the brain responsible for processing fear—jumps in activity at the sight of everyday objects formed from flat planes and sharp angles. Another found that our comfort with curves extends to shaping interior space as a whole. As in the 2012 experiment I described above, researchers pitted one suite of interior design images against another—picture designer Karim Rashid, the king of the curvaceous contour,

Floating home. Williamette River, Portland, Oregon. Architecture by Robert Harvey Oshatz. Photography by Cameron R. Neilson.

Living room details. Beverlywood, Los Angeles, California. Interior design by Lucie Ayres for 22 Interiors. Photography by Amy Bartlam.

in the ring with architect Mies van der Rohe, a man who never met a straight line he didn't like—to see if the difference in morphology made any difference in the subjects' assessment of their aesthetic qualities. Indeed it did: subjects judged the curvilinear environments the more beautiful of the two by a noticeable margin. Using the fMRI scans, researchers were able to trace the source of these judgments to the section of the brain responsive to reward, aesthetic appreciation, and emotion.

Now let's connect the dots. Straight stuff puts us on edge, so to speak. Being on edge makes a person classically convergent, which is to say, wary, trepidatious, and neophobic, i.e., reluctant to delve further into the new and unknown until the perception of threat passes. Curved stuff and spaces, by contrast, relax us because their rounded contours present no sharp edges or pointy corners to do us harm. Relaxed, we let down our guard, defocus our attention, and enter into a divergent, creative frame of mind.

When it comes to shaping the optimal idea space, the choice is clear: choose curved over straight.

HOW TO DO IT

For ground-up and remodeling projects:
Design your creative environment with curved walls, soffits, ceiling shapes, openings, and other non-rectilinear architectural features. Avoid butting flat planes against each other without any mediating elements (e.g., walls meeting other walls, floors, and ceilings).

In an optimally curvaceous world, the only thing that would be continuously straight would be the floor.

For retrofitting an existing space: Let's say you already occupy a boxy space with squared-off openings and straightened details galore. What can you do to soften the rectilinearity of your surroundings without having to call for a dumpster?

Here's a suggestion: find opportunities to add curved or flexible elements of a decorative or applied nature. Hanging a window valance in a swag, for instance, will turn a horizontal element into a graciously curved one. Placing a wavy room divider fashioned from pliable bamboo forward of a wall might moderate its flatness. Installing a cove molding at the top of a bare wall could relax the harsh angularity of its abutment to the ceiling plane.

Graphic solutions are another option. Hire a trompe l'oeil painter to transform your blank walls into convincingly curved Baroque phantasms of architecture. Or grab a brush and apply some DIY patterning of your own.

Get round stuff. New or renovated, populate your space with objects that are rounded in profile, detail, section, and plan. Ditch everything else.

RELATED TACTICS AND EXPLAINERS

#2. Look at something blue.
#7. Embrace detail and complexity.
#11. Gather in a circle.
#14. Bring nature in.
#16. Make it beautiful.
Explainer II: We Are Who We Have Always Been

Kitchen. Paradise Valley, Arizona. Architecture by Jon C. Bernhard, AIA, for Swaback Architects + Planners. Interior design by Studio V Interiors. Photography by Dino Tonn.

TACTIC #13
STAND UP FOR YOURSELF

WHAT TO DO
Stand instead of sit while in creative mode.

WHY DO IT?
Sitting in a chair for long periods of time diminishes health. Diminished health jeopardizes creativity (not to mention survival).

WHY DOES IT WORK?
I imagine a lot of health experts would love to stick a label on the side of every desk chair manufactured in the world. The label would read something like this: "Warning: The majority opinion of the scientific community is that extended use of this product could be injurious to your physical and psychological well-being."

In all likelihood, the first person to volunteer to apply the labels will be Dr. James Levine. He's the author of *Get Up! Why Your Chair Is Killing You and What You Can Do About It,* and director of the Mayo Clinic-Arizona State University Obesity Solutions Initiative.

Levine minces few words when it comes to proclaiming the dark side of desk life. "Sitting is more dangerous than smoking, kills more people than HIV and is more treacherous than parachuting. We are sitting ourselves to death," he writes.

Or, if you like your sentences short, "Sitting is the new smoking."

Sounds bad. But the arguments against prolonged sedentariness are well-substantiated. One study showed that men who spend at least six hours a day in a chair had a 20 percent higher death rate than those sitting under three hours. Women

suffered worse, with a 40 percent increase. Another found that men who sat for at least twenty-three hours a week during leisure time were 64 percent more likely to die from heart disease than those topping out at eleven hours per week.

And that's just the beginning of our problems (or worse, their end). A chair-based lifestyle threatens us with a menu of malicious maladies, including weight gain, high cholesterol levels, high blood pressure, back pain, and risk of diabetes and cancer.

It's enough to scare you sitless.

You have to wonder, though: why is sitting so bad for us when it's such a natural, everyday pose?

Let's begin with the fact that it isn't all that natural. One glance at the kind of landscape from which our species emerged a couple of hundred thousand years ago shows why: there weren't an abundance of places to sit the way we sit in chairs (Fig. 17 and Explainer I). Nor would it have mattered much if there were; early *Homo sapiens* were too busy hunting and gathering and fleeing from hungry animals to have enjoyed them. Life was consumed with survival, and our ancestors' minds, muscles, and skeletal structure

Fig. 17: Evolution or devolution? A stage model of human posture.

Kitchen. Wells, Maine. Interior design by Deborah Farrand for Dressing Rooms. Photography by Eric Roth.

were engineered through evolution to satisfy this imperative. Standing, walking, and running advanced that goal. So did squatting, insofar as it allowed humans to rest in place free of external supports (and still does in many parts of the world). Sitting? Not so much.

What, then, can today's chair-bound creatives do to avoid literal and figurative death by desk?

One solution is to switch from a traditional to a standing desk. Standing desks have a long and distinguished pedigree. Thomas Jefferson designed an adjustable six-legged version so he could read, write, and draw architectural plans in one place. Ernest Hemingway, Napoleon, August Wilson, Winston Churchill, Kierkegaard, Maxwell Perkins, Oscar Hammerstein, Otto von Bismarck, Virginia Woolf, Stan Lee, and Oliver

Wendell Holmes Jr. did some of their finest work at them. Michael Dell and Jimmy Kimmel swear by them. In fact, it's the sheer number of notable figures who've availed themselves of this particular piece of equipment over the years that validates its worth as an idea engine.

That said, the scientific evidence linking active desks to *immediate* improvements in creative productivity is mixed. A 2017 study, for instance, found that people working at standing desks demonstrated increased interest and enthusiasm in their efforts to solve creative problems, but failed to register measurable gains in task performance.

A 2014 experiment conducted in a workplace environment was more positive. Researchers observed that employees who had to stay on their feet for lack of enough chairs collaborated with greater efficiency on their creative exercises than those who found seats. The authors of the paper speculate that being free to move around activated a sense of group belonging among those who stood, similar to the psycho-spatial response to circular seating arrangements described in Tactic #12. However, if that were the cause, then the boost in creativity is less attributable to being upright per se than to the mobility that came from being unshackled from chairs and tables (see #9).

Still, it's hard to argue with the roster of high achievers who've stood up for standing desks (by the way, did I mention Lewis Carroll, Philip Roth, Johannes Brahms, Edward R. Murrow, and Vladimir Nabokov in my earlier list?). It might just be one of those situations where a thousand geniuses can't be wrong. Or look at it this way: any mechanism that can lift us out of our ass-magnets for even a few hours a day has to benefit our health, our brains, and our butts. And that's good enough for me.

HOW TO DO IT

Get a standing desk. Standing desks are man-ufactured in a broad range of styles, configura-tions, and price points. Some are designed to be placed on top of a conventional desk, others are freestanding. There are fixed-height desks, adjustable height and angle desks, and desks that can move up and down on lifts for toggling back and forth between standing and sitting positions.

You could also design a standing desk as part of a larger built-in.

Then there's the DIY option. In truth, any desk can be made for standing simply by posi-tioning the tabletop at the appropriate height. (If you're on a computer, that's the height where your forearms are level with the floor when your hands are at the keyboard.) Desktop converters, lecterns, and monitor mounts that can be set on top of a standard desk when needed to elevate

Fig. 18: Interior From Amaliegade with the Artist's Brothers, *by Wilhelm Bendz. Danish. c. 1829. Hirschsprung Collection, Copenhagen.*

your work surface and equipment to the required heights can be bought or built as well.

Cushion your sole. Standing in a static position for prolonged periods can cause muscle and joint pain. Relieve pressure and fatigue by standing on an air-cushioned floor mat. Or try a balance board. They're small platforms resting on four cushioned feet pliant enough to let you rock back and forth while you work.

Hop on a treadmill desk. Treadmill desks, also known as exercise desks, are bulkier and usually more expensive than their stationary counterparts owing to the addition of pricey machinery. Then again, you might find the expense to be less than the cost of a recurring gym membership.

Take a look at seated alternatives. If the idea of a standing or treadmill desk doesn't get you up in the morning, consider alternatives like pedal desks, wobble stools, and exercise balls. They can counteract the injurious effects of static seating by inducing physical movement.

Diversify. The best seating plan is a diverse seating plan. Avoid the physical harm and mental lethargy that stem from sitting in the same position hour after hour by changing your stance throughout the day. A simple method is to push your chair or stool behind you at regular intervals and stand up while you work. Or set up multiple workstations,

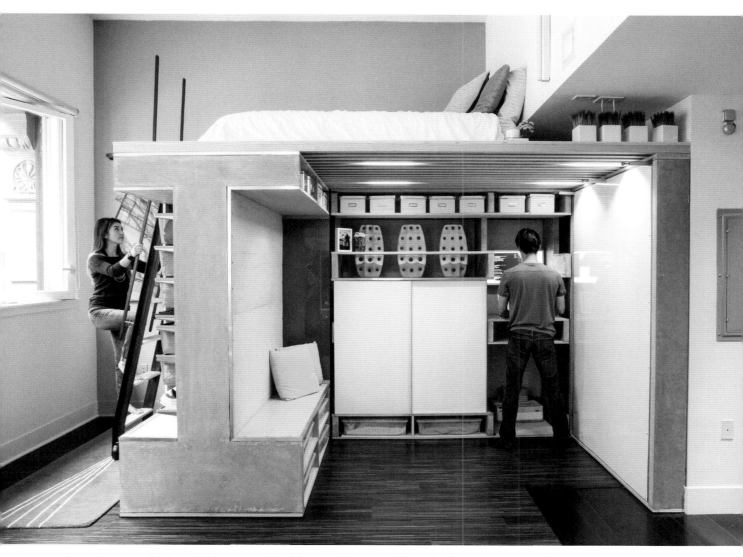

Studio. San Francisco, California. Architecture by Charles Irby for ICOSA Design and Peter Suen for FifthArch. Photography by Brian Flaherty.

one of which could be stand-biased. Regular breaks (#37) and walks (#38)—even if only taken around the room—can help too.

Find something else to do. Still can't extract yourself from your chair? Maybe it's time to take up a new hobby (#42). Easel painting, cooking, and gardening are three creative pursuits guaranteed to keep you on your feet.

RELATED TACTICS AND EXPLAINERS

#9. Be flexible.

#11. Gather in a circle.

#12. Choose curved over straight.

#37. Take a break.

#38. Go for a walk.

#42. Pursue a hobby.

#47. Get out of the house.

Explainer II: We Are Who We Have Always Been

EXPLAINER II:

We Are Who We Have Always Been

RELATED TACTICS

#2. Look at something blue.

#3. Work under a lofty ceiling.

#4. Take in a view.

#10. Face your space.

#12. Choose curved over straight.

#13. Stand up for yourself.

#14. Bring nature in.

#19. Let in natural light.

#20. Be smart with your lighting.

#29. Make a fire. Or look at a picture of one.

#38. Go for a walk.

Prospect-refuge. Approach-avoidance. Locus of control. Biophilia. Circadian cycle. Cavemen. The African savanna. With so many references to creatures, concepts, and conditions rooted in the prehistoric era sprinkled throughout this book, you could be excused for wondering whether you've picked up a primer for brain-based design or a textbook on the early evolution of mankind.

Truth be told, this book is about both, though not in equal measure. The intersection of home design and idea birthing is clearly the focus. But it's nearly impossible to explain why many of the tactics I present in these pages have their effect on human cognition without resorting to scientific theories regarding the evolutionary development of the human mind. My dependence on this information springs from an existential paradox: our bodies might be born in the present, but parts of our brain think we're still in the primordial past.

How far back in the past is subject to debate. Some scientists believe the human brain reached the size and shape it is today about 190,000 years ago. Others agree with that assessment, but take issue with the implication that the brains of first generation *Homo sapiens* therefore functioned more or less the same as ours. They posit instead that the brain only attained its current cognitive capacity about 50,000 years ago, around the time that the first flowerings of human culture began to emerge in Africa and Europe. Still others take the opposite tack, going back a whopping 2.5 million years to locate the foundations of our psychological framework among the earliest hominids.

Personally, I'm happy to let the experts duke it out at their leisure. Whatever they ultimately decide, the fact remains that our neural circuitry is remarkably similar to the wiring that made our ancestors tick eons ago. From this it can be inferred that our responses to certain external stimuli should be the same too. But here's the rub: the external world we live in has changed dramatically over the millennia. Our storehouse of knowledge and insight has grown enormously. Most of us are in far less danger of being hurt or starved by external forces. Life expectancy is off the charts compared to times past. And yet, despite our progress, we're still directed by outmoded impulses for preservation and perpetuation, whether it's sitting with our back to the wall in a coffee shop, happily exploring the boundaries of a blue room, or inwardly tensing at the sight of a sharp-edged piece of furniture.

The branch of science that studies the earliest development of human thought, emotion, and behavior is called *evolutionary psychology*. Think of it as

Ngorongoro Crater, Ngorongoro Conservation Area, Tanzania. Photography by Blaine Harrington III.

the psychological equivalent of classic evolutionary theory, as served up by Mr. Darwin and his followers, except that instead of exploring human development through the medium of the human body, it does so through the lens of the human mind.

Now, if there's one thing that all evolutionary scientists do agree on, it's that evolution moves very slowly. Really, really slowly. So slowly, that our brains haven't had sufficient time to adapt to modern conditions. This begins to explain why we react to environmental cues in ways that on the surface seem to defy rational analysis, and why it's possible to reverse engineer the knowledge gleaned from evolutionary psychology to shape happy, healthy, and creative places.

It also begins to explain why incorporating elements of organic nature into your home is one of the most powerful techniques for optimizing creativity at your disposal. I explore this tactic in the next section.

TACTIC #14
BRING NATURE IN

WHAT TO DO
Integrate nature into your creative space.

WHY DO IT?
Scientists have uncovered substantial evidence that exposure to organic nature boosts creativity.

WHY DOES IT WORK?
Theories abound.

One school of thought is founded on the notion that our brains have limited capacity to sustain the high level of concentration needed to perform challenging tasks, such as conceiving novel and useful ideas. By some estimates we can maintain this level of cognitive intensity for only about twenty to twenty-five minutes at a time. After that our minds begin to grow weary and our ability to screen out competing sensory inputs weaken. We need a brain break. What to do?

According to several studies, we can recharge our brain batteries by turning attention away from the task at hand and directing it toward nature instead. A brief period of undirected reflection should be sufficient for us to return to our activity with renewed energy.

The reason? Simply that it takes far less mental exertion to take in natural scenography than it does to hunker down on a taxing problem. Being able to indulge in unfocused consciousness gives our cognitive circuitry a chance to replenish itself

Kitchen. Hilton Head island, South Carolina. Architecture by Frederick + Frederick Architects. Interior design by Emily Mahoney. Photography by Richard Leo Johnson/Atlantic Archives.

before revving up for the next round of directed attention. Hence the name given by researchers to explain the connection between plant matter and psychological revitalization: Attention Restoration Theory, or ART for short.

Well, duh, you're probably thinking to yourself. Of course we're going to feel rejuvenated after we stop banging away on demanding work so we can vegetate for a spell. Nothing magical or scientifically revealing about that.

Except that not all respites are created equal. Researchers have compared the physiological responses among people passively experiencing natural settings to those observing built environments, including relatively placid and attractive settings. I'm sorry to say that nature wins hands down for the depth of its restorative effect (sorry, because I've always assumed good architecture could solve all problems). That goes for human-made objects too. Mindlessly staring at an ashtray for several minutes isn't going to resuscitate you to the same extent that gazing at foliage, flowers, and forests will. So the question remains: what gives organic forms their unique power to reinvigorate the human mind?

One possible answer is that nature is often fractal. A fractal is a shape that repeats at different scales, as for example on the inside of a nautilus shell, the diminishing stems of a fern, and the recurring wave patterns in the sea. Because the shapes are similar it doesn't take a lot of mental energy to visualize them en masse. Stand in the middle of Times Square, on the other hand, and you're bombarded with a battery of disparate visual, audible, and olfactory

Entry hall. Albemarle County, Virginia. Architecture and interior design by Dagliesh Gilpin Paxton Architects. Photography by Philip Beaurline.

inputs, straining your mental capacity to process them simultaneously.

Another camp points to the survival urge imbued in early humans. For our ancestors roaming the savannas of Africa, the sight of lush, verdant vegetation was a welcome sight indeed. It signified the promise of food, a means to attain shelter and shade, and favorable climatic conditions amenable to the sustenance of life. Evolutionary psychology (Explainer II) suggests that the memory of that positive association has been genetically seared into the human race so deeply that it still influences our behavior today. It's a compelling argument, considering that 99.99 percent of the total time our species has spent on the planet has been within purely natural environments.

Still others maintain that stress reduction is the principal mechanism by which nature positively influences our mental state. They believe that that the sights, sounds, and smells of organic growth lift our spirits and elevate our mood by triggering our long-standing association of vegetation with survival. After all, it's intrinsically comforting to feel you won't be starving any time soon, even if the origins of that fear bear no relationship to present-day reality.

Putting stress and mood arousal at the center of the discussion about nature's influence on us would fit Ulrich's observation that hospital patients who glimpsed trees through their windows recovered better than those who saw only hardscape (see the Introduction). It would also explain why several studies show employees are more productive and creative when the workplace contains plants. As many of us are aware, the pressure to devise paradigm-shifting products or services on a regular basis can be emotionally and physically trying, especially when we rely on creative work product to make a living. Anything we can do to alleviate that stress will be a boon to original thinking, because stress is the enemy of idea creation. Stress, which is caused by the release of cortisol into our system, leads us to freeze up, narrow our focus, and become risk-averse—all conditions inimical to the open embrace of freewheeling ideas.

A symbolic connection between nature and creativity might play into our response to it as well. Plant matter, and nature in general, signify the emergence of life-forms—that is, the bringing forth of things that were previously unknown or absent.

Human creativity is cut from the same conceptual cloth. Out of thin air we conjure up objects and concepts that were formerly nonexistent (only we do it at a much faster pace than the glacial crawl of evolution). Unconsciously equating plants and flowers with themes of fertility and production could be fueling our motivation to engage in creative undertakings ourselves.

Yet another interpretation of the data stems from the aesthetic properties of natural form, in contrast to industrially manufactured products. Imagine, for example, looking at a wall finished in Sheetrock and painted a flat color. What's your eye going to do? Most likely, it's going to come

Living room. Carmichael, California. Architecture and interior design by Mark Dziewulski Architect. Photography by Keith Cronin.

Greenhouse. Emmitsburg, Maryland. Architecture and interior design by Jim Rill, AIA and Rich Rossi for Rill Architects.

quickly to a rest, there being no incentive for it to travel anywhere particular along its uniform surface. Now imagine you're looking at the same wall except that it's clad in stone or naturally finished wood; what does your eye do now? That's right—it jumps around all over the place, lured by the non-repetitive and variegated grain or texture of the surface.

Scientists call these ocular motions *saccadic eye movement*. What makes saccades of interest to us is that when we look left, the right side of our brains becomes activated, while looking right does the same to the left hemisphere. Rapidly darting our eyes back and forth in different directions has the consequent effect of strengthening the neural connection between the two hemispheres. This is naturally very good for creativity, which relies on the interplay of both "left-brain" (divergent)

and "right-brain" (convergent) thinking to stir up ideas that are both novel *and* useful, creative *and* purposeful.

Happily, there's reason to believe that saccadic effects can be immediate. A 2009 experiment in which subjects performed rapid eye shifts for thirty seconds found them to exhibit greater aptitude in solving creative problems than a group that stared straight ahead before doing the same exercises. Developing strong inter-hemispheric connections over the long haul could be equally beneficial, if a recent report on Albert Einstein's fabled brain is any indication. Exceptional for his ability to think both visually and analytically, the famous scientist was discovered to have had an exceptionally large corpus callosum—the bundle of nerve fibers that bridges the two halves.

Bosco Verticale apartment towers. Milan, Italy. Architecture by Boeri Studio. Photography by Chris Barbalis.

You'd think with so many avenues of confluence binding human well-being, happiness, and creativity to the natural world, someone would have invented an overarching term that embraced these many lines of thought. Well, someone has. It's called *biophilia*—literally, a love of living things. Coined in 1973 by the psychoanalyst Erich Fromm, the concept was later popularized by the biologist Edward O. Wilson in his 1984 book of the same name. Wilson defines biophilia as "the urge to affiliate with other forms of life." From there it was a short step to the idea of *biophilic design*, a design strategy that applies the concept of biophilia to buildings, spaces, and places. No mere theory, biophilic design has been credited with a 15 percent jump in creativity among employees in workplace environments crafted in accord with its principles.

With a modicum of effort, that same cognitive benefit could accrue to you.

HOW TO DO IT

Open up. Depending on where you live, you might find nature in greatest abundance right outside your window. If so, open up your idea room to natural light, air, sounds, smells, and views as much as possible and practical.

Connect inside and outside. Diminish the physical barrier that separates in from out by selecting colors, upholstery and fabric patterns, floor and wall coverings, lighting, furnishings, architectural trim, artwork, and decorative pieces that evoke the natural world in form and principle. As much as possible, make choices that relate directly to your context. For instance, if you're in a verdant or wooded environment, adopt a

Kitchen extension. Enmore, Sydney, New South Wales, Australia. Architecture and interior design by Danny Broe Architect. Photography by Karina Illovska.

Living area. Nashville, Tennessee. Building and interior design by David Latimer for New Frontier Tiny Homes. Photography by StudiObuell.

material palette dominated by greens and browns and naturally finished woods to suggest trees and plants. Botanic prints, a landscape painting, a piece of old-style furniture with supports carved in the shape of animal legs, or a sisal area rug would fit right in too. You urbanites might look to regional characteristics for design guidance, even if visible signs of nature are in modest supply in your immediate surroundings.

Use natural materials, or their simulacra. Next time you're stymied by a creative block, don't beat your head against a wall. Look at it instead. It could lift you out of your rut.

That's the takeaway from a number of surveys and clinical studies showing that interiors constructed or finished in natural materials provide greater mental and physical stimulation than spaces fashioned out of products having a uniform or blatantly mass-produced appearance. Remember, though: as far as generating ideas goes, it's perception that counts. Cultured stone, faux wood laminates, trompe l'oeil painting, and other instances of biomimicry can cue the same primal associations as the real deal.

Be an indoor gardener. Slather your space with indoor plants, mosses, and flowers. Search out species that give off a scent; the smell as well as sight of plant matter can add to the natural ambience.

As for style, the choice of containers these days is nearly endless, having expanded far beyond the classic terra-cotta variety. Living walls are another increasingly viable option.

Go green. I'm not referring to the sustainability movement, although recycling, up-cycling, adaptive reuse, energy conservation, the patina of craftsmanship, and nontoxic building products go hand in hand with biophilic design. I'm talking about the color. Results from several experiments showed that subjects who saw green ink on paper or a green rectangle on-screen before undertaking creativity assessment exercises excelled in comparison to those who first glimpsed other hues or neutrals. A green color scheme, accent wall, or softscape could do the same for you. Feel too limited by monochromatic decor? Try a dyadic palette that mixes blues (#2) with greens instead.

Master bedroom. Yonkers, New York. Architecture by Gary Brewer for Robert A.M. Stern Architects. Photography by Francis Dzikowski/Otto.

RELATED TACTICS AND EXPLAINERS

#2. Look at something blue.

#4. Take in a view.

#5. Display art.

#7. Embrace detail and complexity.

#12. Choose curved over straight.

#15. Get with your pet.

#19. Let in natural light.

#20. Be smart with your lighting.

#24. Pick up the scent.

#29. Make a fire. Or look at a picture of one.

#38. Go for a walk.

#47. Get out of the house.

Explainer II: We Are Who We Have Always Been

TACTIC #15
GET WITH YOUR PET

WHAT TO DO
Bring an animal companion into your home.

WHY DO IT?
Pets deliver a plethora of cognitive and health benefits that nurture creativity.

WHY DOES IT WORK?
Let me count the ways:

1) *Pets help control blood pressure and relieve stress.* Have you ever wondered why so many dentists install fish tanks in their offices? It isn't because the little creatures are good for cleaning dentures. Or so no one will notice that the pile of magazines in the waiting room hasn't been updated in three years. It's because watching fish be fish can reduce anxiety and relieve muscle tension. And as we all know, there are few things in life more certain to make us anxious than climbing into the dentist's chair.

A growing body of research affirms the calming effects that domesticated animals instill. In 1999 a scientist at the University of Buffalo discovered that hypertensive and unmarried New York stockbrokers who kept a dog or cat at home had lower blood pressure and heart rates than those who lived entirely alone. Similarly, a research team from Virginia Commonwealth University observed that stress among the employees of a North Carolina dinnerware company who brought their dogs to work dropped an average of 11 percent over

Foyer. Hong Kong. Interior design and photography by Y. C. Chen for hoo.

the course of their day. Tension among their canine-deprived coworkers, in contrast, shot up by as much as 7 percent in the same stretch. I suppose it's a small miracle that those people made it in at all.

Mental strain is bad for our health under most circumstances, but as I note throughout the book, it's a particularly dangerous suppressant of iconoclastic behavior.

2) *Pets promote touch and transmit warmth.* Among the reasons pet owners enjoy lower stress levels than the general population is that positive touch experiences release hormones into our bloodstream that suppress our psychological sensitivity to threat cues. This gives us greater confidence to take up the sort of explorative and risk-taking ventures that lead to creative breakthroughs.

Your feelings of safety could be magnified if your pet is warm-blooded. Researchers have found that coming into physical contact with objects exuding warmth lights up a slab of brain tissue called the insula, part of which connects physical sensations to feelings of trust.

3) *Pets elevate mood.* Pet companionship generally make us happy (save for the distress of the occasional broken lamp or soiled rug). Happiness breeds creativity as sure as animals breed animals.

4) *Pets promote social interaction.* Dog owners are the ultimate social animals. They have to be. Out there every day of the year rain or shine, bumping into fellow dog walkers along their route, they're invariably thrust into the very sort of close human interaction from which

Entry. Toronto, Ontario, Canada. Architecture and interior design by Gloria Apostolou for Post Architecture. Photography by Arnaud Marthouret for Revelateur Studio.

many a unique idea has flowed. Pet owners of all varieties can accrue similar networking benefits by joining virtual and physical communities populated by like-minded animal aficionados.

5) *Pets promote movement, play, and exercise.* Whether it's playing fetch with a dog, chasing a cat around the sofa, or hurtling after a bird that's flown the coop, pets get us up and moving. Movement and creativity are closely intertwined, as several of the related tactics listed below attest.

6) *Pets distract.* In a good way, that is. Think of your animal companion as a live version of Einstein's violin—not that you'd ever pick up Fido and pluck him as the renowned physicist often did to his musical instrument when he found himself stuck on a difficult problem. No, the value of pets lies in their being there for you when you want or need to take a break from the work, giving your ideas a chance to productively percolate in the nether regions of your brain that function without conscious

Pantry. Austin, Texas. Architecture and interior design by Tim Cuppett Architects. Photography by Whit Preston.

8) *Pets take us out of ourselves.* Virginia Woolf, Kurt Vonnegut, John Steinbeck, Gertrude Stein, and scores of other illustrious creatives have been pet people. Woolf even wrote a biography of Elizabeth Barrett Browning's dog, demonstrating how pets can push us to see the world empathetically through another creature's eyes.

HOW TO DO IT

Make your pet at home. If I had to offer a single word of design advice for bringing animals successfully into the home, it's *integrate*. Seek out furniture, toys, and equipment designed with an eye toward enhancing the decor, rather than eroding it with incongruent materials, colors, and shapes. Explore opportunities for built-ins, should resources allow.

For the ultimate in visual integration, consider coordinating your decor with your pet. For example, you could base the colors and patterns of your pet's favorite lair on that of your creature companion. Or maybe it's the other way around, and you find yourself an animal friend whose appearance and character harmonize with your existing home. However far you take it, just remember: it's your house too.

RELATED TACTICS AND EXPLAINERS

#14. Bring nature in.
#29. Make a fire. Or look at a picture of one.
#33. Exercise.
#37. Take a break.
#38. Go for a walk.
#43. Play.
#47. Get out of the house.
Explainer II: We Are Who We Have Always Been

intervention. Of course, sometimes it's your pet who compels you to step away from your pursuits by demanding to be fed, walked, or have its hygiene attended to. But that's okay too—planned or unplanned, mental downtime can be enormously productive for triggering an idea stream (#37).

7) *Pets bind us to the natural world.* See Explainer II and Tactic #14 for details.

HARRIET BACKER.

TACTIC #16
MAKE IT BEAUTIFUL

WHAT TO DO
Design your creative space to be beautiful.

WHY DO IT?
A 1956 study revealed that people enter into a more positive state of mind when they're inside a beautiful setting than in unsightly or average-looking surroundings. Later neuroimaging data suggest that our favorable response to attractiveness is encoded into our brain structure.

WHY DOES IT WORK?
Abraham Maslow is best known as a founding father of positive psychology, a scientific discipline that focuses on the brighter side of the human psyche—in contrast, say, to Freudian preoccupations with its dark underbelly. Somewhat forgotten in Maslow's corpus, however, is a paper he published in the 1950s that explored the impact of environmental aesthetics on our state of mind. Which is too bad, because it deserves to be better known.

To produce the study, Maslow teamed up with fellow Brandeis professor Norbett L. Mintz and, somewhat unusually for the academic world, with his own wife (her contributions are uncredited in the paper, an omission not at all unusual in the academic world). Mrs. Maslow evidently had an aptitude for art and interior decoration, skills that the two men needed to help them answer an important question: does the aesthetic quality of space matter?

Blue Interior by Harriet Backer. Norwegian. 1883. National Gallery of Norway, Oslo.

Three experimental sites were set up to find out: 1) a Beautiful Room—Maslow's own office—featuring large draped windows, soft lighting, a piece of sculpture from the hand of Mrs. Maslow, a comfortable chair, bookcase, mahogany desk, and handsome rug; 2) an Average Room, neat and clean but otherwise workaday in its decor; and 3) an Ugly Room, a repurposed basement space staged like a janitor's closet, with dirty gray walls, a couple of straight-backed chairs, a bare-bulb light fixture with a torn shade, tin-can ashtrays, mops, a disused box spring, and bare mattress strewn haphazardly around the room.

Proctors ushered student volunteers into one of the three rooms. Each received a stack of black-and-white photographic headshots and instructions to rank the anonymous faces on a numerical scale for their "energy" and "well-being."

Now, you might expect that the scores turned in would fall within a relatively narrow range regardless of setting. After all, the picture sets were identical. Surely a nice-looking floor covering or a touch of mood lighting wouldn't impinge on our consciousness sufficiently to alter our judgment. At the end of the day, decoration is just eyewash, right?

Actually, wrong. Subjects who evaluated the photos in the Ugly and Average Rooms were noticeably more negative in their scoring than persons in the Beautiful Room. Even less expectedly, the experiment also adversely affected the proctors. Examiners stationed in the basement space were observed to be more irritable, fatigued, and prone to complain about the assignment

Interior with a Young Man Reading *by Vilhelm Hammershøi.*
Danish. 1898. Hirschsprung Collection, Copenhagen.

found that the beautiful works heightened activity in a particular part of the subjects' brain—the medial orbito-frontal cortex (mOFC), if you're keeping score—while the ugly inputs fired up the amygdala and left somato-motor cortex.

Why is this significant? In part, because the mOFC happens to be associated with positive, rewarding, and emotional experiences, such as love, whereas the two neural centers correlating with exposure to visual and audible unpleasantness are linked to fear, anger, and movement, as if our brains were urging us to flee from the offending stimulus. These opposing reactions bring us back once again to the recurring dichotomies of approach-avoidance motivation (#2). Sensory inputs that promise pleasure move us toward the relaxed, trusting, flexible, and inquisitive mind-set conducive to imaginative exploration. Those that raise the prospect of harm narrow our focus and close our mind to untried ideas—about the last thing you want to experience in a space devoted to creative pursuits.

HOW TO DO IT

Teach yourself about design. Realizing a beautiful space can be daunting to the nonprofessional. It doesn't have to be. Design is a creative skill, and like any skill, it can be taught and learned. Read books, take classes or webinars, scrutinize the work of acknowledged master practitioners to analyze what makes their portfolio beautiful in your eyes and the eyes of people whose opinion you respect. Sure, some experts believe in a 10,000-hour rule, which prescribes the minimum amount of time it takes a person to master a domain. But you're not aiming to get into the pages of *Architectural Digest*; you're simply trying to fashion an environment that rewards your senses, elevates your mood, and lights up your medial orbito-frontal cortex. So practice with sketches, swatches, and simulations—and

than those performing their duties in Maslow's well-appointed office.

Conclusion: the visual quality of our environs does indeed influence how we think, feel, and act. We tend to be happier with ourselves, more affirmative in our outlook on the world, and more energized by our work in an aesthetically appealing setting than in a mediocre or chaotic environment.

In other words, design is good for us.

Maslow, of course, didn't have access to brain-scanning technology at the time of his experiment, nor was it widely available by the time of his passing in 1970. But it's safe to say that he would have been intrigued by recent neuroimaging studies that suggest our predilection for the beautiful is deeply rooted in brain biology. In one study, volunteers encased in an fMRI machine viewed pictures of paintings and listened to musical excerpts they'd rated earlier as beautiful, indifferent, or ugly. Researchers

The Actor Kristian Mantzius in His Study *by Carl Bloch. Danish. 1853. Hirschsprung Collection, Copenhagen.*

don't be afraid of falling short at first. "Creativity is allowing yourself to make mistakes," *Dilbert* cartoonist Scott Adams once declared. "Art is knowing which ones to keep."

Hire a professional. Beauty is what we do. If resources permit, bring aboard a designer who shares your vision. The return on your investment can be enormous.

RELATED TACTICS AND EXPLAINERS

#2. Look at something blue.

#3. Work under a lofty ceiling.

#5. Display art.

#7. Embrace detail and complexity.

#12. Choose curved over straight.

#14. Bring nature in.

#19. Let in natural light.

Explainer II: We Are Who We Have Always Been

CREATIVITY TACTICS
GROUP TWO:
AMBIENCE

TACTIC #17
MAKE NOISE

WHAT TO DO

Fill your space with ambient noise of seventy decibels to optimize idea generation.

WHY DO IT?

A 2012 study found that subjects attained peak creative performance when subjected to moderate noise levels.

WHY DOES IT WORK?

To remark that the French writer Marcel Proust was sensitive to auditory distraction would be an understatement. The man was positively neurotic about it. He treated the bedroom in his Paris apartment where he wrote like a sensory deprivation chamber—shutters closed, drapes drawn, the walls lined with sound-absorbing cork. It still wasn't enough. He wore earplugs too.

Proust was hardly alone in craving silence. Charles Darwin, Anton Chekhov, and Richard Wagner were similarly beset by hypersensitivity to sound. So was fellow obsessive Franz Kafka, who described his condition in his signature surreal style by saying that "I need solitude for my writing; not 'like a hermit'—that wouldn't be enough—but like a dead man." Sadly, by the time he got his wish, it was too late to do anything with it.

The correlation between high-level inventiveness and difficulty in filtering out sensory inputs is

understandable, given that open-mindedness is a hallmark of the creative personality. The problem for off-the-chart geniuses like Proust and Kafka was that their minds were a bit *too* open. Everything got through. Hence the extreme measures they took to avoid being immobilized by incoming stimuli.

Then again, most of us aren't Marcel Proust. According to research data from 2012, we creative mortals actually reach our peak performance under moderately noisy conditions—70db (decibels), to be precise. This is roughly equivalent to the chatter in your local coffee shop or restaurant on a reasonably busy day (Fig. 19). As to why this is the case, the scientists who authored the study have a theory:

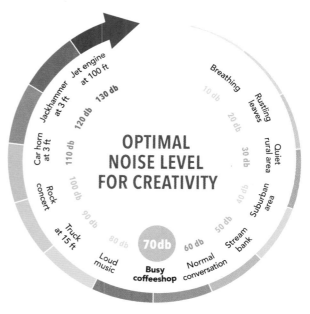

Living room and fountain details. Bellevue, Washington. Architecture by David Coleman Architecture. Interior design by Elizabeth Stretch for Stretch Design. Photography by Paul Warchol.

Fig. 19: Optimal noise levels for creative processing compared to other conditions. After Ravi Mehta, Rui (Juliet) Zhu, and Amar Cheema (2012).

Living area and deck. Malibu, California. Architecture and interior design by Mark Dziewulski Architect. Photography by Nico Marques.

We theorize that a moderate (vs. low) level of ambient noise is likely to induce processing disfluency or processing difficulty, which activates abstract cognition and consequently enhances creative performance. A high level of noise, however, reduces the extent of information processing, thus impairing creativity.

Translation: silence isn't as golden as it sounds. Absolute noiselessness tends to focus our attention, which is helpful for tasks that entail accuracy, fine detail, and linear reasoning, such as balancing our checkbook or fixing a Swiss watch. It's less supportive of the broad, big-picture, abstract mind-wandering that leads to fresh perspectives. On the other hand, excessive noise overwhelms our sensory apparatus and hinders our ability to properly process information at all. In between lies the sweet spot—noise not so loud that we can't hear ourselves think, and not so quiet that we can't help but hear ourselves think.

There's a caveat to the data, however: the noise has to be white. Otherwise you're prone to tune into the source of the sound, which diverts too much of your conscious attention from your task to be a useful distraction. (Music, being a special type of sound rather than noise, is exempt from this requirement, as I discuss in the upcoming tactic.)

HOW TO DO IT

Get the app. Yes, Virginia, there really is an app for everything. Use the search term "noise" to bring up dozens of sound-generating programs in your smartphone's app store. You'll also see a

Courtyard. La Quinta, California. Architecture by Frank Stolz for South Coast Architects. Photography by Eric Figge.

Get or hack a sound generator. Another option is to purchase a desktop appliance designed to emit white noise. They're smallish devices, typically placed on night tables and in babies' rooms to help occupants fall asleep. For an architectural solution, think about installing an indoor or outdoor fountain—few things in life are as pleasantly hypnotizing as the mellifluous whoosh of water descending onto water. Price points run the gamut from low cost store-bought products to sky's-the-limit custom installations.

DIY contrivances also abound; consult the Internet for guidance.

Let in or keep out external noise. City dwellers and people who reside along busy highways might have a ready-made noise machine right outside their window: road traffic. Open your windows to varying degrees or use sound muffling, such as drapery, to see if you can calibrate ambient noise to fall within the optimal range.

A less cacophonous but perhaps costlier strategy for harnessing exterior sounds would be to relocate to within earshot of ocean waves. It's like having an always-on fountain, only bigger.

Find a sound sanctuary. Avail yourself of a bustling coffee shop, eatery, hotel lobby, railroad station, or oceanside perch when you're in need of a noise fix or on the road.

RELATED TACTICS
#18. Make music.
#35. Take a shower or bath.
#47. Get out of the house.

broad selection of metering apps for measuring decibel levels at home.

Some of the app companies operate websites that let you download audio files of white noise soundtracks onto your computer or play them directly through a browser. A couple of my favorite sites include Raining.fm, which offers tracks simulating—what else?—downpours, rolling thunder, and heavy thunderstorms, and Coffitivy, which specializes in—what else?—coffee shop buzz.

TACTIC #18
MAKE MUSIC

WHAT TO DO
Listen to music or play a musical instrument.

WHY DO IT?
Music enhances creativity.

WHY DOES IT WORK?
In 1993 a team of researchers tested the spatial reasoning skills of a group of undergraduates after first listening to a recording of a Mozart sonata. They put another group through the same drill but without the musical prelude. Music teachers everywhere must have smiled when they heard the results: students who heard the Mozart piece scored higher than the control group. The phenomenon became known, fittingly, as the Mozart Effect.

Most reports of scientific experiments come and go in the popular press. This one, however, struck a chord among the public by intimating that anyone with ears could get smarter simply by listening to classical music. That was all a certain class of entrepreneurs had to hear. Mozart-branded audio discs, cassette tapes, booklets, and other pseudo-educational paraphernalia soon flooded the market. Many went far beyond the scope of the original findings by heralding every conceivable improvement in health and mental well-being. "Innovative and experimental uses of music and sound can improve listening disorders, dyslexia, attention deficit disorder, autism, and other mental

and physical disorders and injuries," proclaimed an overly fervent booster vying for admission to the snake oil salesman hall of shame.

Then the bottom dropped out of the Mozart market. Scientists attempting to replicate the original findings discovered that listening to any musical genre you liked could yield similar results. Doubts also piled up about the strength and long-term effects of the stimulus. The original researchers eventually backed off from some of their purported conclusions, insisting they'd been misrepresented by the media. By the following decade, the Mozart Effect had become the Mozart Myth.

Still, to discount the power of music to alter fundamental brain activity would be to throw the Bach out with the bathwater. There's abundant anecdotal and clinical evidence that the sound of music can indeed amp up creative output—provided the conditions and extent of its influence are understood.

The first prerequisite is that you like the music you're listening to. A die-hard classical music fan forced to endure the Sex Pistols is likely to be in poor temper after a few bars of "God Save the Queen." Temper, in turn, has a huge impact on cognitive style; a positive outlook encourages our minds to roam more freely by imbuing us with an inward sense of comfort and safety, while negative emotions can quash our curiosity.

A second condition for enhancing creativity through music is that it feel familiar. Deviant music that's outside your usual repertory might draw too much of your attention away from the task at hand

Living room. Calgary, Alberta, Canada. Architecture and interior design by Richard Davignon and Doris Martin for Davignon Martin Architecture + Interior Design. Photography by Eymeric Widling.

Studio. Marblemount, Washington. Architecture by David Coleman Architecture. Photography by Ben Benschneider.

as your brain tries to decode the auditory patterns underlying the unfamiliar sounds.

Third, the music should be appropriate to the subject matter. Tempo, mood, and genre are key in this regard. Research commissioned by the music streaming service Spotify in 2013 observed that upbeat pop and rock music benefited students studying subjects in the humanities, while slower tempo pieces in classical and other genres boosted learning skills in math and science. On the other hand, mournful folk or pop tunes might just be the thing if you're writing a poem or novel about a lovesick character, whereas a Wagnerian opera could get you sufficiently pumped up to finally attack that difficult coding problem you've been putting off. The fact is, most musical genres accommodate a range of cadences and characters, so you should have little trouble finding the right

beat and emotional timbre for any task regardless of your musical tastes.

You might also find it helpful to stick with instrumental music. Songs with lyrics can siphon off too much mental energy as our brains labor to decipher their meaning. If you prefer to listen to music with words, choose tracks you've heard a thousand times before so the lyrics fade from conscious awareness.

Just as rewarding for creativity as listening to music is making it yourself, especially when you need to cut through a creative logjam. In fact, two of the greatest problem solvers in history and literature made music for this purpose—Albert Einstein and Sherlock Holmes. Biographer Walter Isaacson writes about the importance of music to Einstein's problem-solving methodology:

Music room. Westchester, New York. Interior design by Robin Baron Design. Photography by Phillip Ennis.

Music was no mere diversion. On the contrary, it helped him think. "Whenever he felt that he had come to the end of the road or faced a difficult challenge in his work," said his son Hans Albert, "he would take refuge in music and that would solve all his difficulties." The violin thus proved useful during the years he lived alone in Berlin, wrestling with general relativity. "He would often play his violin in his kitchen late at night, improvising melodies while he pondered complicated problems," a friend recalled. "Then, suddenly, in the middle of playing, he would announce excitedly, 'I've got it!' As if by inspiration, the answer to the problem would have come to him in the midst of music."

There's now data to suggest that playing a musical instrument can bring you long-term gains in creative prowess in addition to short-term breakthroughs. A recent neuroimaging study found that a group of professional musicians scored higher on tests measuring divergent thinking than a competing group of non-musicians. Brain scans taken during the experiment revealed greater blood flow between the left and right hemispheres of the musicians' brains, raising the possibility that the performers had developed stronger neural connections as a result of rigorously practicing their craft.

HOW TO DO IT

Install a source for recorded music. Equipment for delivering music run the gamut from an old-fashioned desktop boombox or shelf-mounted stereo components, to architecturally integrated whole-house hardwired multi-zone programmable sound systems. Costs range accordingly.

Set up a music room or studio. You have an equally broad range of options for fitting out a space for making music of your own. A low-key approach is to simply store your instrument near where you play it, whether by hanging it on a wall, placing it on the floor, or leaving it on display in its case or on a stand. At the other end of the spectrum is the dedicated music room, complete with appropriately engineered acoustics and decor to match the character of the music. Even without the luxury of a separate space, you can still modulate the quality and intensity of sound by means of plants, drapery, wall and floor coverings, and shelved books.

RELATED TACTICS

#17. Make noise.
#37. Take a break.
#43. Play.

TACTIC #19
LET IN NATURAL LIGHT

Architecture is the masterly, correct, and magnificent play of masses brought together in light.
—Le Corbusier

WHAT TO DO
Optimize the amount and quality of daylight entering your space.

WHY DO IT?
Natural light feeds creativity.

WHY DOES IT WORK?
Here's a gloomy statistic. According to the US Environmental Protection Agency, people living in developed countries spend upward of 90 percent of their time indoors. Gloomy, because study after study shows that a low daylight diet is detrimental to physical and mental health. A 2014 workplace survey, for instance, found that staffers laboring in windowless rooms slept forty-six fewer minutes a night on average than colleagues with access to windows. They also reported lower scores on seven other measures of health and productivity. Another study from the same year linked a dearth of sunlight to higher blood pressure. Still others have found correlations between shortfalls in daylight and diminished visual acuity, color differentiation, vitality, happiness, social and cognitive development, and academic performance.

As if that weren't depressing enough, light-starved settings also come with environmental and financial costs. Less interior daylight means

Master bath. Hilton Head island, South Carolina. Architecture by Frederick + Frederick Architects. Interior design by Emily Mahoney. Photography by Richard Leo Johnson/Atlantic Archives.

more electric illumination and therefore increased energy consumption and higher household bills. Given that electric lighting amounts to 15 percent of total energy use in the United States, that's no small potatoes.

In light of these statistics, the expression "you've got to get out more" takes on greater urgency. Wholesale changes in lifestyle are easier said than done, of course. In the meanwhile, you can bolster your creative productivity and overall well-being by optimizing the quality and quantity of daylight entering your home.

HOW TO DO IT
Aim primarily for indirect rather than direct light. Direct light comes straight from the sun. It's bright, warm, invigorating, and facilitates plant growth. In cold climates it can heat interior space and reduce energy use. Carried to excess, however, unfiltered sunshine can bring with it serious downsides, chief among them glare, unwanted heat gain, deep shadows, and damage to artwork, finishes, fabrics, and furnishings.

A successful design balances direct sunlight with ambient light.

Ambient light is light reflected off surfaces both inside and outside the home. Unlike direct light, it's diffuse and generally moderate in intensity. Also unlike direct light, it's hard to get too much of it when properly controlled.

Determining how to best maximize ambient light while modulating direct sunshine depends

Guitar studio. Okatie, South Carolina. Architecture by Frederick + Frederick Architects. Photography by John McManus.

on a variety of factors, including your home's geographic location, the orientation of your creative space relative to the solar trajectory, type and size of openings, how much exterior and interior shading you currently have in place, and the existing landscaping.

The first step is to assess your light conditions. Do you currently get too much direct sun at times?

Or is your space so hopelessly dark that you have to leave the lights burning from morning to night? Depending on your observations, consider implementing some of the following techniques to improve present conditions. Keep in mind that a good lighting design balances competing objectives. Energy consumption, task appropriateness, personal comfort and visibility, and research into

Screen porch. Lexington, Massachusetts. Architecture by Sally DeGan for SpaceCraft Architecture. Interior design by Deborah Farrand for Dressing Rooms. Photography by Michael J. Lee.

ideal lighting intensity for idea streaming (#21) should all play into your choices.

To bring and disperse light in the interior:

- Move furniture out of the way of exterior openings.
- Pull back on window treatments that block light, such as heavy drapes and curtains, or replace them with products and materials having greater adjustability and translucency.
- Hang mirrors on walls or stand them on floors to bounce light back into the room. The optimal location for a mirror is directly across from a source of outside light. Mirrors reflect about 95 percent of the light that strikes them.
- Choose light colors for walls, floors, or ceilings. Pale hues reflect more light than darker ones. When painting, check to see if the can's label lists a light reflectance value (LRV). Recommended values are 60 to 90 for ceilings, 35 to 60 for walls, and 20 to 30 for flooring.
- Choose reflective materials and finishes for non-painted surfaces, including furniture. Generally, the higher the gloss the higher the reflectivity.
- Keep your space clean! Dust hinders light bounce.

Breakfast area. Richmond Hill, Georgia. Architecture by Donald M. Rattner for Ferguson Shamamian & Rattner, Architects. Interior design by Donna Rukin. Photography by Richard Leo Johnson/Atlantic Archives.

- Replace interior and exterior solid doors with glazed units and/or add transoms and sidelights.
- Replace solid interior walls with glazed partitions, shoji screens, or space dividers that steal light from adjacent areas while allowing for privacy and sound attenuation.
- Enlarge doorways and interior openings.
- Enlarge existing (or add new) windows, glazed door units, projecting bays, and skylights.

- Specify paving and decking materials with high reflectivity for surfaces outside your creative space, if applicable.
- Relocate, replace, or trim back landscape elements that impede the passage of light at times of year or day when it's wanted.

To modulate the influx of direct light:
- Install interior shutters, louvered blinds, roll-down shades, or translucent curtains on windows and glazed doors.

- Install awnings, shutters, and light shields above exterior openings to block the sun at appropriate times of day.
- Configure porches, deeply projecting eaves, balconies, and other overhanging architectural features to do same.
- Plant seasonally appropriate landscaping to filter out direct light in warm months and allow it to enter in cool months.
- Look into window film, double-glazing, or low-E glass to reduce dangerous ultraviolet radiation and heat gain through windows subject to direct sunlight.
- Explore translucent exterior cladding systems specially designed to filter in evenly diffused daylight, such as those made with polycarbonates.

RELATED TACTICS AND EXPLAINERS

#4. Take in a view.

#14. Bring nature in.

#20. Be smart with your lighting.

#21. Dim the lights.

#22. Switch on a filament bulb.

#25. Sleep.

#26. Nap.

#38. Go for a walk.

#47. Get out of the house.

Explainer II: We Are Who We Have Always Been

Kitchen. Mill Valley, California. Architecture by YAMAMAR Design. Interior design by Jenny Gamble for gamble + Design and Nagisa Yano for YAMAMAR. Photography by Bruce Damonte.

TACTIC #20
BE SMART WITH YOUR LIGHTING

WHAT TO DO

Use programmable lighting to replicate the intensity and color temperature of the daily solar cycle.

WHY DO IT?

Aligning interior lighting conditions with the path of the sun speeds mental processing, elevates mood, and improves well-being.

WHY DOES IT WORK?

Once upon a time, humans rose with the sun and slumbered with the stars. Now, we need an alarm to roust us out of bed in the morning and struggle to stay remain asleep in it once we climb back in at night.

Something clearly happened to disconnect our daily routine from the ebb and flow of natural light. Was it a change in the sun's rays? No, the sun remains the same as it ever was (Fig. 20). It still throws a warm amber light into the sky every day at sunrise before slowly transitioning into a cooler, brighter light during the morning and early afternoon. It still changes back to amber by evening. It still disappears below the horizon at night, only to repeat the cycle starting at nearly the same time the following morning.

Was it something with how our eyes function? Again, no. Like those of our ancestors, our eyes contain photoreceptors, called rods and cones, which can sense changes in the color of the sun's rays and their intensity. The rods and cones still send signals to the pineal gland in our brain that trigger the release of various hormones at specified times of day—among them, serotonin (the body's natural antidepressant) in the morning,

Fig. 20: Solar trajectory. Copyright 2017 Kelvin S. do Prado under MIT License.

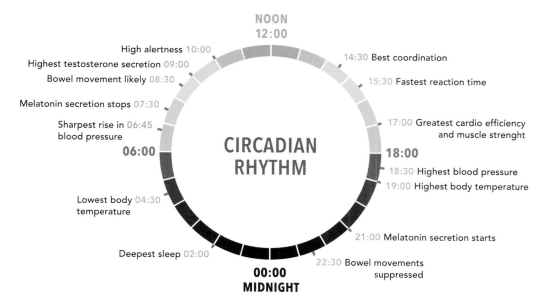

NOON
12:00

High alertness 10:00
Highest testosterone secretion 09:00
Bowel movement likely 08:30

Melatonin secretion stops 07:30

Sharpest rise in 06:45
blood pressure
06:00

CIRCADIAN
RHYTHM

14:30 Best coordination

15:30 Fastest reaction time

17:00 Greatest cardio efficiency
and muscle strenght
18:00
18:30 Highest blood pressure
19:00 Highest body temperature

Lowest body 04:30
temperature

21:00 Melatonin secretion starts

Deepest sleep 02:00

22:30 Bowel movements
suppressed

00:00
MIDNIGHT

Fig. 21: Bodily states mapped to the circadian rhythm.

and melatonin (a hormone signaling the need to sleep) at night. These and other hormones are still able to regulate bodily states through the daily cycle, from bowel movements to tiredness. From this regular cycle comes the circadian rhythm on which our mental and physical health, mood, and energy continues to depend (Fig. 21).

So if there's nothing new under the sun, what caused the disruption to our internal clocks?

In a word, modernity.

First we invented the industrial economy, which relocated large numbers of people from sunlit fields to darkened factories and offices. Then we came up with the electric light bulb, which brought day into night, thoroughly confounding our circadian rhythm. Other creature comforts, from air-conditioning to modern kitchen appliances to home entertainment systems, soon followed, enticing us to spend still more time in artificial indoor environments.

And just when it couldn't get any worse, we invented computer monitors, tablets, and smartphones, all of which emit a steady blue light that further scramble our biological timekeeper,

hurtling us into a sleep and health crisis of epic proportions.

The road back to a harmonious relationship between body and sun will not be easy. But there is one thing you can do almost immediately to begin the healing process: get rid of the static lighting system in your home that's exacerbating the problem, and replace it with something better.

HOW TO DO IT

Install human-centric lighting. Circadian lighting systems suitable for residential use comprise two basic elements: a programmable color-changing bulb, and a smartphone or desktop app for controlling the light. Some systems also include a hub, which is a piece of hardware that sends commands to the bulb, and a keypad. Others pack the hub function inside the bulb.

Installation and setup are comparatively easy; the hub—if one is required—connects to your wireless network, the bulb gets screwed into your fixture, and the app gets loaded onto your smartphone or computer. No special wiring is required, although you need to program the lights to perform the

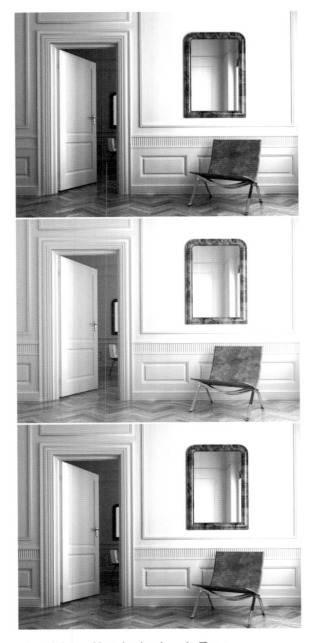

Electric lighting calibrated to the solar cycle. The top frame corresponds to morning light, the middle to midday, and the bottom to evening hours.

color-changing bulbs run around sixty-five watts. This could be a problem should you seek higher light levels. They're also only available in limited configurations. Swapping out a classic A19 pear-shaped bulb or a four-inch-diameter floodlight is no problem, but larger floods and other specialty items are presently unavailable in color-changing models. However, market conditions change rapidly, so scope things out periodically to stay abreast of this fast-evolving technology.

Then there's the question of money. Compared to conventional products, the up-front costs for smart lighting are as you'd expect—higher. Fortunately, you can offset some of that outlay by replacing old heat-generating energy-sapping incandescent bulbs with the energy-efficient longer-lasting LED variety. And of course, you can't put a price on better health and creative flow.

Smart lighting accrues further value by providing you with a nearly limitless menu of other programming opportunities besides mimicking the circadian cycles. Set your lights to go off or on whenever you leave or enter your house or apartment. Have them change colors in time with the music at your next party. Flash red whenever it's about to rain, or make them glow green on your birthday. Create lighting presets for watching movies, dinner parties, and of course, brainstorming sessions.

Or just have fun, because now you can.

RELATED TACTICS AND EXPLAINERS

#4. Take in a view.
#14. Bring nature in.
#19. Let in natural light.
#21. Dim the lights.
#22. Switch on a filament bulb.
#25. Sleep.
#26. Nap.
Explainer II: We Are Who We Have Always Been.

desired functions. Some product lines integrate with native or third-party apps that automatically change bulb color to mimic the solar cycle.

There are a few constraints to be aware of. Currently, the maximum wattage of off-the-shelf

TACTIC #21
DIM THE LIGHTS

WHAT TO DO

Maintain low levels of light to promote innovative thinking.

WHY DO IT?

In 2013, German researchers determined that peak idea formation occurs at a lighting level of 150 lux.

WHY DOES IT WORK?

Two tactics back (#19) I sang the praises of natural light as a means of enhancing creativity and psycho-physical states generally. In the next section I celebrated light as a central metaphor for creativity itself.

Now I'm going to give you mental whiplash by suggesting that there are times when being a bit dim is actually the bright thing to do.

It all has to do with the effect of light levels on cognitive style.

There are three possible explanations for the paradox. The first is that just as highly illuminated surfaces tend to draw the eye toward them and therefore to the world outside ourselves, so too does the absence of light lead our thoughts inward by depriving the eye of anything to occupy it. As I noted in the Introduction, internally directed cognition is allied with mind-wandering and creativity, externally directed attention with convergent and analytic mental processing.

The same holds true in terms of our perception of interior space. Think how difficult it is to assess the dimensions of a room shrouded in darkness. Now imagine the same room, but brightly lit. The

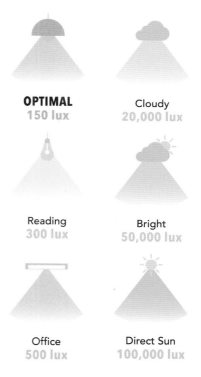

OPTIMAL	Cloudy
150 lux	20,000 lux
Reading	Bright
300 lux	50,000 lux
Office	Direct Sun
500 lux	100,000 lux

Fig. 22: Standard indoor and outdoor light levels in lux.

extent of the spatial envelope suddenly becomes fully discernible and measurable. Recalling my earlier thesis that our mental space grows and shrinks in direct proportion to our sense of physical space (#2), it follows that dimness expands our idea space, while brightness narrows it.

A third potentially contributing factor involves surveillance. Whether it's in an overlit office or in a prison complex subjected to the unforgiving beam of searchlights, being under the spotlight often stresses us out. Why? In part because it makes us feel that we're not in control of ourselves, that we're under the thumb of another party—which is literally the case

Library. Abbotsford House, residence of Sir Walter Scott. Architecture by William Atkinson. 1821–1822, 1853. Melrose, United Kingdom. Photography by Michael D. Beckwith.

with prison inmates, and which can be figuratively true of organizations that fail to convey a sense of autonomy among employees. Creativity demands freedom, the freedom to take risks without censure or threat of dismissal or demotion; absent that feeling of empowerment, we will simply refrain from trying. True, if you're a home-based creative, you exert the highest degree of influence over your surroundings and actions you're likely to enjoy anywhere, and are therefore somewhat immunized against the motivational constraints brightness places on what scientists call our *locus of control*. Nonetheless, the impact of high-intensity lighting on cognitive style and spatial determinacy I outlined above would still apply.

Having stated all this, I don't want to give the impression that you should operate within perennially murky surroundings. That's neither practical nor healthy, as numerous studies attest. Balance dimness with task appropriateness. Keep lighting low when you're trying to put as many ideas on the table as possible, or when you're aiming to break a creative logjam. Turn up the juice after you've progressed deeper into the creative process or need to perform visually demanding tasks.

HOW TO DO IT

Get a light meter. Sticklers who want to know how much light is bouncing off their desk or easel or countertop can either get themselves a piece of handheld hardware, which ranges from moderately to very expensive, or load an app on their smartphones for free or nearly free. Unsurprisingly, the cheaper alternative is less accurate, although for our purposes close enough might be good enough.

Parlor. French Quarter, New Orleans. 1832. Photography by Mitchell Hollander.

Another course of action is to use the light meter on your SLR digital camera. Consult the Internet for details.

For reference, one lux equals the amount of light that falls on a one square meter surface positioned one meter away from a candle outputting one lumen. A lumen is a unit of emitted light. The light bulbs you buy in a store are now commonly measured in lumens.

Turn lights off or filter incoming light during the day. Start by switching off all electric lights and assessing the ensuing brightness. Then either add light back by turning on some or all of your lights, or reduce brightness by tempering the amount of daylight entering the space. Be aware that daylight can vary from 1,000 to 100,000 lux, depending on weather and atmospheric conditions, so be prepared to manage a wide range of ambient conditions.

Install dimmers. Regulate electric lighting by installing dimmers. Swap out existing wall switches or add dimmable lamp cords to table and desk lamps as needed. You might want to also check out the type of switch that offers multiple preset options, allowing you to jump to predetermined light levels with a single tap.

Smart and Z-wave controlled lighting do a great job of regulating brightness as well, as outlined in Tactic #20.

RELATED TACTICS AND TACTICS
#2. Look at something blue.
#3. Work under a lofty ceiling.
#4. Take in a view.
#14. Bring nature in.
#19. Let in natural light.
#20. Be smart with your lighting.
#22. Switch on a filament bulb.
Explainer I: Space, Time, and Creativity

TACTIC #22
SWITCH ON A FILAMENT BULB

WHAT TO DO

Place an unshaded filament bulb in a light fixture in your creative space. Turn it on to unleash a torrent of ideas.

WHY DO IT?

Scientists found that subjects who saw a standard A19 light bulb switched on prior to completing a creative task outperformed subjects who either viewed a different type of bulb or a bulb concealed by a shade.

WHY DOES IT WORK?

The lingo of creativity and light are inextricably linked. Think of the command "let there be light" to mark the biblical account of the world's creation. Or phrases like "a flash of brilliance" to describe the sudden revelation that strikes us at "moments of illumination." Or an era of momentous scientific and cultural advancement called the Enlightenment.

The list is long. Suffice to say that equating light with creativity has a rich history. The visual metaphors that people have invoked in analogizing the two, however, have changed over time. In the preindustrial era, lightning bolts, the sun, and fire were among the images commonly deployed to represent a sudden burst of ideas. In the late nineteenth century, a new trope emerged. This image came courtesy of Thomas Edison, a master marketer who flooded the press with pictures of himself holding his newly perfected light bulb.

Inventiveness and bulbs soon coalesced in the public consciousness. From there it was only a matter of time before someone transformed the bulb into a metaphor for creative insight in its own right.

That moment arrived in 1942 when the first true idea bulb graphic popped up over Goofy's head in a Disney cartoon (an embryonic version had appeared seven years earlier in a Betty Boop short). Since its cinematic debut, the idea bulb—and its accompanying sound blip, the idea "ding"—have become authentic cultural memes, visual shorthand for creative epiphany.

Thanks to science, we now know that the idea bulb does more than simply symbolize the pop of revelation; it actually promotes it.

The finding comes courtesy of a study led by Michael Slepian, then at Tufts University. Slepian and his team arranged to have students complete a variety of insight problems in rooms lighted from overhead by either a standard twenty-five-watt incandescent bulb or a fluorescent tube. They also instructed the proctors who administered the experiment to comment on the initial state of darkness in the room, and to flip on the light switch on their way out. This ensured that subjects took notice of the bulb overhead.

The results were enlightening, so to speak. The incandescent group solved 70 percent more insight problems involving spatial, verbal, and mathematical reasoning than subjects seated under the fluorescent tube. And faster too.

Another round of experiments pitted two incandescent bulbs against each other, one bare

Library. Greenwich, Connecticut. Architecture by Peter Ogden Kinnear. Interior design by Gaby and Donald M. Rattner. Photography by Donald M. Rattner.

and the other shaded. The naked bulb won that contest as well.

In light of these results (sorry, can't help myself), it's safe to say that it was the image of the traditional bulb, rather than the quality of the illumination it emitted or the appearance of the fixture that held it, that primed the concept of creative insight in the minds of the winning subjects.

The idea bulb is just one of many primes associated with creativity that operate on a metaphorical level. For instance, how often have you been advised to "think outside the box" when solving a creative problem? Or to "look at both sides of the coin"? Like the idea bulb, these phrases are meant as allusive stand-ins for imaginative nonconformity. They've also proven to be potent catalyzers of creativity when enacted in physical form: in the previously mentioned 2012 experiment, scientists discovered

that subjects who took their creativity assessment tests sitting just outside an open cardboard carton scored higher than those who sat inside it during the exercise.

Yet a metaphor doesn't have to relate specifically to creativity to jump-start our imagination. Metaphors by definition fuse dissimilar concepts into new wholes, helping us see things from a fresh perspective. "All the world's a stage" equates life with a play. A "table leg" likens a furniture element to human or animal anatomy. A "loud tie" meshes aural shrillness with apparel. Each turn of phrase wrenches us out of our literal mind-set and into a make-believe world of imaginative possibility.

Some very significant innovations came about because of our ability to think metaphorically. Velcro is a classic example. On a summer day in 1941, a Swiss inventor named George de Mestral

Rear yard, kitchen, and living room. San Francisco, California. Architecture by YAMAMAR Design. Interior design by Alison Damonte for Alison Damonte Design. Photography by Bruce Damonte.

took his dog out for a nature walk. Returning home, he noticed that both he and his dog had burrs clinging to their legs. De Mestral removed a few of the seedpods and put them under his microscope. There he discovered that the seeds had attached themselves by means of tiny hooks. Most people would have left it at that. But de Mestral was an inventor. He had the mental chops to make the conceptual leap from a tiny piece of bioengineering into an enormously enterprising idea for a removable fastener. The key to his success? Thinking metaphorically (i.e., divergently) rather than literally (i.e., convergently).

"Metaphor is the lifeblood of all art," writes dancer and choreographer Twyla Tharp in her book *The Creative Habit: Learn It and Use It for Life.* Tharp goes on:

The process by which we transform the meaning of one thing into something different is an essential part of human intelligence. Without symbols, and the ability to understand them, there would be no writing, no numbers, no drama, no art. Everything you create is a representation of something else; in this sense, everything you create is enriched by metaphor.

Developing a spine is the first step in building what I like to think of as your MQ, or metaphor quotient. In the creative process, MQ is as valuable as IQ.

Being attuned to metaphor can help you be more creative in your work, in your pastimes, and in play. But, like any skill, it requires exercise to develop. Author Daniel Pink (a home-based business thinker who operates out of a converted garage) suggests maintaining a log for jotting down any provocative metaphors you encounter in the course of your day. Try perusing your list when you're faced with a knotty problem; the entries might jar your mind just enough to shed some light on an answer.

HOW TO DO IT

Use a filament bulb. An unshaded standard incandescent bulb can be visually discomfiting. I recommend utilizing a filament, or what's alternatively called an Edison or Vintage bulb, in its place. They come in both LED and incandescent versions.

Insert the bulb into a desk lamp, sconce, or ceiling fixture designed for exposed lighting. Hanging them singly or in multiples from ceilings and walls with exposed cords makes for an equally handsome presentation.

Display a graphic image of the idea bulb. As with most primes, a pictorial representation of the stimulus can yield the same results as the real thing. Hang a poster, attach a wall decal, or paint a stencil of an idea bulb in your creative space.

RELATED TACTICS
#5. Display art.
#19. Let in natural light.
#20. Be smart with your lighting.
#21. Dim the lights.
#29. Make a fire. Or look at a picture of one.

Advertisement for IBM. Text at bottom reads "Every man with an idea has at least two or three followers[.] Brooks Atkinson[.] Management Development IBM." Graphic design by Ken White. [1974]. Library of Congress.

TACTIC #23
ADJUST THE THERMOSTAT

WHAT TO DO
Regulate indoor temperature for optimal productivity.

WHY DO IT?
Creative performance is sensitive to ambient temperature levels.

WHY DOES IT WORK?
Forget those tired clichés about frostbitten writers cranking out literary masterpieces in unheated Parisian garrets. Real people know that suboptimal environmental conditions lead to diminished productivity, not a book contract.

So what is the ideal room temperature and humidity for peak creativity, you ask?

I wish I knew.

It isn't for lack of data. The problem is that the figures that have been published to date are all over the map, and sometimes only partially relevant to our purposes. A study out of Cornell University, for example, found that workers in a Florida office scored the fewest keyboard errors and typed the most words at 77°F (25°C). That's a helpful data point for assessing analytic task performance, but it's unrevealing in determining conditions suited to abstract mental processing. Meanwhile, another study found nearly the exact opposite of Cornell's, subjects showing a steady *decline* in proofreading skills as the temperature *rose* from 68 to 77°F (20 to 25°C).

Then there's the experiment that purported to fix the ideal temperature for creative tasks at 80.6°F (27°C), and 78.8°F (26°C) for logic-based problems. Given that our brain consumes greater amounts of glucose to cool us down than it does to warm us up, the narrow margin strikes me as a bit suspect. Both figures seem high overall as well, the first because it borders on a temperature range that many would find uncomfortable, and the second because it rubs against the idiomatic characterization of analytic thinking as the "cool light of reason."

Adding to the challenge is the surfeit of variables that influence body temperature. Let's start with attire; who knows how those employees in Florida were dressed? Were the men wearing shirts and ties, or polo shirts? What about the women, whose metabolic rates differ significantly from their male colleagues? Both gender and

Honeywell T-86 Round Thermostat. Product design by Henry Dreyfuss from concept by Honeywell engineer Carl Kronmiller. American. 1953. Photography by Honeywell International.

clothing impact our response to temperature. So does age. So does context; a Floridian entering conditioned space after passing through 90°F (32°C) heat and 90 percent humidity outside is going to find 77°F (25°C) downright balmy. Not so for colleagues in Alaska transitioning in from the frozen tundra.

Finally, there's color. Researchers have documented several instances where the palette of a room influenced feelings of thermal comfort among occupants. One account tells of an air-conditioned factory cafeteria with light blue walls. Employees insisted they felt cold during meals despite a room temperature of 72°F (22°C). Management raised the thermostat to 75°F (24°C), but the complaints kept coming. Then somebody hit on the idea of painting the walls orange. Within short order the staff clamored to take the room back down to 72°F (22°C), a rare success story in the often acrimonious struggle to achieve collective thermostatic bliss.

Conclusion: it's impossible to speak definitively or precisely of an ideal temperature for creative cognition at a macro scale. On this one, you're on your own.

Nest Learning Thermostat. Product design by Tony Fadell, Ben Filson, and Fred Bould for Nest Labs. American. 2011. Photography by Nest Labs.

HOW TO DO IT (NONETHELESS)

Find your personal sweet spot. Try to discover what works best for you by experimenting with different temperature settings. Measure your output objectively by keeping a journal of time, temperature, humidity, dress, time of year, and work product. Be exacting in your records; a single degree difference in temperature can sway results.

Use a smart thermostat. Consider replacing older analog devices with a programmable thermostat that allows for variable settings at different times of day. Look into getting a "learning" thermostat, which gradually assimilates your temperature preferences and controls for them without prompting. Both types can automatically adjust the temperature when they detect a residence is unoccupied, saving energy and money. In tandem with third-party apps, the possibilities grow more numerous and granular.

Smart systems that can control old-style radiators and through-wall or window A/C units are now on the market as well.

Use low-energy mechanical devices to maintain comfort. Running a ceiling fan brushes heat away from your skin, leading you to feel more comfortable while reducing the cooling load. But you probably knew that. What you might not have known is that a ceiling fan can also lower your heating bills if you install a model that pulls air upward by spinning in a clockwise direction as well.

Integrate passive heating and cooling. From an environmental and cost perspective, the best mechanical system is the one that never runs. You can achieve this goal by constructing your residence to third-party energy standards and by shaping it in accord with the natural environment, a practice known as passive house design. A core principle of this approach is to allow the sun's energy to enter only to the extent that it's needed to heat or cool the space. I review some of the techniques for solar control in Tactic #19. Go deeper in your research if you're interested in taking passive design to the next level.

Den and office. Toronto, Ontario, Canada. Architecture and interior design by Gloria Apostolou for Post Architecture. Photography by Arnaud Marthouret for Revelateur Studio.

RELATED TACTICS

#14. Bring nature in.

#19. Let in natural light.

#20. Be smart with your lighting.

#21. Dim the lights.

#29. Make a fire. Or look at one.

#30. Have a drink.

TACTIC #24
PICK UP THE SCENT

WHAT TO DO
Infuse the home with scent.

WHY DO IT?
Certain aromas are believed to improve mood, mental processing, and idea formulation.

WHY DOES IT WORK?
Do you live with someone who doesn't feel the normal rules of tidiness apply to them? A teenager perhaps? A slovenly spouse? If so, the solution to your problem could be right under your nose: citrus-scented cleaning fluid.

Kudos to the team of Dutch psychologists who discovered the cure. How did they do it? By hiding a bucket of cleaning liquid under a desk in a lab room, putting subjects through a stealth exercise, and then secretly watching them eat a crumbly cookie handed out afterward as a snack. I say stealth, because the psychologists had zero interest in the exercise per se; what they really wanted to know was if the fumes from the bucket affected how the subjects dealt with the cookie crumbs that invariably fell onto the table during consumption.

They certainly did. Subjects who unwittingly breathed in the scent were three times more likely to wipe the bits of cookie off the table than a control group who went through the same routine but without the concealed bucket.

Foyer details. Hong Kong. Interior design and photography by Y.C. Chen for hoo.

The causal relationship between olfactory stimulus and behavioral outcome seems plain enough in the case of the Dutch experiment. Other attempts to pin down cause and effect among various fragrances have been less decisive. One reason is that variations in gender, ethnicity, race, nationality, culture, age, and, most of all, personal experience among subjects can lead to very different associations between scent and memory. This person's sweet smell of success might be the next person's odor of horror because of diverging events in their respective pasts. Adding to the general unpredictability of the data are the facts that men are statistically less sensitive to smell than women, and that some people have a less acute sense of smell by nature.

Nevertheless, we can draw a few general deductions about the efficacy of aromatherapy for fostering creativity. Let's begin with the premise that scent influences mood in a manner similar to music (#18) and other hedonic inputs. By that logic, pleasing fragrances put people in a good mood, while bad odors put them in a bad mood. Positive affect nourishes our creativity. Down states inhibit it.

That's a start, though a bit broad. Has anyone run laboratory experiments or collected data to correlate a particular smell and improved creative performance? Yes; in 2012 a research group from the Netherlands (what is it about the Dutch that gets them stoked by smell tests?) discovered by way of an experiment on nocturnal task activation that having subjects inhale an orange-vanilla fragrance during sleep increased problem-solving skills and

made them more accepting of innovative ideas. Design scientist, consultant, and author Sally Augustin also cites cinnamon-vanilla as having been linked to heightened creativity.

More research is needed to determine if other scents would bring about the same results. In the interim, it's safe to say that scent can nurture creative capacity indirectly through mood arousal, stress reduction, steadier sleep cycles, and improved physical well-being.

HOW TO DO IT

Dr. Augustin offers a number of useful prescriptions for applied aromatherapy in her book *Place Advantage: Applied Psychology for Interior Architecture*. Here are just a few:

To improve performance on mental tasks in general: Lemon and jasmine.

To improve mood: Lemon and cinnamon-vanilla are particularly associated with a positive mind-set, although almost any scent you personally find pleasant can do the same.

To relax: Options includes lavender, rose, almond, cedar/pine, bergamot, chamomile, marjoram, heliotrope, sandalwood, vanilla, muguet, ylang-ylang, and spiced apple. The last has been shown to reduce blood pressure in subjects by three to five points. Lavender works by sedating the central nervous system.

To reduce tension: Lavender and cedar.

To reduce anxiety: Orange, vanilla, lime, marjoram, rose, lavender, bergamot, cypress, and floral scents generally.

To improve sleep: Jasmine will boost cognition after sleep by helping people sleep more soundly and wake up feeling less anxious. Interestingly, the benefits of overnight inhalation have been found to linger into the following afternoon.

To feel healthier: The aroma of baby powder, assuming you like babies. (Scent only; never inhale the powder itself!)

Master bedroom details. Palos Verdes Estates, California. Interior design by Lucie Ayres for 22 Interiors. Photography by Amy Bartlam.

A few closing remarks to keep in mind. First, the cognitive and physiological benefits of a scent will remain in effect even after you've stopped detecting it because of prolonged exposure. So don't be too quick to jettison your stock the moment its strength seems to dissipate.

Second, aromatherapy can help propel good ideas while you're outside your main creative space, especially in places where creative ideas tend to flow most often, such as bedrooms (#25) and baths (#35).

As for how to transmit scents, options include candles and sticks, liquids poured into open containers or spray bottles, diffusers, scent jars, potpourri, soaps, and machines. Natural and organic matter, such as plants, flowers, spices, and fruits can emit aromas too. Avoid synthetic scents if possible, as they can be injurious to your health.

Homes heated or cooled through ductwork offer the added possibility of distributing scents through the HVAC system by clipping air fresheners designed for cars onto supply vents.

You'll find dozens more homespun hacks on the Internet.

RELATED TACTICS
#14. Bring nature in.
#18. Make music.
#30. Have a drink.
#32. Cook.
#38. Go for a walk.

CREATIVITY TACTICS
GROUP THREE:
ACTION

TACTIC #25
SLEEP

To sleep, perchance to dream.
—William Shakespeare

WHAT TO DO
Get a good night's sleep.

WHY DO IT?
Sleep is idea time.

WHY DOES IT WORK?
A bedroom is good for more than just conceiving children. It's also good for conceiving ideas.

Just ask Paul McCartney where he was when the melody for his song "Yesterday" popped into his head. Or, if you could travel back in time, ask the same of Mary Shelley and the inspiration for her novel *Frankenstein*. Or Russian scientist Dmitri Mendeleyev, originator of the Periodic Table of Elements. Or Madame C. J. Walker, inventor of a successful hair tonic that made her the first black millionaire businesswoman in history.

"The bedroom," they would answer in unison. "While dreaming during sleep," they would add.

The common conception of sleep as a period of reduced mental activity turns out to be off the mark. Brain biologist John Medina reveals what really goes on in our braincase while dozing in a section of his book *Brain Rules* titled "You Call This Rest?"

Bedroom. Bolling Hall, Bradford, United Kingdom.
Photography by Michael D. Beckwith.

If you ever get a chance to listen in on someone's brain while its owner is slumbering, you'll have to get over your disbelief. The brain does not appear to be asleep at all. Rather, it is almost unbelievably active during "rest," with legions of neurons crackling electrical commands to one another in constantly shifting, extremely active patterns. In fact, the only time you can observe a real resting period for the brain—where the amount of energy consumed is less than during a similar awake period—is during the phase called non-REM sleep. But that takes up only about 20 percent of the total sleep cycle. This is why researchers early on began to disabuse themselves of the notion that the reason we rest is so that we can rest. When we are asleep, the brain is not resting at all.

Instead, as lab studies and fMRI scans demonstrate, the brain is turning over information acquired during the day, integrating it with what you already know, and looking for potential connections among the bits of collected data in an effort to work through lingering problems. One experiment, for example, found that rats who started to learn how to get through a maze during a daytime experiment figured out a solution more adeptly after a night's sleep than another group of rats who tried to crack the puzzle uninterruptedly. Scientists believe that

Master bedroom. Seaside, Florida. Architecture by Gary Brewer for Robert A.M. Stern Architects. Photography by Peter Aaron / Otto.

the rats allowed to snooze used their downtime to consolidate memories of what they'd learned earlier so as to continually rerun the problem in their brains overnight. That gave them a leg up when they were thrown back into the maze the following day.

Humans use sleep for similar purposes. Barack Obama had all the information he was likely to get from military intelligence when asked for final authorization of the raid on Osama Bin Laden's compound in Pakistan in 2011. Were he a character in a movie, he no doubt would have shouted "Let's do this!" after the appropriate dramatic buildup—or something to that effect. In real life, his response was quintessentially anticlimactic. Obama told stunned officials that he was going to sleep on it. He gave the go-ahead the next day after a sixteen-hour interval.

Science aside, the notion that our brains can gain insights into certain issues more effectively at night than during daytime is commonsensical. During the day we tend to be conscious of being conscious. That is, we're relatively controlled and inhibited in our thinking, in part because we're expending a great deal of mental energy processing incoming information while screening out irrelevant inputs. At night we're no longer bombarded by sensory stimuli, nor are we in conscious control of our thoughts. Our brains are freed up to purposefully churn information.

The challenge we face today is getting enough quality shut-eye to give free rein to the brain's capacity for "offline" creative problem-solving. There's little debate as to the root causes of epidemic sleep deprivation. High on the list are the electronic devices we immerse ourselves in at all hours, along with electric illumination and indoor living. Thanks to these conveniences, we're no longer hindered from carrying on the day's activities into night for lack of light. Add to this the pressures of modern life in general and you've got a perfect storm for restless sleep.

I can't do much to reform the state of the world. I can, however, suggest steps you can take in designing your bedroom that can further sleep quality and, by extension, nocturnal idea generation.

HOW TO DO IT

Temper the lighting. Get into the habit of lowering the lighting levels in the room about three hours before sleep. The simplest way is to gradually turn off fixtures, leaving only low wattage lights on by bedtime. Inexpensive dimmer switches are another option. Tech junkies will want to look at the many wireless technologies and smart bulb systems that can dim lights automatically. Close your curtains, blinds, or shades fully. By the time you've shut your eyes to sleep you should be in total darkness.

Fixture types matter too. Lamps or overhead fixtures that cast light downward over limited areas are best. Avoid large fixtures that flood the room with diffuse light characteristic of the outdoors, such as center-mounted ceiling lights that bounce light off the ceiling. At a minimum, limit such fixtures to daytime use.

For reading a book in bed (no back-illuminated e-books please!), use a lamp that focuses light within a limited range so as not to spill illumination onto your partner's side of the bed or into the room. A

Sleeping loft. Nashville, Tennessee. Building and interior design by David Latimer for New Frontier Tiny Homes. Photography by StudiObuell.

desk lamp with a telescoping or swivel arm is ideal; swing-arm lamps or sconces can work too.

Some people go so far as to light candles before bed while extinguishing their electric lights. The safety conscious might consider battery-operated candles or tea lights as an alternative.

Mute color and pattern. The last thing you want to do in decorating a bedroom is shock your nervous system. Avoid fire-engine reds, over bright yellows, bold chevron patterns, or any other visually intense surface treatment that will send your senses into hyperdrive. Stick with broad areas of warm and neutral tones and appropriately scaled patterns. Maintaining warmth harmonizes with the change of light at day's end and generates an aura of cocooning by drawing in the surrounding space.

Then again, there is some evidence that the reverse might be equally true when it comes to choice of hue. A survey by a British hotel chain found that on average people at home in the UK sleep longer in a blue room than any other color. They also wake up happier. Researchers theorize that blue's calming effect and propensity to lower blood pressure and heart rate might be the cause. Perhaps the contradictory nature of the finding can be explained by the offsetting properties of the warm electric lighting commonly used in domestic interiors, which can alter the optics of a color quite drastically. Hard for me to say. Such is the complex and messy nature of the human mind.

Whether you go warm or cool, it's probably best to stay with muted and pastel shades of your chosen colors for walls, rugs, bedding, upholstery, and drapery in order to encourage sleep.

Furnish right. Other than the bed, the most important piece of furniture in the room is a nightstand or prop on which to place a pad and pen or other recording device for capturing all the ideas you'll be putting out with your newfound sleep. Don't rely on memory; we forget most ideas shortly after having them. A bed shelf hung from the side of the bed or mounted on a wall, or a built-in ledge running behind the bed, are fine alternatives as long as you can reach your record keeper easily.

Avoid any pieces that conflict with sleeping and dressing functions. Televisions most of all. Watching TV before bed is precisely what you shouldn't do if you want to maintain healthy sleep patterns. Even when the set is off it can have the unwanted effect of stimulating your brain by virtue of its association with wakefulness. If you must have a television, place it inside a cabinet or behind doors. Or treat yourself to the model that turns itself into a nicely framed reflective mirror when switched off.

The same advice pertains to desks, exercise equipment, computers, printers, and assorted other nonessential furnishings that sneak into sleeping quarters. I understand this is not always possible in dwellings where space is tight or if you live in a dorm room, loft, or open-plan abode. Just do the best you can to pare down or conceal ancillary belongings.

Speaking of extra baggage, you would do well to control clutter by storing as much stuff as you can in drawers, cabinets, and closets. The more spare and calming the decor, the less there is to overstimulate the brain before bed. Think along similar lines when choosing artwork for the room. Landscape and nocturnal scenes, minimalist abstract art, art built on muted color palettes, and other pieces conducive to quiet contemplation will serve you best.

Try selecting furnishings and decorative elements that can be arrayed symmetrically, especially in relationship to the bed. Balance denotes repose—precisely what the sleep doctor ordered.

Keep cool and quiet. The ideal sleeping temperature for the broadest segment of the population falls between 64 and 70°F (18 to 21°C). Put

Photography studio of Nicholas Yarsley. Gloucestershire, United Kingdom. Architecture, interior design, and photography by Nicholas Yarsley.

in a ceiling fan, crack a window, or adjust heating and cooling levels to meet this target. To mitigate noisy environments, lay down a plush rug and provide a generous supply of pillows in the room to absorb sound. Thick drapes and upholstery can help as well. Reduce audible and visual noise in the first place by banishing alarm clocks and other devices that tick, beep, blink, or burp.

Thread count counts. As sleep expert Michael Breus points out, tactile experience influences sleep quality as much as stimuli received through other senses. He recommends putting on the softest and highest quality bedsheets you can afford. Use natural fibers such as wool, cotton, linen, and silk instead of synthetics, which could trap heat and moisture.

Try aromatherapy. I mention in Tactic #24 that cinnamon-vanilla scent was found to have

positive effects on ideogenesis when administered to subjects during sleep. Research indicates that lavender can be relaxing and reduce morning sleepiness as well. Or follow your own instincts in choosing an aroma. "Any fragrance that makes you calm and relaxed can promote sleep," explains Dr. Natalie Dautovich of the National Sleep Foundation. "Your olfactory system is directly linked to the emotional center in your brain, so when you sniff something that brings back a good memory, your body releases feel-good, relaxing chemicals that can set the stage for great sleep."

You've got multiple options for releasing scents into the room. Fragrant plants and flowers emit their bouquets naturally. Other vehicles include sprays, scented candles, sachets, and mechanical diffusers. Liquid products can be bought commercially or cooked up on a stovetop.

Seed ideas. In addition to shaping your sleep environment for optimal restfulness, there are actions you can take prior to bedtime to spawn ideas overnight. One widely practiced technique is to "seed" your dreams by pondering the creative challenges you're currently facing. It could be an assignment at work or a personal project you've taken on at home. If you're a writer, you could reread the last several hundred words you wrote earlier that day so as to prime your brain for the content to follow. If you're a coder, you could ruminate on the algorithm you're hoping to nail down next before turning in.

The story of Elias Howe is a classic instance of inadvertent idea seeding. In 1845 the inventor was struggling to finalize his design for a modern sewing machine. Problem was, he couldn't figure out how to get the thread to penetrate the fabric and come back up again to complete the stitch. It was only after he fell asleep at his workbench one night that a dream led him to a solution: bore the hole for the thread at the bottom of the needle rather than at the top, where it traditionally sits in handheld needles. Like the aforementioned rats decoding the secret of a maze, his mind had picked up right where it left off.

Entrepreneur and LinkedIn co-founder Reid Hoffmann has self-institutionalized idea seeding by jotting down during the day issues that he wants his mind to address overnight. Being a seasoned creative, he frames his queries as questions: What are the key things that I want to think about? What do I want to solve creatively? What might be constraining a solution? What are the tools or assets I might have to bypass these constraints?

Keep a journal or voice recorder at the ready. I can't stress enough that ideas caught mid-sleep must be captured before they evaporate in the fog of night. Keep that pencil or voice recorder within arm's reach.

RELATED TACTICS

#2. Look at something blue.
#20. Be smart with your lighting.
#21. Dim the lights.
#23. Adjust the thermostat.
#24. Pick up the scent.
#26. Nap.
#27. Exploit the groggies.
#28. Lie down or recline.
#37. Take a break.
#39. Daydream.

TACTIC #26
NAP

WHAT TO DO
Nap for ten to thirty minutes a day.

WHY DO IT?
Napping restores cognitive capacity, and more.

WHY DOES IT WORK?
If I told you that performing a certain activity for twenty to thirty minutes a day could help you formulate ideas, kick-start productivity, quicken motor reflexes, sharpen perception, strengthen stamina, hone decision-making, bolster memory, lower stress, promote weight loss, lessen chances of cancer, heart disease, and diabetes, and elevate mood, would you do it?

Of course you would.

So why aren't you taking regular naps?

I know, I know—you're busy getting the job done during the day. Emails and texts are flooding in, the phone rings incessantly, the cat needs to be fed, and someone's screaming for that presentation/memo/drawing/rewrite/proposal/post/fill-in-the-blank you've been working on for hours.

Sorry, but no excuse. Scores of highly successful creative individuals and organizations manage to pull off naps. Thomas Edison, hardly anyone's picture of a slacker, dozed midday for up to three hours. The decorator Sister Parish, namesake of top-drawer New York decorating firm Parish-Hadley, retired to her apartment every day for a post-lunch doze, after which she carried on with her work with renewed energy. The doyenne of decorators maintained this habit into her eighties. Margaret Thatcher, Ronald Reagan, Salvador Dalí,

Master Bedroom. Mill Valley, California. Architecture by Michael Rex Architects. Interior design by Anamar Interiors. Photography by Michael Keeney.

Aristotle, and Lyndon Johnson followed a similar routine. Nor is napping confined to the uber-achiever class; employees at companies like Google, Apple, Nestle, AOL, Time Warner, Facebook, GlaxoSmithKline, Procter & Gamble, Intuit, and Nike can choose to snooze in dedicated napping facilities without being canned for slacking off.

Alcove. Muharraq, Bahrain. Photography by John Grummitt.

Scientific research confirms the empirical and anecdotal evidence. For instance, a 2009 experiment in which subjects who took a creativity test in the morning followed by a nap scored higher on a follow-up test in the afternoon than a second group who took both tests without intervening rest. Brain scans generated in a study at Georgetown University a few years later showed that the parts of our brain associated with convergent thinking rested quietly during afternoon slumber, while regions linked to divergency continued to plug away. And those are just two among many studies affirming the cognitive value of naps.

As is often the case, one of the reasons supplementary sleep periods are so good for us is that nature bioengineered them into our daily cycle from the get-go, as sleep scientist Sara Mednick notes in her book *Take a Nap! Change Your Life:*

Let's look at the rest of the animal kingdom. Do any other species [besides humans] try to get all their sleep in one long stretch? No. They're all multiphasic, meaning that they have many phases of sleep. *Homo sapiens* (our modern industrialized variety, anyway) stand alone in attempting to satisfy the need for sleep in one phase. And even that distinction is a relatively recent development. For most of our history, a rest during the day was considered as necessary a component of human existence as sleeping at night. As A. Roger Ekirch, one of the few historians to study sleep, put it, "Napping is a tool as old as time itself."

Curiously, the realization that napping is built into our biorhythms only came to light in 1986, when researchers sequestered volunteers in a converted World War II underground bunker for weeks at a time. Isolated from clocks or windows to the outside, the volunteers were free to sleep whenever they wanted. Subjects soon fell into an unforced rhythm: a long sleep period at night and a shorter stretch in the afternoon.

Of course, we don't help ourselves by doing things like eating carb-heavy lunches, which can lead to what's popularly known as a "sugar crash." Coffee drinkers might also suffer the effects of caffeine withdrawal after intake (#30). Add in the stress that typically mounts in the course of the workday, as well as possible sleep deprivation (#25), and you've got the perfect ingredients for a mid-afternoon falloff.

The only remaining question is how to turn a need into a nap.

Children's bedroom. Seaside, Florida. Architecture by Gary Brewer for Robert A.M. Stern Architects. Photography by Peter Aaron / Otto.

HOW TO DO IT

Find your spot. Optimal napping depends on two factors: identifying the right place, and the right furniture.

Many creatives opt to catnap in their workspace. Others retire to another part of the home. Either strategy works. The only restriction I would impose is to avoid using your bedroom for the purpose so as to draw a clear distinction in your mind between the different phases of sleep.

As for furnishings, sofas, recliners, long banquettes, and perhaps best of all, daybeds are all designed for short-stint slumber. Comfortably upholstered armchairs are fine for those who prefer to nap upright.

Pieces can be either freestanding or built-ins. Built-in sleepers are commonly fitted into nooks. A nook is a secluded or sheltered space set off from the room into which it faces. Nooks can project outside the structure of the home or be contained within its walls. A bay window or dormer are examples of the former. A recess framed by built-in cabinetry or flanking interior walls falls into the latter category.

Projecting nooks and nooks positioned on exterior walls generally have windows, which helps with daytime reading, but can interfere with napping. Install blinds or shades to block out windows if you're light sensitive.

Windowed nooks have the potential to afford you all the psychophysical creativity boosters that come with exterior openings: daylight (#19), glimpses of greenery (#14), long vistas (#4), and so forth. But daybeds embedded in blind (i.e., windowless) nooks have something of their own to offer: the inner sense of security that accrues from being sheltered in a space situated at the edge of another space and protected from behind and above (see #4).

Keep it ten to thirty. Resist the temptation to nap beyond a half hour to avoid sinking into a deeper phase of sleep that leaves you groggy rather than refreshed on wakening.

Stay regular. Break at a consistent time of day. Morning people tend to dip in the early hours of the afternoon (1:00 to 2:30 p.m.), night owls in later periods (2:30 to 4:00 p.m.).

RELATED TACTICS AND EXPLAINERS

#2. Look at something blue.
#20. Be smart with your lighting.
#21. Dim the lights.
#23. Adjust the thermostat.
#24. Pick up the scent.
#25. Sleep.
#27. Exploit the groggies.
#28. Lie down or recline.
#30. Have a drink.
#37. Take a break.
#39. Daydream.
Explainer II: We Are Who We Have Always Been

TACTIC #27
EXPLOIT THE GROGGIES

Guy Raz: Did you think of yourself as a creative person when you were younger?

Sting: I was actually allowed to dream a lot as a child. I worked with my father every morning as a milkman. And he would get me up at five in the morning when all of my school friends are in bed. And we'd drive around the streets and deliver milk. And he wouldn't say very much to me, apart from, you know, two pints here and three pints there. We didn't talk. And so I was allowed—in this very creative time in the day, you know, as light was coming up—to dream. And I dreamt and dreamt and dreamt about futures I might possibly have, fantasized I suppose. So I was in that creative mode from the very beginning, just by being left alone.

—Host Guy Raz interviewing composer, singer-songwriter, actor, author, and activist Sting on the TED Radio Hour, October 3, 2014

WHAT TO DO
Harvest ideas when you're tired.

WHY DO IT?
Subjects in a 2013 study exhibited superior skills in solving insight problems at nonoptimal times of day.

WHY DOES IT WORK?
In Tactic #1, I stress the importance of maintaining a regular creative routine. In Tactic #25, I advocate getting a good night's sleep. In Tactic #26, I promote naps as vital to creative performance. Throughout this book, I underscore the interconnection of peak physical and mental health, scheduling consistency, and productive ideation.

I'm now going to contradict much of what I state elsewhere: sometimes we're at our creative best when we're at our mental and physical worst.

This happens at three times of day in particular: 1) in the minutes just prior to dozing off, which scientists call the hypnagogic period; 2) when we'd prefer to be asleep; and 3) when we're prematurely rousted from our slumber—in other words, those moments of drowsiness right before, during, and shortly after the sleep or nap cycle when we're groggy and zonked out.

Why would this be the case? The scientists who put together the landmark 2013 study linking improved problem solving to off-hour activity surmise that the brain regions responsible for regulating the flow of information normally needed to manage real-time activities are operating at reduced capacity during sleep or near sleep. They're able to power down because being dormant lessens our need to pay close attention to what we're actually doing. Freed from having to filter out data and stimuli deemed nonrelevant to performing a deliberate task, our mental floodgates open up to let in ideas, memories, and bits of stored information that hitherto were held back so as to avoid distracting us from the job at hand. Out of that swirling mélange emerges the sort of serendipitous idea collisions that might otherwise elude us during periods of full wakefulness.

With the diminished level of top-down control also comes a weakening of mental and behavioral constraints and less obeisance to the status quo. "Exhaustion," explains creativity blogger Tanner

Study. Lilyfield, Sydney, New South Wales, Australia. Architecture by Danny Broe Architect. Interior design assisted by Toby Andrews. Photography by Karina Illovska.

Christensen, "can spur creativity because, frankly, you just don't give a damn." Christensen tracks these feelings of insouciance to the flow of chemicals in our brain. In particular, he describes how the frontal cortex—the region that handles executive functioning, among other tasks—begins to lose its power to keep our whims in check as tiredness causes the supply of dopamine going to our head to diminish. The result? An increasingly devil-may-care attitude to what we're doing or thinking—precisely the kind of rebellious mentality that gives birth to nonnormative ways of looking at the world.

HOW TO DO IT

Discover your chronotype. A good first step in harnessing brain fog for creative ends is to determine your chronotype. A chronotype is a personal biological rhythm. More granular and individualized than the universalized circadian cycle, your chronotype specifies the optimal times of day for you to undertake various types of activities.

There used to be two commonly accepted categories of chronotype—early birds and night owls. Then clinical psychologist Michael Breus, author of *The Power of When,* expanded the number to four, renaming them lion, dolphin, bear, and wolf. (Breus offers an online quiz for calculating your animal alter-ego. Mine is a dolphin, which puts me in the same class as Dickens, Shakespeare, and Richard Branson, thank you very much.) Once you learn where you fall on the biorhythmic spectrum, the thinking goes, you'll be able to more finely coordinate your problem-solving pursuits with your sleep and nap timetable.

Your chronotype can also guide task scheduling during waking periods. For instance, according to Breus, as a dolphin I'll be at my best if I write this book (a divergent form of mental processing) between 8:00 and 10:00 a.m., and proofread it (a convergent process) from 4:00 to 6:00 p.m.

Capitalize on found moments of delirium. If you're like most adults, you probably wake up at least once in the night as a matter of course. Capitalize on the hiatus to capture any ideas that might have taken shape in the intervening hours.

Disrupt yourself. You can also create your own opportunities for mining the interstices between consciousness and unconsciousness.

Thomas Edison, who was as inventive in finding ways to be inventive as he was in inventing things, devised a particularly idiosyncratic method for doing so. He'd first place metal saucers underneath whatever seat he chose for his nap. Then he'd take hold of a couple of steel balls in each hand, close his eyes, ponder the problem he was currently grappling with, and let himself nod off. Eventually his grip would loosen, leaving the balls to drop onto the saucers. Jolted from his reverie by the ensuing clatter, Edison would grab a nearby pad and pencil to scribble down whatever was coursing through his mind before the interruption.

Cumbersome, but effective. You, on the other hand, could simply set a timer to go off at an appropriate interval after settling down to rest. Or rouse yourself out of bed an hour or two earlier than you'd care to in the morning, and then devote the time to idea jamming.

Tiny home. Nashville, Tennessee. Building and interior design by David Latimer for New Frontier Tiny Homes. Photography by StudiObuell.

Cabin and studio. Marblemount, Washington. Architecture by David Coleman Architecture. Photography by Ben Benschneider.

You also could induce grogginess by having a drink. Like sleep deprivation, alcohol consumption can open the door to deviant thinking by inhibiting activity in the frontal lobe. (Before you go scurrying to the liquor cabinet, however, I suggest reading what the experts have to say on the subject in Tactic #30.)

Whatever method you practice, it's crucial that you download any resulting insights into a notebook or device as soon as possible after emerging from your stupor. Forget about trying to retrieve your musings later on; it's estimated that about 90 percent of sleep-induced content evaporates within ten minutes of its occurrence.

RELATED TACTICS
#19. Let in natural light.
#25. Sleep.
#26. Nap.
#28. Lie down or recline.
#30. Have a drink.
#37. Take a break.

TACTIC #28
LIE DOWN OR RECLINE

WHAT TO DO
Assume a recumbent position while performing creative tasks.

WHY DO IT?
Scientists have discovered that people can solve creative problems 10 percent faster while reclining than when standing up.

WHY DOES IT WORK?
Lying down on the job turns out to be a good thing—if your job requires you to be creative, that is.

In 2005, Australian psychologists Darren Lipnicki and Don Byrne observed that subjects laying on a mattress scored higher on insight problems involving anagrams than a group noodling the same puzzles on their feet.

Why the difference? Richard Wiseman, author of *59 Seconds: Think a Little, Change a Lot*, explains the finding:

Reclining furniture. From top to bottom: MVS Chaise by Maarten Van Severen for Vitra, 2000. Eames Lounge Chair ES670 and Ottoman ES671 by Charles and Ray Eames for Herman Miller, 1956. Couch attributed to the workshop of Duncan Phyfe, 1837. Metropolitan Museum of Art, New York.

The answer, according to Lipnicki and Byrne, might have to do with a small section of your brain referred to as the *locus coeruleus* (Latin for "the blue spot"). When activated, this region produces a stress hormone called noradrenaline that, in turn, increases heart rate, triggers the release of energy, and raises blood flow around the body. When you stand up, gravity draws blood away from the upper body, which subsequently increases activity in the locus coeruleus, whereas lying down decreases its activity. Some researchers think that noradrenaline may also impair the brain's ability to engage in certain types of thinking, including the creativity and flexibility required to solve anagrams. It seems that the act of adopting an upright or supine (Latin for "can't be bothered") position dramatically affects the chemicals racing through your body and causes your brain to operate in quite different ways.

Living room. Carmichael, California. Architecture and interior design by Mark Dziewulski Architect. Photography by Keith Cronin.

This could well be a situation where science is simply confirming what idea makers have long understood or capitalized on intuitively. Recall Marcel Proust, the reclusive French novelist who penned all 1,267,069 words comprising his seven-volume fictional tour de force *Remembrance of Things Past* while sequestered in bed (#17), or the story of Archimedes, who was kicking back in the bath when he birthed the original eureka moment (#35). Closer in time is the American novelist Michael Chabon, no slouch himself when it comes to turning out a word barrage; he works leaning back and with his feet up in Herman Miller's classic Eames lounger and ottoman (as am I right now). His near contemporary, Truman Capote, was of a similar bent. Confessed Capote: "I am a completely horizontal author. I can't think unless I'm lying down, either in bed or stretched on a couch and with a cigarette and coffee handy. I've got to be puffing and sipping." (Between puffing and sipping, you've got to wonder where Capote found the time to write.)

Writers, psychoanalysts, digital nomads, and general deep thinkers naturally count among the creative types most inclined to be reclined. Not every creative pastime and profession is as accommodating. Cooks, athletes (except those careening downhill on a luge), and orchestra conductors are rarely in a position, shall we say, to lie down on the job.

HOW TO DO IT

Find your place. Settle into a recliner, lounger, chaise, recamier, daybed, sleeper chair, sofa, divan, futon, fainting couch, bench, window seat, hammock, or any other piece of furniture that can cradle your outstretched body. Alternatively, you could lie on the floor with or without a mat and pillow, depending on the floor surface and your tolerance for pain, or on the ground outside.

Some rather nifty high-tech contraptions combining a motorized recliner with desk and computer apparatus have lately appeared on the market as well.

Unless you're confident you're the next Marcel Proust, for reasons put forth in Tactic #25 I suggest you utilize a sleep bed for extended creative stints during waking hours only if it's dressed for daytime use with cushions, bolsters, throws, and the like.

RELATED TACTICS
#13. Stand up for yourself.
#25. Sleep.
#26. Nap.
#34. Do yoga. Or meditate.
#39. Daydream.
#46. Read.

Living room. Toronto, Ontario, Canada. Architecture and interior design by Gloria Apostolou for Post Architecture. Photography by Arnaud Marthouret for Revelateur Studio.

TACTIC #29

MAKE A FIRE. OR LOOK AT A PICTURE OF ONE.

WHAT TO DO

Position yourself in view of an open fire, perhaps with a warm drink in your hand.

WHY DO IT?

The impression of fire lowers blood pressure, encourages reflection, induces dream states, and elevates mood.

WHY DOES IT WORK?

It's a curious thing. Property owners and real estate agents looking to sell or rent a home will happily tout the presence of fireplaces in their pitch, despite their having long outlived their usefulness as a source of heat or for preparing meals. In fact, most older fireplaces are environmental disasters in terms of energy efficiency, leaking streams of cool air into the interior while directing torrents of warm air up the flue.

So why are people willing to pay an average premium of over a thousand dollars per fireplace for such an impractical anachronism?

The short answer is that a good fire is hedonic, meaning it affords pleasure. And if there's anything we like to spend our money on, it's pleasure. But there's a deeper reason as well. According to a number of scientists, fire might be mapped to our evolutionary DNA, and by extension to our ability to survive by solving problems creatively.

A starting point for this theory lies in the supposition that fire enabled our early hominid ancestors to remain awake after nightfall. Staying alert and active for a greater part of the daily solar cycle put them on a different evolutionary path than their ape cousins, who were consigned to sleep or lie dormant in the dark. Not only did the brain development of the hominids accelerate as a result of prolonged periods of mental activity, the artificial light also protected them from nocturnal predators who might have threatened their existence altogether.

That heightened sense of nighttime security brought a complementary benefit to our forebears: better sleep quality in the form of increased REM duration. Copious experimental data links the kind of rapid eye movement associated with REM sleep to nonlinear thinking. A Harvard Medical School study, for instance, reported a 30 percent jump in abstract problem-solving proficiency among subjects tested shortly after waking from dream-rich REM, versus those coming off non-REM sleep or no rest at all. A similar investigation at UC San Diego registered a 40 percent spike.

Some scientists attribute the results to the brain's propensity to forge associations between unrelated ideas during REM sleep—the fusion of disparate concepts into new wholes being a defining characteristic of creativity (#32). Another intriguing possibility is that the rapid back-and-forth motion of the eye known as saccadic movement, such as occurs during dreams or while following the flickering flames in a fireplace, might stimulate mental breakthroughs by encouraging whole-brain thinking (see #14 and the Introduction).

Study. Chester, Connecticut. Architecture by Donald M. Rattner for Ferguson Shamamian & Rattner, Architects. Interior design by Linda Chase Associates. Photography by Durston Saylor.

Certainly, some world-changing brain pops have come into being by the hearth. Most famously, the nineteenth-century German chemist August Kekulé told of having arrived at a key insight into molecular structure after drifting off in front of a blaze in his darkened study in Ghent, Belgium.

There's evidence that fire can have a sedative effect beneficial to creativity even without lulling us to sleep. Researchers at the University of Alabama recorded a 5 percent drop in blood pressure after student volunteers watched videos of logs burning in fireplace and campfire environments (setting real conflagrations inside university lab buildings generally being *verboten*). This suggests that fire can put us into a creative frame of mind in the same ways that the color blue (#2), pets (#15), yoga

Covered outdoor living area. La Quinta, California. Architecture by Frank Stolz for South Coast Architects. Photography by Mark Davidson.

Living room. Calgary, Alberta, Canada. Architecture and interior design by Richard Davignon and Doris Martin for Davignon Martin Architecture + Interior Design. Photography by Eymeric Widling.

(#34), and other assuasive primes do: by lifting our spirits, relaxing our survivalist fear of the unknown, and spurring psychological wanderlust.

Speaking of spirits, there's also reason to believe that grasping a hot toddy or other heated refreshment while you bask in your inferno could supercharge your creative mojo still further. I put this out there because several experiments have found that we become more open, friendly, and generous after touching something warm. Although these particular studies didn't examine the priming effects of palpable warmth on creative task performance directly, I wouldn't be surprised if future research revealed a correlation, given the interrelationship of mood arousal, receptiveness to novel experience, and creative cogitation evident with other primes.

But why stop there? Down that spiked drink and you could really go into ideation overdrive. Find out why in the upcoming tactic.

HOW TO DO IT

Install a fireplace or freestanding stove. Or use one you already have. Those blessed with a working fireplace in their current abode should continue to enjoy it, especially in concert with their creative pursuits. Those who lack the amenity or believe the cost of acquiring one to be prohibitive might wish to reconsider their options. Retrofitting fireplaces into existing environments or furnishing them in new builds has become easier and more affordable than ever before, thanks to some inventive products having entered the market.

Consider ventless fireplaces, for example— so-called because they require no flue to exhaust off-gases to the outside. Instead of wood or coal, these units emit heat by means of natural gas, propane, alcohol-based gels, or electricity. They're particularly suited for urban dwellings, where building costs are high and post-construction installation often impossible. These products have engendered a degree of controversy regarding occupant health and safety, however, and are subject to local building codes, so research them thoroughly before proceeding.

Both ventless and vented fireplaces and stoves now come in prefabricated versions. They're less expensive than traditional masonry fireplaces and

Tiny home. Nashville, Tennessee. Building and interior design by David Latimer for New Frontier Tiny Homes. Photography by StudiObuell.

offer greater variety in configuration, including wall-hung, suspended, and freestanding units.

Take it outside. Gathering around a fire pit or campfire at night can be an immensely pleasurable and socially rewarding experience. Great for group brainstorming sessions, with or without marshmallows. Review pertinent building ordinances for restrictions.

Watch the video. Barring all else, you can always watch log-burning videos to spark your imagination. Viewed full-screen and with the volume on, some are surprisingly convincing—and an easy ticket to a 5 percent reduction in blood pressure.

RELATED TACTICS AND EXPLAINERS
#23. Adjust the thermostat.
#25. Sleep.
#26. Nap.
#27. Exploit the groggies.
#30. Have a drink.
#32. Cook.
#34. Do yoga. Or meditate.
#46. Read.
Explainer II: We Are Who We Have Always Been

TACTIC #30
HAVE A DRINK

Write drunk, edit sober.
—Ernest Hemingway

WHAT TO DO
Drink alcohol or coffee in prescribed quantities.

WHY DO IT?
Studies indicate that alcoholic and caffeinated beverages can provide a creative jolt when imbibed in controlled amounts.

WHY DOES IT WORK?
Finally, proof that drinking can solve your (creative) problems.

So a person might conclude from a 2012 query into the effects of alcohol on creativity. According to the research, men who downed the equivalent of two pints of beer or two glasses of wine before solving knotty brainteasers not only got more questions right, they also were quicker to deliver their answers than the temporary teetotalers who performed the exercises sober.

So next time someone tells you that there's no drinking on the job, just point them to this study.

Before you grab that bottle off the shelf, though, be mindful that you need to calibrate your intake so as to maintain a blood alcohol content of 0.075 percent. Above or below that figure, your creative powers rapidly fall off or fail to accelerate from standard measures.

For reference, the legal limit for driving under the influence in the United States is 0.08 percent.

STACT modular wine wall. Product design by Eric Pfeiffer for Pfeiffer Lab. 2012. Photography by STACT.

The delta between danger and creative nirvana is apparently very thin.

Why does alcohol lubricate our creative cogs? One theory is that it reduces the mind's working memory capacity. Working memory refers to our ability to concentrate on something specific, and to remember one thing while thinking about another. Those abilities are helpful when it comes to dealing with analytical problems that require focus, rational thought processes, and useful information we've already retained. These same capabilities, however, can be inhibitive when the task calls for out-of-the-box thinking and free-wheeling imagination. In those instances, it's best to let our minds go off on tangents rather than narrow their focus.

There are serious long-term downsides to hunting inspiration in a bottle, of course. Addiction. Weight gain. Organ deterioration. Among the short-term risks are slurred speech, proneness to injury, and a propensity to doze.

True, the last isn't necessarily a downer when it comes to creativity. After all, sleeping (#25) and napping (#26) can do wonders for idea conception. Even grogginess has its upsides on occasion (#27). Thing is, you can't continually operate in a daze. Nodding off in the middle of a conference call or while dicing tomatoes as a result of throwing back a glass or two or three at lunch just won't get you where you want to go.

So what do many do when they need to rescue themselves from mental stupor? That's right—they resort to drink again. Only this time, the magic tonic is coffee.

Now, you might figure that coffee—or more precisely, the caffeine it contains—would cramp creativity, given what you just learned about liquor. Yet there's evidence that suggests that caffeine can actually fuel the imagination, if used right.

The science behind the chemistry is rather intricate. Suffice to say that in the process of allaying sleepiness, caffeine also permits the flow of two chemicals connected to free thinking. The first is dopamine, which has been found to heighten receptivity to untried experiences and atypical ideas, traits integral to divergency. The second is glutamate. This chemical forges stronger and longer-lasting signals among neurons, which in turn enable us to draw ever more connections among ideas already nested in our brains. Since the core of creativity is the fusion of disparate concepts, glutamate must count among its elixirs.

The sheer number of creative caffeinators throughout history testifies to its potency. Bach adored the drink so much that he wrote a comic opera about a coffee-loving father and daughter called *The Coffee Cantata*. Beethoven and Mahler incorporated it into their daily routines. Simone de Beauvoir, Margaret Atwood, and Gertrude Stein are among known fiends. American icons Benjamin Franklin and Teddy Roosevelt practically drowned in the stuff. David Lynch reportedly drinks seven cups a day. Balzac clocked in at fifty. We probably all know people who verge on criminal insanity if they don't get their fix.

Coffeepot with stand and burner. Designed and fabricated by Bennewitz & Bonebakker, Silversmiths. Dutch. 1815. Rijksmuseum, Amsterdam.

And why not? Caffeine can be a highly effective motivator, a liquid call to action. It can get us off the sofa and into the productive quarters of our idea room. It's a particularly good antidote to the personal inhibitors of self-doubt and lack of initiative. It tastes good.

Now, the fine print. First, the effects of caffeine can be short-lived. Moreover, as the effects wear off, your body tends to veer toward a crash-and-burn condition because you used up a lot of your energy reserves while under the influence of the drug. That initiates a potential vicious cycle that prompts you to drink more coffee as you start to feel drowsy, then another when the drowsiness returns, then another and another. Before long you've set up a permanent encampment at the coffee station. Physical addiction is just a mug away.

Second, for some people, caffeine alters thinking in ways adverse, even opposite to those recommended for peak creative performance. For instance, I noted that openness of mind is a precondition for creative insight, yet drinking coffee can serve to narrow attention rather than broaden it. Focus adds value to other productive activities, to be sure, but might detract from your ability to address problems and tasks that permit a heterodox approach.

My advice on creativity-friendly libations? Drink coffee or alcohol because you like them, not because you're angling to be the next Simone de Beauvoir.

Studio. Girona, Spain. Architecture and landscape design by Co Govers and Joana Ramalhete for Zest Architecture. Photography by Jesús Granada.

HOW TO DO IT

Set up a bar or coffee station. Find a place for your preferred potions. Caffeination stations can range from a countertop percolator to elaborate built-in machines and storage units. The design possibilities for bars are similarly diverse.

Consider DIY and hack solutions. Freestanding or existing built-in bookshelves could be readied for use almost instantly. Repurposed furniture is another affordable option if construction is out of reach.

The key design factors to account for are appliances, storage, drinkware, counter space, cleanup, plumbing and power, portability, appearance, transporting the beverage to users, and budget.

Location has an impact on decor as well. Provide seating nearby if your facility is in a social space or is intended to engender social interaction, as bars, wine cellars, and coffee centers often do.

RELATED TACTICS

#27. Exploit the groggies.
#29. Make a fire. Or look at a picture of one.
#31. Eat brain food.
#32. Cook.

TACTIC #31
EAT BRAIN FOOD

Feed your head.
—*Grace Slick*

WHAT TO DO
Eat foods that nourish creative thinking.

WHY DO IT?
Food intake affects cognitive performance.

WHY DOES IT WORK?
Remember how your parents would admonish you to eat your fruits and vegetables as a child? Well, I do. And now I'm glad they did; according to a 2014 self-report study of over 400 young adults, we're likely to experience greater curiosity, creativity, and personal happiness after helping ourselves to copious and daily helpings of these two food groups than people who push their plates aside or feed them to the dog instead.

Take particular note of the term *curiosity* in the paragraph above. The link between creativity and inquisitiveness doesn't get as much press as it should, in my opinion. Yet experts in the field like the psychologist Todd Kashdan call curiosity "a fundamental motive in facilitating industry and creativity." Without it, he and others say, we lack the drive to pursue our creative goals, open our minds to novel experiences, and learn what we haven't already learned.

Funny thing is, curiosity is an innate trait. The proof is in the pudding; we're never more curious about the world than while growing up. We had to be, in order to learn how to survive in it. Yet by the time we attain adulthood, a lot of the curiosity has been talked out of us. "Curiosity killed the cat," goes the old saw, the speaker almost always conveniently omitting the follow-up line "but satisfaction brought it back." Instead, we're taught to seek certainty and security in our life and work choices. Unfortunately, this attitude carries severely negative repercussions for individual creativity. A disinclination to take risks. A fear of following our fascinations. An atrophied skill set. Intellectual stagnation. Indifferent subservience to the status quo.

So what can we do to ameliorate the pressure to play it safe? Apparently, eat our fruits and vegetables. What else? How about play (#43)? Or read (#46)? Maybe get out of the house (#47). Better still, *really* get out of the house (#48).

There's a larger lesson here, of course. What we put in our stomachs goes right to our head. And since our brain is the seat of creativity, it's natural to presume that food intake affects mental and physical output. We certainly know it affects productivity. Eat foods that release glucose into the bloodstream quickly, like pasta, bread, cereal, and sodas, and we'll ride high for a short stint before plummeting back to earth. Foods that release glucose more slowly, like beans, lean meats, yogurt, and oats, sustain us for longer periods.

Size matters too. Big meals slow us down. Smaller repasts keep us chugging along.

And let's not forget the pleasure principle. As long as we're not pulling the rug out from under ourselves by overindulging in delectables, food that makes us happy gets our creative juices flowing.

That said, the science of correlating specific foods with improved insight is still in its infancy. Additional study is needed to verify the relationship between certain nutrients and both short- and long-term creativity. In the meanwhile, be mindful of what's on the plate or in the glass. It could make all the difference.

HOW TO DO IT
Eat the right stuff.

- Omega-3 fatty acids help build the neural highways that link the various areas of the brain, potentially furthering your capacity to synthesize disparate ideas and perspectives into coherent wholes. They're also believed to increase neural communication by rebuilding brain cells. Salmon, halibut, flaxseed, peanut butter, walnuts, kale, and leafy greens are rich in omegas.

- Like our parents told us (and a team of professors confirmed), get your fill of fruits and vegetables.
- Speaking of fruits, be up for blueberries in particular. They carry high doses of antioxidants found through laboratory experimentation to reduce stress, promote brain plasticity, and sharpen spatial navigation.
- Dark chocolate contains flavanols, a nutrient found to increase blood flow to the brain by dilating circulatory vessels. It also delivers moderate amounts of caffeine and magnesium, both of which can lower stress and elevate mood by releasing "feel-good hormones" such as serotonin and endorphins into the bloodstream. Red wine and green tea are other sources of flavanols.

Deck and living area. Greenwich, Connecticut. Architecture by Peter Ogden Kinnear. Interior and deck design by Gaby and Donald M. Rattner. Photography by Gordon Beall.

- The most plentiful ingredient in brain matter is water. Hydrate regularly.
- Other foods believed to contain substances favorable to creative cognition include avocado, eggs, broccoli, Brussels sprouts, brown rice, and various whole grains.

(Note: This is just a small sampling of foods believed to spawn ideas. As with most food guidelines, you should coordinate their consumption with your individual health and dietary needs.)

Modulate. Allowing yourself to grow famished can send images of dancing bagels into your head instead of creative solutions to the problem at hand. It also encourages you to quash the discomfort by stuffing yourself silly, which then diverts energy from mental processing to food processing. Avoid the roller-coaster ride in blood-glucose levels that results from waiting too long to eat or eating too much after waiting too long by taking food at regular intervals. Modulate amounts accordingly—it's

Summer kitchen. Jupiter, Florida. Interior design by JMA Interior Design. Photography by Brantley Photography.

generally best to graze several times over the course of the day than to gorge once or twice.

Be inventive. Come up with ways to incorporate other tactics from the book into your meals and snacks—like baking cookies in the shape of an idea bulb (#s 22, 32).

Be brave. Dipping your toe and your tongue into thoroughly unfamiliar cuisines and dishes (tuna eyeballs, anyone?) will widen your perception of the possible and move you out of your comfort zone, both of which incite explorative behavior.

RELATED TACTICS
#22. Switch on a filament bulb.
#30. Have a drink.
#32. Cook.
#43. Play.
#46. Read.
#47. Get out of the house.
#48. Really get out of the house.

TACTIC #32
COOK

WHAT TO DO
Cook as often as possible.

WHY DO IT?
Cooking exercises and encapsulates the core attributes of creativity.

WHY DOES IT WORK?
Anyone who eats these days knows how popular food culture has become. Television and the Internet abound with cooking shows. Foodie websites and blogs score millions of visits a day. Celebrity chefs open restaurants around the world. Daring feats of culinary imagination are lapped up by those lucky enough to land coveted reservations. At home, we stock up on exotic ingredients in order to emulate the wizardry of our professional heroes. People everywhere seem to be in a collective feeding and cooking frenzy.

To quote Martha Stewart, this is a good thing. Cooking counts among our most creative pursuits. It stimulates our imaginations, affords pleasure, and reinforces social bonds in the act of consumption. It's accessible and accommodating to everyday life. Basic operations are simple enough that most of us can learn and practice them with a modicum of instruction, regardless of whether we ever attain expert status. Our normal routines build in time for it.

Just as valuable is what cooking can teach us about the nature of creativity itself. For more than any other single activity, cooking embodies the central characteristics of human invention. I call these characteristics the Seven Attributes of Creativity because,

well, there are seven of them. It is by scrutinizing the parallels between cooking and creativity that we can learn a great deal about both.

Here they are, in no particular order:

Cooking and creativity are combinatorial. Cooking is nothing if not the judicious blend of ingredients. Sometimes a simple pairing is all it takes to fashion a new food product; witness Harry Reese's happy marriage of chocolate and peanut butter in the 1920s. Complex configurations, like Julia Child's Boeuf Bourguignon, offer even

deeper satisfaction. Her list of ingredients runs several pages long.

That cooking and creativity are inherently combinatorial is irrefutable. But some experts go further, arguing that there's nothing truly new under the sun, *all* creative ideas being amalgams of things that already exist.

Given the often substantial size of their egos, you'd think that more than one creative would take umbrage at the notion that invention is merely a remix of old ideas. Somehow that doesn't sound as momentous as making something out of nothing. Yet no less a narcissist than Steve Jobs acknowledged the validity of the proposition in a 1996 interview with *Wired* magazine:

> Creativity is just connecting things. When you ask creative people how they did

something, they feel a little guilty because they didn't really do it, they just saw something. It seemed obvious to them after a while. That's because they were able to connect experiences they've had and synthesize new things.

Jobs should know something about connecting things. He played a starring role in the greatest essay in conglomerative creativity of our time—the smartphone. Though he didn't really invent the mother of all mash-ups so much as improve on it (a form of creativity in its own right), Jobs fully acknowledged its synthetic character while introducing the iPhone in 2007.

He began by announcing to the audience that he was about to unveil three revolutionary products. The first was "a new widescreen iPod with touch

Kitchen. Battleground, Oregon. Building design by Blondino Design. Interior design by Garrison Hullinger. Photography by Blackstone Edge Studios.

controls," the second "a revolutionary mobile phone," the third "a breakthrough Internet communications device." He repeated his descriptions of the three products several more times until the crowd realized what he was getting at. Only then did he reveal to thunderous applause that Apple had fused all three products into a new whole, one having far greater value than the sum of its parts.

Ideational bricolage is hardly reserved for physical products alone. Albert Einstein forever changed our understanding of the world by combining three factors that were previously known into the elegantly simple equation $E=mc^2$. Like Jobs, Einstein was fully cognizant of the composite nature of his and other discoveries, writing in 1945 that "combinatory play seems to be the essential feature in productive thought."

Most combinatorial innovations are qualitatively closer to Reese's peanut butter cups than to the theory of relativity. But a lot of very valuable additions to our economic and cultural landscapes continue to be launched by consolidating formerly disassociated ideas, goods, and services into new wholes. The Internet has been a particularly effective medium for joining traditional business models to the novel technology of the web to give people choices they didn't have before. The virtual hotelier Airbnb, to take one recent example, connects homeowners with spare rooms to rent and travelers looking for same, to the financial benefit of both.

Artists have long opened up new avenues of investigation by combining previously existing things and ideas. Marcel Duchamp planted an upright bicycle wheel on a wooden stool and turned the foundation of art on its head. Picasso picked up on Duchamp's use of industrial products by fusing a bicycle seat and handlebars in his 1942 sculpture *Bull's Head*. American-born painter James McNeil Whistler sought inspiration from diverse sources in composing his paintings, including

influences from faraway Japan. Victorian, beaux arts, and postmodern architecture reveled in eclectic juxtapositions of elements from historic styles.

Creativity, you might say, is all about getting it together.

Cooking and creativity are social and collaborative. "The kitchen is a function of man's social nature," writes German design visionary Otl Aicher. By virtue of that quality, he went on, "cooking is only a pleasure when others join in eating. And cooking is even more of a pleasure if others join in the cooking."

I don't know about your household, but in mine getting people to join in eating is rarely a problem.

To be fair, neither is encouraging others to join in the cooking. From a young age my son has happily engaged in kitchen activities with parents and friends. Some of his earliest concoctions were thoroughly inedible, but as parents we knew better than to rely on him for sustenance. Our real purpose was to give him space to cultivate his creativity and imagination, teach him visual, math, and communication skills, develop manual dexterity, elevate self-esteem, learn how to work in tandem with others, and have fun. The most fun came for us when he turned old enough to cook without adult supervision, preferring instead to

Kitchen. Nashville, Tennessee. Building and interior design by David Latimer for New Frontier Tiny Homes. Photography by StudiObuell.

team up with sleepover friends to prepare shockingly flavorful breakfasts. That's where inedible leads.

I hope he carries his fondness for teaming up into his later working life, because the reality is that collaboration and innovation are inextricably entwined. Unfortunately, our present popular culture reinforces the opposite message. Rather than celebrate alliance, we spin tales of Lone Creators, people who miraculously achieve imaginative heights entirely on their own.

I'm as guilty as the next in perpetuating this mischaracterization of creativity. Being an architect, I know that I have to pull together a team of employees any time a project exceeds a certain scope. There's simply too much to be done for

me to do it alone. I hardly mind; a lot of my best ideas come from them. But that doesn't stop me from marveling at the number of points recorded by Michael Jordan without a moment's thought about the teammates who set him up to score, or prattling on about Steve Jobs as if he built Apple single-handedly.

It doesn't help that some Lone Creators seek to perpetuate the myth of their loneliness. Jobs was notorious for claiming credit for everything that ever rolled out of Apple studios. So self-absorbed was he that a few years ago somebody made a mockumentary film titled *iSteve*.

Maybe he was channeling Thomas Edison. In 1878 the inventor announced to the newspapers

that he had solved the problem of the electric light. To this day people all over the globe consider him its inventor. Just one problem—it isn't true. In point of fact, he was years away from a successful product. Twenty-two other inventors came up with working versions before he filed a single patent. They've been largely forgotten.

None of this is meant to take away from the accomplishments of great artists and innovators. On the contrary, it should open our eyes to the fact that some of the world's most fruitful insights have come from people working cooperatively rather than competitively.

Collaboration isn't incumbent on scale. Joshua Wolf Shenk, in his book *Powers of Two: Finding the Essence of Innovation in Creative Pairs*, explores how human chemistry and the nature of creativity combine to make the well-matched duo a powerful engine of innovation. Indeed, some of history's most creative people have been twofers. Think Simon and Garfunkel, Jobs and Wozniak, Martin and Lewis, Gilbert and Sullivan, Masters and Johnson.

There's little question that in each case the partners produced work they would not have done alone.

Ultimately, however, creativity transcends the individual, the pair, and the team altogether for the simple reason that ideas do not emanate out of an informational vacuum. Rather, they are part of a continuous flow of human creativity and social interaction in which we are all immersed. Every idea a person has, every innovation a company produces, can be traced in some fashion to the ideas and innovations that came before and will come after. No one works alone, in fact or in spirit.

So next time you're up for some houseguests, take a page from some leading hedge-funders and throw an idea dinner. Invite people you think could contribute to a lively conversation about creative projects you're working on, or you on theirs. Or simply make it a routine event for your household occupants. Who knows? The stuff that comes out of the meal could be the beginning of a breakthrough.

Cooking and creativity are fun. Yes, cooking can be a chore at times. And yes, creativity can be tremendously frustrating too. But they're also often fun. And making something fun is how nature makes you want to do it more—kind of like sex.

Cooking and creativity are serendipitous. Dr. Percy Spencer, a scientist working on a defense contract for the Raytheon Corporation, was testing some radar technology in his laboratory one day in 1946 when he noticed that a chocolate bar in his pocket had mysteriously melted. Since he had been examining a new vacuum tube called a magnetron at the time he discovered he had goo in his clothes, Spencer had a hunch there might be a connection between the two events. So he got hold of some popcorn kernels and put them next to the vacuum tube to see what would happen. In amazement he watched as the kernels started to pop and explode on the laboratory table, seemingly all by themselves. A colleague joined him in his laboratory on a following day. This time they tried the experiment with an egg. At first the egg started to tremor and shake. Intrigued, Spencer's colleague moved in for a closer look. Just then the egg burst open and splattered all over his face.

Dr. Spencer had discovered the microwave. Leftovers have never been the same.

A great many innovations have come about under equally accidental circumstances. A short list includes the Slinky toy, Post-it Notes, Play-Doh, and stainless steel.

The image of inventors, artists, and scientists acting deliberately for predefined ends predominates our popular perception of creativity. Somehow the thought of an unsuspecting individual stumbling on an unanticipated discovery that turns into something big uncomfortably deflates the myth of the prescient mastermind. Yet in truth that is often exactly how new things arise.

Food is a natural medium for happy accidents. There are so many potential combinations of ingredients and so many different ways of processing them that the chances of coming across an edible arrangement on the fly are pretty good. They were certainly good enough to lead to the ice cream cone. The year was 1904 and an ice cream seller at the St. Louis World's Fair named Arnold Fornachou had run out of cups at his popular stand. A food vendor nearby offered to come to his rescue by rolling up one of his waffle pastries to form a cone. Fornachou purportedly plopped a scoop of ice cream into it and presto! the ice cream waffle-cone was born.

Potato chips, chocolate chip cookies, crepes Suzettes, Slurpees, cornflakes, pink lemonade, nachos, and Worcestershire sauce are just a few of the other foods attributed to creative serendipity. The most widely known delectable to emerge via domestically discovered happenstance? I nominate the Popsicle. Eleven-year-old Chicagoan Frank Epperson was searching for a new dessert to satisfy his sweet tooth when he unthinkingly left a bucket of gooey mix he had been toying with on his porch overnight. A mixing stick remained sitting upright in the bucket. That night temperatures dropped to freezing. Come morning, the Popsicle was born.

Here's the thing, though: all of these inventions came from people already primed to invent them.

Percy Spencer was a trained laboratory scientist. Fornachou knew his ice cream. Even Popsicle pioneer Frank Epperson had become immersed in the subject of sugary desserts by the time he stumbled on his recipe. The takeaway is that serendipitous solutions are more likely to come to those who've geared themselves to be creative in a particular arena in the first place. As the French microbiologist Louis Pasteur famously put it, "chance favors the prepared mind." Without mental preparation, opportunities for unplanned leaps of imagination could well pass by unnoticed.

The kitchen is an environment rich with occasion for chance discoveries. Open your refrigerator and scan your pantry shelves. What do you see? Dozens of ingredients and foodstuffs probably purchased independently of each other with little thought as to their eventual combination or method of preparation. Perhaps our affinity for serendipitous discovery explains the pleasure we get when we successfully "throw something together" for a meal by instinctively grabbing random ingredients from whatever happens to be in the refrigerator.

Cooking and creativity are heuristic. Many baseball fans know that Babe Ruth held the record for most career home runs for nearly forty years until it was finally broken by Hank Aaron. Fewer know that Ruth also struck out a lot. More than just about everybody who ever played the game, in fact. The number one strikeout king of all time as

of now? Reggie Jackson, another former Yankee slugger known for the long ball.

It's human nature for people to view their heroes in a positive light. Failure is often overlooked, foibles excused.

Steve Jobs is a classic case in point. We marvel at his uncanny aptitude for coming out time and again with innovative products we had no idea we needed. Lost in our extolments of his triumphs, however, are the many failures he precipitated on the road to his successes. Flawed products like the Apple Lisa, Newton, Apple III, NeXT, and Macintosh TV. Strategic mistakes, like recruiting John Sculley as CEO, or trying to prematurely unload Pixar at fire-sale prices.

The truth is that a high percentage of creative efforts on the scale of a Ruth or Jobs are going to fail. It's what happens when people swing for the fences. Even if you're merely looking to hit the proverbial double, the odds of creatively connecting on the very first swings are slim, whether in baseball, business, or basket weaving. The key is to not view failure as a failure, but as part of a process. Unfortunately, we're taught in school and occasionally at home that failure is inevitably bad and never an option. That's a difficult mind-set to overcome.

Creatives are compelled to redefine failure by the nature of their work. Famed playwright Samuel Beckett asked "Ever tried? Ever failed? No matter. Try again. Fail again. Fail better." Will do, Sam!

One of the antidotes neophytes deploy to overcome the drag of failure is to be prodigious in their output. Frank Lloyd Wright, whose shortcomings generally leaned personal rather than professional, was extraordinarily prolific, turning out nearly a thousand designs in his lifetime. Picasso cranked out canvas after canvas, some good, some not so good. Edison was an invention machine. Jeff Bezos at Amazon tries and fails constantly, and

Kitchen. The Greenbrier, West Virginia. Architecture by Donald M. Rattner for Ferguson Shamamian & Rattner, Architects. Interior design by Victoria Hagan for Victoria Hagan Interiors. Photography by Mick Hales.

is proud of it. Serial entrepreneurs are labeled serial for a reason.

Failure in the domestic kitchen is unlikely to take you to the edge of despair, unless you happen to leave a pot on the stove unattended and burn your house down as a result. More likely your setbacks will occur at the level of an imperfect effort or temporary setback. Toast burnt? Fiddle with the toaster settings until you get the desired results. Soup too bland? Add a little salt or seasoning. Pie crust too doughy? Next time adjust the amount of water or flour, increase the baking time, or both. Like Edison, you keep making adjustments until you find the solution.

There's a term for a method that utilizes trial and error: it's called a *heuristic*. A heuristic is an approach to problem solving that enables people to discover or learn something for themselves. Other heuristic methods are rules of thumb, educated guesses, intuitive judgments, industry standards, stereotyping, and common sense. Think of them as mental shortcuts to use when a definitive answer to a question is too distant or difficult to be immediately useful or attainable.

Heuristics are often considered the opposite of algorithms in problem solving. When you use a formula or rule to solve a problem you're expecting a precise, reliable, and internally consistent answer

to each question. A heuristic, on the other hand, might work one time but not the next, and it will often yield imprecise or different answers depending on the question. A recipe from Julia Child is akin to an algorithm, a taste test to a heuristic. A set of construction drawings is in theory algorithmic; what gets built is definitely heuristic.

Heuristics are intrinsic to innovation. How else could it be otherwise? If you've already got the answer to a problem by means of an algorithm there's nothing left to invent. And what do you think is one of the main ways algorithms are invented in the first place? By a lot of trial and error, that's how! Even then, they're

not necessarily final or definitive. Google is constantly refining the algorithms it uses for its famed search engine to improve performance or accommodate user trends. Much of the Internet itself is built on the premises of testing, testing, and more testing. If Darwin was right—and I hear he was—that makes the Internet very much like Nature herself, which the scientist discovered to be one long trial-and-error session known as *natural selection*.

So don't be too quick to buy into the old saw that "failure is not an option." Sometimes it is, and sometimes the world is better for it. "I make more mistakes than anyone else I know," Edison once declared, "and sooner or later, I patent most of them."

Cooking and creativity are destructive. You've heard the old adage that you can't make an omelet without breaking some eggs. Well, it's true. I've tried it myself. In fact, to prepare almost anything in the kitchen you've got to destroy, or to phrase it less ominously, transform food to make food.

In 1942, an economist named Joseph Schumpeter coined the phrase *creative destruction* to describe a similar correlation of omelet to egg in innovative economies. Schumpeter's idea was that market-place innovation necessarily entails the destruction of the old in favor of the new. A prime example of the cycle of supersession from our day is the personal computer. Look around—do you see any typewriters? Probably not, because this onetime mainstay of the industrial era has been almost entirely supplanted by its more powerful cousin, just as quill and metal nib dipping pens yielded to fountain pens years before.

A similar oscillation between new and old happened with modern recorded music. First there was the vinyl record. That gave way to the eight-track, which in turn was superseded by the cassette tape, which died a slow death as the compact disc emerged, which has since withered away thanks to the popularity of the more convenient MP3 digital format—which is now threatened by streaming services.

It's not every day that you or I are going to be involved in a personal or professional project with the potential for creative destruction on a grand scale. The real issue is whether we resist it on a personal level, as is our common nature as human beings. The cause is invariably habit—we are by nature creatures of it. The problem with habit is that it's habit forming; once we settle into a routine we don't easily give it up. From a practical standpoint our reliance on habit to get through the day is entirely understandable. We would

simply not get anywhere if we had to reinvent the wheel each time we were faced with a task or call to action. Unfortunately, this dependence often turns habit into the enemy of the new.

Resistance to creative destruction can be far more injurious to businesses. The sad fate of companies like Kodak and Polaroid reflects the downside to creative destruction known as the *innovator's dilemma*. Harvard business school professor Clay Christensen originated the concept in a 1997 book of the same name. In a nutshell, the innovator's dilemma occurs when large companies and organizations are reluctant to pursue innovation out of concern it will undermine their own present success. Neither of the two aforementioned camera and film companies, for example, could wrap their corporate heads around the idea that a nascent digital photography industry would soon render their flourishing film-based technology obsolete. As a result the people in charge failed to take the necessary steps to capitalize on market evolution (despite the fact that Kodak was itself a pioneer in digital cameras). The leadership of Netflix, on the other hand, recognized early on that its customer base was migrating away from renting DVDs of old movies in favor of downloadable and original content. Unlike other companies faced with a changing landscape, it implemented a shift in its business model to avoid a similar demise.

Habit, ritual, the tried-and-true have their place, of course. Not everything we do in the kitchen or elsewhere in a residence has to be ruthlessly discarded every time someone pops up with a novel gadget, design concept, or methodology. But if you're serious about wanting to hone your creative faculties at home, work, or school, then be prepared to break old habits when the time comes. Should new habits form, have the willpower to break them too. Maintain mental agility by constantly trying novel combinations of ingredients, aromas, textures, and ethnic traditions. Explore new tools and techniques wherever you can find them. Share ideas with others. Cook up a storm.

Cooking and creativity are teachable. We know that cooking is teachable because plenty of people learn to do it, whether by self-instruction, family interaction at home, reading books and watching videos, or attending cooking classes.

But what about creativity generally?

Back in the day, people thought that the mental wherewithal to be creative was reserved for the few, either the result of divine favor or genetic inheritance. Most scholars, psychologists, and educators now take the opposite view: that nearly everyone is born with the innate ability to develop novel and useful ideas. Writes creativity expert Tina Seelig of Stanford University:

We are all naturally creative and, like every other skill, some people have more natural talent than others. However, everyone can increase his or her creativity, just as everyone can increase his or her musical or athletic ability, with appropriate training and focused practice. We can all learn tools and techniques that enhance creativity, and build environments that foster innovation.

Amen.

Conclusion. Given the many commonalities of creativity and cooking, it's unsurprising to find that the kitchen counts among the home's most intense idea spaces for personal expression and exploration. Equally importantly, this room is the source of our sustenance, the social heart of the home, and a harbinger of the future. It's a place where ideas are born, businesses are conceived, lives are planned. It's a teaching space for the young, a life classroom where they can learn about teamwork, experimentation, the acceptance of failure and the rewards of persistence. As the most spatially elaborate and elaborately detailed room in the home, the kitchen also presents unparalleled design challenges and opportunities to architect, designer, builder, and home dweller. For those wanting to both understand and exercise their creativity, it is clearly the place to be.

RELATED TACTICS

#30. Have a drink.
#31. Eat brain food.
#41. Make stuff.
#44. Make a mess. Or not.

TACTIC #33
EXERCISE

WHAT TO DO
Exercise regularly.

WHY DO IT?
Exercise has been found to boost creativity, cognitive flexibility, memory, and learning, in addition to providing multiple health benefits.

WHY DOES IT WORK?
You might have noticed that a number of the tactics in the book incorporate body movement and non-sedentary behavior—walking (#38), standing up, and using a treadmill desk (#13), for instance. But what about exercise in its own right? Do activities pursued principally for the purpose of fitness accrue the ancillary benefit of jump-starting creativity?

According to the evidence, it does. A 2005 paper, for example, notes that subjects scored higher on Torrance Tests for Creativity after moderate aerobic exercise, both immediately afterward and two hours later.

Scientists offer several reasons to explain the bump, starting with an increase in heart rate brought on by exercise. The result of this extra blood flow are a series of chemical and hormonal responses in our body and brain that result in lower stress, higher energy, and elevated mood, all of which prime the pump for greater creativity.

Then there are the endorphins. Endorphins are chemical substances released by the central nervous system during exercise and other physical activities. I think of them as our happy hormones because they reduce our perception of pain and lead

Via Elevado Presidente João Goulart, São Paulo, Brazil. Photography by Davidson Luna.

to a euphoric feeling known to fitness aficionados as "runner's high"—a peak experience believed by some to typify Mihaly Csikszentmihalyi's "flow state." Besides general mood arousal, endorphins also boost our self-esteem and confidence, two ingredients essential for neophytes aiming to venture into the unknown and untested.

Finally, there's evidence that exercise fosters neurogenesis, meaning the growth of new brain cells. Most of this growth has been found to occur in the hippocampus, a region of the brain central to the formation and recall of long-term memory. Since creative ideas are often built by melding thoughts and observations we've previously filed away in our mental database, it's conceivable that hippocampal neurogenesis could also serve to strengthen idea formulation.

All this having been said, quite a few people view the prospect of exercise with something less than euphoria (me, for example). One reason for our reluctance is the painfully repetitive nature of the

Gym and party space. Piedmont, California. Architecture by Studio Bergtraun Architects. Photography by Treve Johnson.

activity (that's why they call them "reps"), a form of mindless behavior that can be excruciatingly tedious. I offset this negative by reminding myself that repetitive action is a blessing when it comes to creativity; relieved of the need to focus on what we're doing, our thoughts are free to meander and our ideas to percolate. In that regard exercise can be as ideationally productive as showering (#35), but without the soap and water.

HOW TO DO IT

Repeatedly. Most experts recommend at least a thirty-minute regimen of aerobic exercise three to five times a week, depending on your fitness level. Pierce Howard, author of *The Owner's Manual for the Brain*, defines aerobic exercise as "any physical activity that keeps the heart pumping at elevated levels continuously for twelve to thirty minutes." According to this definition, running in place, riding a stationary bike, or continuous calisthenics qualify as aerobic.

Get a room. It's easy to adopt an exercise regimen at home. The real challenge is where. If you've got the space, a dedicated exercise room is ideal. You can sweat profusely without sullying fine finishes. You can grunt and groan without ruining anyone's concentration or dinner. You can cluster your equipment. You can shape your surroundings in accordance with the tenets of creativity-based design.

Converted garages are a perpetual favorite for transforming into workout environments. So

Atrium. Pine Lake, Village of Chenequa, Wisconsin. Architecture by Robert Harvey Oshatz. Photography by Cameron R. Neilson.

are basements, where there's often room for the equipment, sounds and smells are separated from main living areas, and it's naturally cool. Which would be fine, except these subterranean spaces typically have few if any windows, lack daylight and views, can be dank, and routinely suffer from low ceilings. Not exactly the kind of enticing atmosphere that gets you out of bed and onto the elliptical, let alone stimulates insight thinking.

These conditions are surmountable. I review several potential remedies for diminished room height and compromised lighting conditions in Tactic #3. As for the absence of vistas and greenery, how about painting a landscape mural on the wall facing the workout area (#5)? Studies show that gazing at realistic representations of nature,

whether in the form of paintings, photographs, drawings, or even travel posters, can elicit the same psychological outcomes as seeing the actual thing. Botanic-themed decor, be it printed fabrics, floor and wall coverings, accessories, or color schemes provoke similar reactions. So will low-light plants (#14). Thanks to decorative treatments like these, that stimulus-deprived dungeon you thought you owned can be made over into an attractive and psychologically responsive space.

Or use what you have. Wrestling with the decor in your exercise room is a good problem to have. Some of you are probably more preoccupied with finding a spot to squeeze equipment in at all, or how to better manage the machinery currently gobbling up space in your bedroom or living space.

Home gym and basketball court. San Francisco, California. Architecture by Verner Architects. Photography by Matthew Millman.

Good news: there's no rule that you must have fitness machinery to exercise. Sometimes the best and freest equipment for home fitness activities lies in the fabric of the dwelling itself. Stairs, for instance. You'd be surprised how rigorous and varied a cardio workout you can put yourself through using this everyday architectural feature as a platform. Floors and furnishings are other viable substitutes.

And of course, you can always escape to the great outdoors for a walk, run, or ride (#38).

Capture those ideas. Strap it to the handlebars, put it on a bench, or carry it in your pocket. However you do it, be sure to have that notebook or recording device nearby. Remember: when the heart gets pumping, the ideas start jumping.

RELATED TACTICS

#3. Work under a lofty ceiling.
#5. Display art.
#13. Stand up for yourself.
#14. Bring nature in.
#34. Do yoga. Or meditate.
#35. Take a shower or bath.
#38. Go for a walk.
#40. Pick up a pencil.

TACTIC #34
DO YOGA. OR MEDITATE.

WHAT TO DO
Practice yoga or meditate regularly.

WHY DO IT?
An emerging body of scientific evidence suggests that yoga and meditation techniques can stir the wellsprings of creativity.

WHY DOES IT WORK?
What do Carl Jung, Greta Garbo, conductor Leopold Stokowski, soccer star David Beckham, and music icons Sting and Madonna have in common, besides being accomplished innovators in their respective fields?

They are—or were—practitioners of yoga.

Granted, correlation does not prove causation. Skeptics might argue that the affinity of these noteworthy creatives for the yogic arts is merely coincidental. For the hyper-rationalists among us, yoga's semimystical aura and ancient Eastern provenance make any claims of an attendant creativity kick a scientific stretch.

Then again, the skeptics might be wrong.

The counterargument begins with yoga's most salient characteristic—its power to calm the mind and relax the body, to satisfy what Emily Dickinson termed "the appetite for silence." This is no small matter when it comes to creative productivity; time and again, we find in analyzing creativity tactics that a lessening of physical and psychological tension is an a priori condition for optimizing idea flow.

That might be, retort the stubborn skeptics, but can anyone point to objective data beyond purely anecdotal or self-reported information that would bestow on yoga the same stamp of legitimacy as researchers have conferred on other techniques for amplifying creativity?

Journalist William Broad, in a chapter on creativity in his book *The Science of Yoga*, accepts the challenge by reviewing a number of studies that connect yoga to accelerated activity in brain regions associated with divergent thinking. Others, meanwhile, point to brain waves as a potential lead in the search for corroboration.

Brain waves? To the uninitiated, the term smacks of pseudoscience. Yet brain waves are a very real thing, as one writer explains:

> Your brain consists of billions of little nerve cells, known as neurons. In order for your brain to work, these neurons have to talk to each other. The neurons communicate using electricity.
>
> When millions of neurons are communicating at the same time, this all generates a significant amount of electrical activity, which can be detected using sensitive scientific equipment, such as an EEG (electroencephalograph) machine.
>
> This combined electrical activity in the brain is known as a brainwave pattern. It's called a brainwave due to its wave-like patterning.

According to science, brain waves sort into four categories, based on wave frequency as measured in cycles per second (Hz).

BETA **15 to 40Hz**	**ALPHA** **9 to 14 Hz**	**THETA** **5 to 8 Hz**	**DELTA** **1.5 to 4 Hz**
SUPERCONSCIOUS Awake, alert, active, engaged	**CONSCIOUS** Calm, lucid, reflective	**SEMICONSCIOUS** Deeply relaxed, meditative	**UNCONSCIOUS** Minimally aware
Lively conversation Client presentation	Listening to music Sitting by a fire	Daydreaming REM sleep	Dreamless sleep

Fig. 23: A taxonomy of brain waves.

So where does idea origination fall along the spectrum? Most experts locate it somewhere in the alpha–theta range. Precise categorizations aside, the discovery by researchers that experienced yogis and meditators can overcome distracting surroundings to slow their brain waves from beta to alpha and theta states at will is just one of several findings recommending practiced mind and body control as an inspirational and cognitive tool.

As tantalizing as the confluences between idea genesis and the meditative arts observed to date are, however, it's fair to say that science still has work to do to fully clarify the relationship in terms of cause and consequence. That day might be around the corner; in the meanwhile, you could be well served going to the mats for creativity anyway.

HOW TO DO IT

Dedicate a space to yoga or meditation. In an ideal world, you'd have sufficient space at home that you could custom-design a space solely for yoga or meditation. Otherwise, try using movable furniture, screens, storage solutions, and other flexible features (#9) to transform an available space from supporting activity to sustaining serenity.

Keep it spare. Maintain a healthy distance between objects. Decorate in muted colors and patterns. Close off views of your work life. Banish devices except to funnel music. Declutter without hesitation—unlike other types of creative spaces, it's best to tamp down on sensory stimulation in areas dedicated to relaxation and meditation.

Manipulate light, sound, smell, ventilation, and temperature. Filtered natural light (#19) and candles, dimmed electrical illumination, soothing instrumental music (#18) or white noise (#17),

Meditation pavilion. Stowe, Vermont. Architecture and photography by David Coleman Architecture.

Loft. San Francisco,, California.
Architecture by YAMAMAR Design.
Photography by Bruce Damonte.

aromatherapy (#24), fresh air, and moderately heated surroundings (#23) build mood and ambience.

Do it outdoors. A patio, terrace, roof deck, or garden can be a perfect spot for yoga or meditation—especially if within proximity of a view (#4), body of water, or wildlife habitat. An accessory structure detached from a main residence is another coveted option for escaping the hubbub of daily life.

BONUS SECTION:
ON THE CULTURAL CONSTRUCTION OF CREATIVITY

I would be remiss if I ended the discussion without seizing on the uniquely non-Western origins of yoga and meditation to highlight an important aspect of creativity that might otherwise go unmentioned in the book: namely, that it is a culturally variable concept. In other words, the term can mean different things to different people depending on social, geographic, and historical context.

In the West, for instance, we tend to emphasize creativity's progressive dimension, as manifest in our neophilic enthusiasm for the new and unprecedented. We also place great value on craft and skill, consistent with the sentiment that creativity entails fashioning something out of nothing (itself perhaps a legacy of the Judeo-Christian concept of God as material creator of heaven and earth). And of course, we believe almost anything is open to scientific investigation, including creativity itself.

The traditional Eastern view of creativity, in contrast, stresses personal fulfillment over externalized work product. It considers creativity's ultimate objective to be neither novelty nor problem solving, but introspective revelation. In that sense, creativity unfolds in an endlessly repeating loop of self-actualization, rather than in linear time.

Is this to say that practicing yoga or meditation with the goal of developing novel products, services, and systems amounts to a misapplication of technique? No. In fact, researchers have observed that college students taught yoga postures and breathing techniques exhibited subsequent improvements in creative problem solving of the sort cited throughout the book. It might be better, then, to understand these contrasting views as simply two different paths toward realizing human potential, rather than as conflicting perspectives on what it is to be creative.

RELATED TACTICS AND EXPLAINERS
#4. Take in a view.
#9. Be flexible.
#14. Bring nature in.
#17. Make noise.
#18. Make music.
#19. Let in natural light.
#23. Adjust the thermostat.
#24. Pick up the scent.
#25. Sleep.
#29. Make a fire. Or look at a picture of one.
#33. Exercise.
#39. Daydream.

TACTIC #35
TAKE A SHOWER OR BATH

Why is it that I always get my best ideas shaving?
—Albert Einstein

WHAT TO DO
Cultivate ideas while taking a shower or bath.

WHY DO IT?
Seventy-two percent of the 4,000 people polled in a recent global survey said they get new ideas and solve problems while showering. A striking 14 percent of the study group take showers for the sole purpose of problem-solving, with the highest concentration of these respondents falling in the eighteen through thirty-four age group.

WHY DOES IT WORK?
It's the most famous shriek in creativity history. The ancient Greek mathematician and inventor Archimedes, suddenly realizing the answer to a thorny problem he'd been grappling with, shouts "Eureka!" and runs naked down the street in excitement before returning to his quarters to work out the details of his solution.

And what was the great man doing at the precise instant he registered the world's first recorded "Aha" moment?

He was taking a bath.

Archimedes might have been the first to be credited with experiencing a flash of insight while immersed in water, but he certainly hasn't been the last. These days, it's become almost axiomatic that we arrive at some of our best ideas in the shower. It's so effective a milieu for conceiving ideas that many highly accomplished people take showers expressly to tease out their inner muse. Fashion designer Tom Ford does it. So did Benjamin Franklin, John F. Kennedy, Winston Churchill, Victor Hugo, Gustav Flaubert, Einstein, Maya Angelou, and Steve Jobs. (These people were not only creative, but incredibly clean as well.)

Work-at-home comic, filmmaker, actor, and author Woody Allen is another notable aficionado of the power shower. The controversial figure once described in detail how he used the shower to overcome writer's block:

> I'll be at an impasse and what will help me is to take a shower. It breaks up everything and relaxes me.
>
> The shower is particularly good in cold weather. This sounds so silly, but I'll be working dressed as I am and I'll want to get into the shower for a creative stint. So I'll take off some of my clothes and make myself an English muffin or something and try to give myself a little chill so I want to get in the shower. I'll stand there with steaming hot water coming down for thirty minutes, forty-five minutes, just thinking out ideas and working on plot. Then I get out and dry myself and dress and then flop down on the bed and think there.

So what is it about a good soak or shower that enables us to conjure up creative thoughts not readily discoverable in our normal dressed and dry state?

Master bath. Scottsdale, Arizona. Architecture and interior design by Tate Studio Architects. Landscape design by Desert Foothills Landscape. Photography by Thompson Photographic.

Several things. First of all, we're at home, the place we feel most at ease and protected. Second, we're (usually) alone and cut off from life outside the space we find ourselves in. There's relatively little to pull us away from getting into the flow, so to speak—no reports to submit, no lesson plans to write, no canvases to paint. Even our smartphones don't follow us into the stall. With little to do other than lather, rinse, and repeat, we get to enjoy the luxury of a largely stress-free space in which to think and reflect.

Ambient conditions factor as well. Take the white noise produced by the rush of water streaming out of a showerhead and cascading to the floor. Remarkably, this sound typically measures out at seventy decibels, exactly the figure put forth in Tactic #17 as ideal for nudging us out of focused attention and into a less directed, more relaxed mode of thought.

Tactics relating to temperature, and specifically, warmth, similarly contribute to the idea-friendly atmosphere (#s 23, 29). When we're warm we tend to be happy, and when we're happy we're more confident in rebelling against institutionalized norms.

And then there's the automatic nature of the activity. Reflexive, routine, repetitive, uncomplicated, are some of the terms that spring to mind in describing the act of everyday bathing.

That doesn't necessarily make it a bad thing. It makes it a habit.

Master bath. Chester, Connecticut. Architecture by Donald M. Rattner for Ferguson Shamamian & Rattner, Architects. Interior design by Linda Chase Associates. Photography by Durston Saylor.

Habits are mental shortcuts, recurring behavioral sequences seared into our brains through frequent enactment. Everyone has them. In fact, it could be argued that nature deliberately designed us to be creatures of habit for a good reason: it reduces the amount of mental effort needed to perform recurring tasks. Like showering. Imagine if you had to relearn how to bathe yourself every morning. You'd never get into your inspiration room or out the door in time for work or school.

Habitual behavior has another benefit, one with substantial implications for creativity: it frees up the mind to wander where it will.

And wander it does. According to one assessment, our minds stray from whatever we're doing, habitual or otherwise, on average 47 percent of our waking hours. Specific activities run the gamut. Showering is most favorable to random thoughts, which preoccupy us a whopping 67 percent of the time we're under the spigot. Walking falls right behind, at around 52 percent. During exercise it's 40 percent. The activity least consumed by mind-wandering? Sex, coming in at about 10 percent. Well, I should hope so! But then, one hopes that lovemaking never descends to the level of habit.

Mind-wandering enhances problem-solving by simultaneously relaxing activity in the brain's prefrontal cortex, which handles executive functions like decision-making, and by activating a set of circuits known as the default mode network, or what creativity expert Scott Barry Kaufman more aptly terms the imagination network by dint of its connections to idea formation. An intriguing aspect of the imagination network is that it resides mainly in regions of the brain uninvolved with perceiving or responding to the outside world. Shifting awareness away from external stimuli and objective knowledge allows our minds to expend energy randomly rummaging around the storehouse of memories, images, concepts, and information piled up inside our unconscious. Conditions are ripe for us to discover the sorts of unexpected connections and breakthrough insights that are fodder for fluid thinking.

Two caveats on mind-wandering. First, it's a highly potent method for cutting through creative problems already in our mental pipelines, as experience and data reveal. It's a less effectual method for enhancing creativity in general. So have an agenda when you get in the shower. Then put it on a mental back burner and grab the soap.

Second, you don't want to stray so far off the mental reservation that you miss out on your own good ideas. "For creativity you need your mind to wander," says psychologist Jonathan Schooler, "but you also need to be able to notice that you're mind-wandering and catch the idea when you have it. If Archimedes had come up with a solution in the bathtub but didn't notice he'd had the idea, what good would it have done him?"

Not much, I'm afraid. Or us. Fortunately, there are ways to keep your ideas from floating away in the mist. Check out the material below for pointers.

HOW TO DO IT

Take showers or baths daily, or more than daily. Sure, bathing has a hygienic purpose, but feel free to take a page from the creative's playbook and utilize it as often as you like to clear your head or stimulate ideas.

Place a pad of waterproof paper and pencil inside your shower or by the tub. You stand a good chance of losing your ideas shortly after having them—unless you capture them first. Get yourself an inexpensive pad and pencil specially designed for deep-sea divers and creative types who like to wash and think simultaneously, then fix them to the wall or deck of your shower or tub. Grab the pencil whenever something hits you.

Roof deck spa. Newport Beach, California. Architecture by Frank Stolz for South Coast Architects. Photography by Eric Figge.

Warning: resist the temptation to use the note-taking app on your smartphone while bathing, even if it's protected by a waterproof case. The temptation to get sucked into its multifunctional black hole is too great, and will kill off fruitful mind-wandering.

Apply relevant creativity tactics to your bathroom's design. Consider your bathroom to be a second creative space in your home. Treat its physical appearance as you would your principal place for drawing inspiration.

RELATED TACTICS

#17. Make noise.

#23. Adjust the thermostat.

#29. Make a fire. Or look at a picture of one.

#30. Have a drink.

#33. Exercise.

#38. Go for a walk.

#39. Daydream.

#40. Pick up a pencil.

#45. Be alone.

TACTIC #36
DRESS NICELY

WHAT TO DO
Dress presentably and appropriately when doing creative work.

WHY DO IT?
Experimental data indicates that wearing neat attire and task-relevant clothing induces a creative mind-set.

WHY DOES IT WORK?
Once upon a time people got dressed up to do almost anything. Going to work. Going to dinner. Going to a ball game.

Then dress codes began to weaken. In some quarters they disappeared altogether. Stroll into the offices of a Google or Uber these days and you're far more likely to find flip-flops, tank tops, and hoodies than a tie pin from Brooks Brothers or a pair of Christian Louboutin shoes. Even Zappos, a hugely successful online seller of fashionable shoes and clothing, takes a largely laissez-faire approach to employee dress.

Of course, a few basic rules remain in effect in just about every office, unspoken or otherwise. Nudity is generally frowned upon. No pajamas allowed.

At home, you're free to do either.

Which should make you wonder: does going completely casual help, hinder, or have no effect on the work product of at-home creatives?

Many people who work where they live believe instinctively that relaxed dress is an idea accelerant. After all, they reason, feeling at ease facilitates idea streaming. Besides, if an extraordinarily innovative company like Facebook (headed by a billionaire who shows up every day in a T-shirt) manages to flourish with few sartorial constraints placed on staff, why would anyone hoping to fortify their creativity in the comfort of their own homes impose tighter restrictions on themselves?

Here's why: because there's scientific evidence that one size does not fit all when it comes to the relationship between dress and creativity. In fact, research indicates that you'll be doing your creativity some good by dressing up rather than down.

Frank Lloyd Wright. 1954. Photography by Al Ravenna. New York World-Telegram and the Sun Newspaper Photograph Collection, Library of Congress.

Guest bedroom and study. Toronto, Ontario, Canada. Architecture by Gloria Apostolou for Post Architecture. Interior design by Tanya Yeung for Analogue Design Studio. Photography by Arnaud Marthouret for Revelateur Studio.

At the core of the data is the notion that clothing conveys a *social distancing effect*. Social distance is the measure of how close people feel to each other psychologically. Dress has a profound effect on how we gauge that distance. A person decked out in a snappy business suit, tuxedo, or long gown, is liable to be perceived by the casually dressed observer as authoritative and distant, whereas the same person in Bermuda shorts and sneakers will be judged approachable and open. The same holds true for self-image. A 2007 study found that employees felt more productive, trustworthy, and confident in their abilities when they were wore a business suit at work, but friendlier toward their colleagues when in relaxed dress.

That feeling of remoteness from others or oneself, however faint or subconscious, is sufficient

to trigger a change in how you see the world. Instead of focusing on detail, which requires being close to the object of attention, your brain is primed to view things and ideas from a distance. What does that have to do with creativity, you ask? If you've read about Construal Level Theory in Explainer I, or gone through any of the other tactics grounded in the perception of physical or perceived separation (e.g., #s 2–6), you already know the answer: the more distal your sense of time, space, or now, social separation, the more holistic, big picture, and abstract your thinking is prone to be (Table I).

Two other factors come into play here. One is Pavlovian conditioning; just as separating creative from everyday space can produce a cause-and-effect relationship between mind and place (#I),

Dressing area. Nashville, Tennessee. Building and interior design by David Latimer for New Frontier Tiny Homes. Photography by StudiObuell.

professionals. Decking yourself out as if you were going to bed or the beach when you're trying to do serious work sends a mixed message to the brain. Don't confuse yourself; wear clothes that reinforce your sense of self-worth as a committed creative.

Then again, should you prove to be a clone of Mark Zuckerberg or the second coming of Albert Einstein (who hated to wear socks, especially socks that matched), you can disregard everything I've written here and wear whatever you darn please. Such are the prerogatives of genius.

HOW TO DO IT

Be neat. Avoid clothes that you wouldn't dare wear in public, and states of semi-undress.

Dress to suit. Tailor your attire to the task at hand, including messy work and activities with practical or professional dress requirements (e.g., painting, gardening, automobile repair).

Go in or go out. Leave your clothes out on view, stow them behind closed doors and drawers, or store them in walk-in-closets and dressing rooms—clothes storage is a function of space, resources, priorities, and aesthetic preference. Whatever the strategy, treat your garments with the care that an important creative tool (and outlet) deserves.

RELATED TACTICS AND EXPLAINERS

#1. Designate a creative space.
#2. Look at something blue.
#3. Work under a lofty ceiling.
#4. Take in a view.
#5. Display art.
#6. Think back.
#21. Dim the lights.
Explainer I: Space, Time, and Creativity

so too can dressing differently for creative work than for everyday activities prompt your brain to shift automatically into divergent mode when you put on the appropriate duds. The other gets back to self-image, especially with you creative

TACTIC #37
TAKE A BREAK

WHAT TO DO
Schedule regular breaks during creative periods.

WHY DO IT?
Stepping back from creative work for short stretches can improve problem solving, increase productivity, replenish attention, consolidate memory, promote mind-wandering, and elevate mood.

WHY DOES IT WORK?
Here's one of the best pieces of advice I can offer for stoking your creativity:

Don't do it. Or rather, don't do it continuously for hours on end.

Yes, I realize that the notion that you could augment idea output by taking time away from it is paradoxical, but that doesn't make it any less true. Science tells us as much. In one study, researchers observed that humans who took breaks at their own discretion solved more insight problems and encountered fewer impasses than subjects distracted by unscheduled diversions or who worked straight through.

What's to explain this anomaly? Scientists offer a laundry list of possible answers. Fatigue, for starters; our brain is comparable to a muscle, some say, and like any muscle, prolonged

exertion at problem solving inevitably tires it. *Vigilance decrement* is another. This little piece of jargon refers to the gradual decline in sensory perception that occurs when you're exposed to a constant input, such as when you stop smelling a lingering odor after a few minutes. Scientists have proposed that our brains might similarly veer off-task if we stick at something for excessively long stretches.

Still another thesis is that our brains need periodic interludes to digest the jumble of sensory inputs that continuously pile up in our mental inbox. "Almost certainly, downtime lets the brain go over experiences it's had, solidify them and

Entryway. Sherman Oaks, Los Angeles, California. Interior design by Lucie Ayres for 22 Interiors. Photography by Amy Bartlam.

PREPARATION	INCUBATION	ILLUMINATION	VERIFICATION
Acquire information. Build a knowledge base. Assemble resources. Define the problem.	Internalize the problem into the unconscious. Redirect conscious attention elsewhere.	Move the creative idea from preconscious processing to conscious awareness.	Develop the idea. Evaluate it against the initial goal. Validate the final solution by testing its practicability.

Fig. 24: Four-stage model of creative thinking. After Graham Wallas (1926).

turn them into permanent long-term memories," asserts Loren Frank, physiologist and coauthor of a study involving rats endeavoring to solve a maze puzzle.

All of these potential rewards are predicated on one condition, however—that your brain can downshift during the break by your performing activities that require minimal levels of concentrated attention and recall. Exercising, for instance (#33). Having a snack (#31). Going for a walk or bike ride (#38). Shooting pool for fun (#43).

The rationale for this stipulation is similar to what I discuss in the context of showering (#35): turning the mind away from external, goal-oriented tasks allows ideas to gestate in the back of your mind, a form of subconscious mental churn known as *incubation*. Simply put, incubation is a form of passive creative fermentation that occurs when we abstain from thinking about the problem we're working on. Some creativity experts consider incubation a necessary stage in idea development; Graham Wallas's famous four-tier model of creative thinking, for example, dedicates the phase just prior to illumination to this purpose, signaling that the one is a prerequisite of the other (Fig. 24).

Incubation doesn't mean you should do nothing during off-periods. In fact, doing nothing at all might be the least rewarding strategy for extracting the cognitive value of a break. Consider this: a 2012 study found that subjects who sat quietly during a break from a

Living room detail. Yonkers, New York. Architecture by Gary Brewer for Robert A.M. Stern Architects. Photography by Francis Dzikowski/Otto.

Game room. Jupiter, Florida. Interior design by JMA Interior Design. Photography by Brantley Photography.

creativity assessment test scored lower than a comparison group given a memory-intensive activity to do during theirs. Best in show? A third group assigned a simpleminded task. Just as occurs with noise (#17), walking (#38), and most other action-based creativity tactics, a dollop of distraction combined with a dash of physical exertion turns out to enhance creative performance more effectively than pure cerebration.

HOW TO DO IT

Calendar recurring breaks. For some of you home-based creatives, it's less a question about finding opportunities to take a breather than it is to resist them. The siren call of the refrigerator.

The dog gnawing on your ankle in hopes of getting an outing. A baby crying for a change or feeding. Domestic life can occasionally seem like a giant conspiracy to steal you away from your imaginative pursuits.

All I can offer in response is what the research teaches us: breaks want to be voluntary and routine rather than uninvited and erratic. Privacy issues aside, the standard method for achieving this end is to set a timer at regular intervals to signal when you're due for a respite. How long an interval depends on which time management guru or researcher you consult. Recommendations range from every twenty-five to ninety minutes. Length varies from five

Kitchen, pantry, laundry, and home office. Los Feliz, Los Angeles, California. Interior design by Lucie Ayres for 22 Interiors. Photography by Amy Bartlam.

minutes on up. Try out different regimens to determine your optimal work rhythm.

Do mindless chores. Wash the dishes. Water the plants. Fold the laundry. Vacuum. The dumber the task, the more resources become available to your Imagination Network (see #35). Plus, your home will be cleaner and nicer looking afterward.

Perform other action-based creativity tactics. Take your pick from the list below. Or come up with variants of your own.

Sever the digital umbilical cord. As beneficial as technology can be to work and life, getting sucked into cyber world is about the last thing you want to do during downtime. The sensory tsunami that regularly issues from our devices is likely to rouse rather than rest the conscious brain, making it harder to consolidate memory and convert information to usable form.

Go with the flow. On occasion you might become so immersed in your work that you lose sight of the passing hours. In those cases it's best to forgo breaks in order to ride the wave while it lasts.

Give yourself a really big break now and then. I've been speaking here about breaks of short and medium duration. The payoff for retreating from creative work for lengthier periods, such as vacations, is covered in Tactic #47.

RELATED TACTICS

#14. Bring nature in.

#15. Get with your pet.

#18. Make music.

#26. Nap.

#29. Make a fire. Or look at a picture of one.

#30. Have a drink.

#31. Eat brain food.

#32. Cook.

#33. Exercise.

#34. Do yoga or meditate.

#35. Take a shower or bath.

#38. Go for a walk.

#39. Daydream.

#40. Pick up a pencil.

#42. Pursue a hobby.

#43. Play.

#46. Read.

#47. Get out of the house.

TACTIC #38
GO FOR A WALK

All truly great thoughts are conceived while walking.
—Friedrich Nietzsche

When a traveller asked Wordsworth's servant to show him her master's study, she answered 'Here is his library, but his study is out of doors.'
—Henry David Thoreau

Solvitur ambulando.
—Latin phrase meaning "It is solved by walking."

If I couldn't walk fast and far, I should just explode and perish.
—Charles Dickens

My walking is of two kinds: one, straight on end to a definite goal at a round pace; one, objectless, loitering, and purely vagabond.
—Charles Dickens

From walking, something; from sitting, nothing.
—Bulgarian proverb

My grandmother started walking five miles a day when she was sixty. She's ninety-seven now and we don't know where the hell she is.
—Ellen DeGeneres

WHAT TO DO
Take walks regularly to crack open a creative problem.

WHY DO IT?
A 2014 study out of Stanford University discovered that creativity assessment scores as much as doubled after subjects took a walk outdoors.

WHY DOES IT WORK?
"How vain it is to sit down to write when you have not stood up to live!" Henry David Thoreau wrote in his journal in August 1851. "Methinks that the moment my legs begin to move, my thoughts begin to flow."

You didn't know your legs were wired directly to your imagination, did you? Or perhaps you did, like many others before and since Thoreau.

People like Steve Jobs and Mark Zuckerberg, who were once spotted ambling about Palo Alto in close conversation, the two titans of the technocracy by then having integrated walking into their arsenal of entrepreneurial habits. Or Darwin, who perambulated rain or shine on a gravel track he installed at Down House, his country residence south of London (you can follow in his footsteps there today). Or Nikola Tesla, who reportedly first conceived of a brushless alternating electric current motor while sauntering through Prague as a student. Or Gandhi, who weaponized walking for the purpose of national emancipation.

So what's the magic behind this simple activity? Scientists identify several potential contributing factors. Some cite the salutary effects of increased blood flow to the brain, such as occurs during aerobic exercise (#33) and other forms of rigorous

Entry hall. Yonkers, New York. Architecture by Gary Brewer for Robert A.M. Stern Architects. Photography by Francis Dzikowski/Otto.

Mudroom. Andover, Massachusetts. Architecture by Sally DeGan for Spacecraft Architecture.
Interior design by Deborah Farrand for Dressing Rooms. Photography by Eric Roth.

movement. Others point out that walking is automatic, requiring little thought or concentration to pull off. As a result, the prefrontal cortex, which is the part of the brain that manages information and exerts impulse control, can take a breather from its usual regulatory functions and let whatever offbeat and unorthodox ideas have been simmering in the more raucous and freewheeling regions of the mind rise to the surface. Scientists call this condition *transient hypofrontality*. I call it letting the kids out to play after the adults have left the room.

Then there's the evolutionary psychology angle. Scientists estimate that early humans walked upward of fifteen miles a day on the African savanna in the perpetual struggle to solve the crucial problem of survival. It could be argued that walking and creativity have been fused in our neurological profile ever since. A head-turning 2015 Stanford brain imaging study appears to confirm the connection; the study offered evidence that creativity originates in the *cerebellum*, the part of the brain responsible for locomotion, fine motor skills, balance, coordination, posture, and muscle memory.

Then there are the multitude of other conditions favorable to ideation that can be gained from a casual stroll, or for that matter, from a jog or bike ride. The opportunity for solitude (#45) and diffuse, meditative thought (#34). Immersive experience in nature (#14). Increased exposure to daylight (#19). The mental jolt that can occur by stepping away from your regular workspace (#47). The cognitive benefits of putting your work aside for a time (#37).

Last, but not least, is the fact that going outdoors necessitates leaving the boundaries of an interior environment. "I like to have space to spread my mind out in," Virginia Woolf once wrote of her rambles through the chalk hills of southern England, eloquently echoing my earlier premise that openness of mind correlates with the openness of our physical surroundings (#s 2–6, Explainer I).

Entry. Truckee, California. Architecture by John E. Sather for Swaback Architects + Planners. Interior by Studio V Interiors. Photography by Matt Waclo.

RELATED TACTICS AND EXPLAINERS

#2. Look at something blue.
#3. Work under a lofty ceiling.
#4. Take in a view.
#5. Display art.
#6. Think back.
#14. Bring nature in.
#15. Get with your pet.
#19. Let in natural light.
#33. Exercise.
#34. Do yoga. Or meditate.
#37. Take a break.
#45. Be alone.
#47. Get out of the house.
Explainer I: Space, Time, and Creativity
Explainer II: We Are Who We Have Always Been

TACTIC #39
DAYDREAM

They who dream by day are cognizant of many things which escape those who dream only by night.
—*Edgar Allan Poe*

WHAT TO DO
Indulge in daydreams attuned to your creative interests.

WHY DO IT?
Daydreaming is a conduit to breakthrough ideas.

WHY DOES IT WORK?
Daydreaming had a very bad reputation in the early twentieth century. Freud panned it as infantile escapism. Productivity experts dismissed it as symptomatic of an unmotivated workforce. Teachers routinely scolded offenders in the classroom.

Still, a few contrarians bucked the trend. Henry Ford showed himself a maverick in this regard when one day a consultant he'd hired came to him with a recommendation that a certain company executive be fired. Asked why, the consultant said that every time he passed by the man's office, the executive had his feet up on the desk and appeared to be doing nothing. Ford replied that the last idea the man had while in that position earned the company millions of dollars. The executive stayed. It's less clear what happened to the consultant.

Ford's view of daytime reverie as a deceptively productive mind-set has since become more popular. And rightly so; according to a steady stream of research, conscious fantasizing can be a powerful vehicle for bringing insightful ideas to light.

What exactly is daydreaming? One of the first scientists to rigorously investigate the phenomenon, Jerome Singer, described it as a shift in attention "away from some primary physical or mental task toward an unfolding sequence of private responses," a bit like "watching your own mental videos." Another writer called it "a means of eavesdropping on those novel thoughts generated by the unconscious."

Daydreaming has several points in common with its nighttime counterpart. Both are a form of mental play unburdened by realistic constraints and convention. Both traffic in counterfactuals and chimera. Both open a portal into an imagined future, enabling the dreamer to visualize how things could be, rather than how they currently are.

Daydreaming also shares characteristics with mind-wandering, a form of mental meandering that often happens during habitual and repetitive activities, like exercising (#33), showering (#35), and walking (#38). Among other things, they each activate the Default Mode Network (a.k.a. Imagination Network), an interconnected group of brain regions where stored information and memories can incubate, collide, and emerge as viable answers to creative problems (see #35 again).

There are differences as well. For instance, only daydreaming is voluntary, meaning you exert a degree of conscious control over when, where, how long, and about what you fantasize. Sleep-induced dreams and mind-wandering, by contrast, generally occur of their own volition, though in

Swimming pool. Girona, Spain. Architecture and landscape design by Co Govers and Joana Ramalhete for Zest Architecture. Photography by Jesús Granada.

the case of mind-wandering you're awake during the experience.

Essential to successfully incorporating daydreaming into the creative process is spotting and capturing a promising idea the instant it appears. "What we find is that the people who regularly catch themselves—who notice when they're doing it—seem to be the most creative," says psychologist Jonathan Schooler, noted authority on meta-awareness, which is the state of being cognizant of one's own thoughts. Meta-awareness derives from a set of countervailing neural circuits, called the Executive Attention Network, which represents the yin to the Imagination Network's yang in that it serves to regulate and organize our thoughts, rather than let them bounce off the inside of our craniums in randomized patterns.

In other words, daydreaming is a balancing act. Wander too far off the mental reservation, and good ideas could be missed; cogitate too self-consciously, and you might not have them at all.

HOW TO DO IT

Choose the right time and place. There are good times and places to daydream, and there are bad times and places to daydream. Landing an airplane, crossing the street at a busy intersection, and practicing dentistry are bad times and places for daydreaming. Home is a very good place much of the time. Indeed, for savants like Gaston Bachelard, home is tantamount to a personalized temple to daydreaming. "If I were asked to name the chief benefits of the house," he writes in *The Poetics of Space*, "I should say: the house shelters daydreaming, the house protects the dreamer, the house allows one to dream in peace."

Create conditions amenable to desultory thought. Power down the electronic pipeline. Seek out a quiet and secluded spot in your home. Embrace boredom; daydreams will be more likely to rush in to fill the mental void when you're fighting the old ennui. Avoid tasks that demand high levels of concentration, induce stress, or that you enjoy, since we're disinclined to relinquish positive experiences for the purpose of casually rummaging through our mental attic.

Be especially mindful of the haptic and visual qualities of any furnishings you appropriate during daydreaming. Explains author Jordan Ayan:

Daydreaming and even conscious idea generation sometimes work best when you have access to furniture that lets you feel comfortable and completely relaxed. When you are stressed, sitting in a chair that invites you to sink deep into its recesses relieves tension, allowing you to think clearly again. But comfort is not just

Polonyna Runa, Ukraine. Photography by Max Vertsanov.

a matter of softness. The look of a chair or couch, the quality of the covering material, the depth of the cushions, and even the smoothness of wood or metal trim can change the sense of comfort that a piece of furniture imparts to you.

Retreat into nature. Even the most placid residential environment can degenerate into hectic or distracting conditions now and then. Or maybe your abode is like that all the time. If so, consider removing yourself to natural surroundings outside your domicile, whether via a backyard, park, leafy street, or remote rural milieu. Scientists speculate that experiences of nature induce a frame of mind favorable to daydreaming.

RELATED TACTICS AND EXPLAINERS

#4. Take in a view.
#14. Bring nature in.
#28. Lie down or recline.
#29. Make a fire. Or look at a picture of one.
#30. Have a drink.
#35. Take a shower or bath.
#37. Take a break.
#38. Go for a walk.
#40. Pick up a pencil.
#43. Play.
#45. Be alone.
#46. Read.
#47. Get out of the house.

Soap Bubbles *by Thomas Couture. French. c. 1859. Metropolitan Museum of Art, New York.*

TACTIC #40
PICK UP A PENCIL

WHAT TO DO
Write it down. Draw it up.

WHY DO IT?
Writing and drawing help you retain, develop, and execute ideas.

WHY DOES IT WORK?
Sometime in the 1930s a man sat with his young daughter inside a San Francisco soda fountain called the Varsity Sweet Shop. He watched as the counterman set down a milkshake in front of her, two paper straws poking up from the tall glass containing the frothy liquid. The girl beamed happily up at the treat.

But there was a problem: how to drink it? The tops of the straws stood well above the little girl's head. She could try elevating her diminutive frame by placing her hands on the counter and raising herself up, but it would be difficult to sustain the pose for too long. She could grasp the glass with two hands and lower it down to her lap, but it was heavy and uncomfortably cold to the touch. She could bend the straws downward, but the sharp crease resulting would choke off the supply of air and liquid, defeating their purpose. She could ask her father to find a few telephone books to lift her up, except that she might fall off the precarious prop.

In business school, professors call situations of this kind a *pain point*. A pain point is the moment when someone encounters an obstacle preventing him or her from realizing a goal. Fortunes large and small have been built by people keen enough to discern a pain point afflicting a potential customer base, and then to devise a solution consumers were willing to pay for.

Such a person was the girl's father. His name was Joseph B. Friedman. Friedman was a born inventor; he conceptualized his first product, a lighted pencil, at age fourteen. He was awarded the first of nine eventual US patents at twenty-two.

Leaving the fountain parlor that day, Friedman went home and played around with an idea bubbling in his head. An inveterate scribbler, he pulled out a piece of paper and pencil, and began to rough

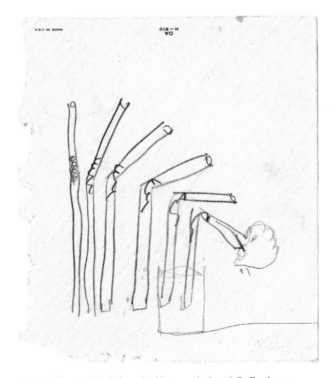

Fig. 25: Concept sketch for a flexible straw, by Joseph B. Friedman. 1930s. Joseph B. Friedman Papers, 1915–2000, Archives Center, National Museum of American History, Smithsonian Institution.

out an idea for a straw that would bend over the lip of the glass, as evident in the sketch reproduced in Fig. 25. He also cobbled together a makeshift prototype out of a couple of straws he'd taken from the sweet shop. From these efforts came his concept for the Flex-Straw, the now ubiquitous drinking tube with the ridged section that allows for bending without crimping.

It would take Friedman another decade to manufacture and ship his first order. The Flex-Straw proved such a hit with the market—hospitals especially—that twenty years later he could sell his rights to the invention to a large corporation for a considerable sum.

The story of Joseph Friedman, a young girl, and a milkshake represents a classic case of opportunity meeting preparation. Integral to that story is the role of Friedman's sketch, undoubtedly one of many he produced in the process of inventing a bendable straw. Together these sketches performed four critical functions in fueling his imagination:

Writing chair. Artisan unknown. American. Early nineteenth century. Cooper Hewitt, Smithsonian Design Museum, New York.

Idea capture. Ideas can be fleeting. Putting down his initial thoughts rapidly lessened the risk of Friedman's forgetting them because of the brain's limited capacity for retaining short-term memories.

Idea development. Few ideas are born fully hatched, like Athena from the head of Zeus. Most require considerable refinement in progressing from concept to executable product. In Friedman's case, his early scratchings would have been followed up with increasingly detailed and precise delineations, culminating in the mechanically drafted documents submitted for his patent application and for machine tooling.

Idea visualization. Externalizing ideas does several useful things. It gives creatives something they can show others to get critical feedback. It builds a memory warehouse they can consult in the future. And it gives them a powerful tool for convincing others to buy into a creative idea. Friedman, for instance, was able to raise venture capital for his scheme by showing prospective investors a solution to a tangible problem. Writers do something similar by submitting queries and proposals to literary agents and publishers. Imagine either trying to achieve their ends merely by waving their arms around or talking a good story. Those are the methods of the huckster, not the visionary.

Brain and body conditioning. Writing and drawing not only advance a project, they also bolster mental and physical states generally. Numerous studies indicate that recurring motions of the hand energize regions of the brain associated with creativity and long-term neurological health.

All this assumes that you can write and draw, of course. Most of us have little trouble with the first, at least at a fundamental level; it's the second that freaks people out. "But I'm no artist," goes the typical refrain from persons told that drawing might help them achieve their objectives. Well, neither was Joseph Friedman, in the strict sense of the term. But then, the type of drawing I'm discussing here has little to do with crafting museum pieces. Rather, it's about finding a visual language that you can use to conduct an internal dialogue with your own ideas, and to convey them to others.

It's hardly surprising that so many eminent neophiles have historically proven themselves avid compilers, filling notebooks, scrapbooks, and digital devices with sketches, doodles, bits of dialogue and narrative, line drawings, diagrams, formulas, mind maps, musical notations, recipes, random thoughts, and assorted other markings of the mind. Creative figures like illustrator, author, conservationist, and scientist Beatrix Potter, graphic design maestro Michael Beirut, comedian Larry David, artist Frida Kahlo, author Charlotte Brontë, filmmaker George Lucas, entrepreneur and author Tim Ferriss, Bill Gates, Sheryl Sandberg, all-around smart person Albert Einstein—the list of inveterate scribblers, scribes, and doodlers decluttering their brains by offloading their evanescent thoughts is impressive indeed.

HOW TO DO IT

Learn how. Draw, I mean. Like riding a bicycle, drawing is a skill that can be taught and learned. Abundant resources exist to help you get started. Sunni Brown's *The Doodle Revolution*, Dan Roam's *The Back of the Napkin: Solving Problems and Selling Ideas with Pictures*, and Betty Edwards's *Drawing on the Right Side of Your Brain* are just three volumes that come to mind. Online and classroom-based courses are valuable sources of instruction too.

Be prepared. Keep the tools for writing and drawing close at hand. Small notebooks and smartphones are universal favorites, since they can be slipped into a pocket for quick access (Fig. 26). A journal on your nightstand (#25) and waterproof paper in the shower (#35) are excellent substitutes

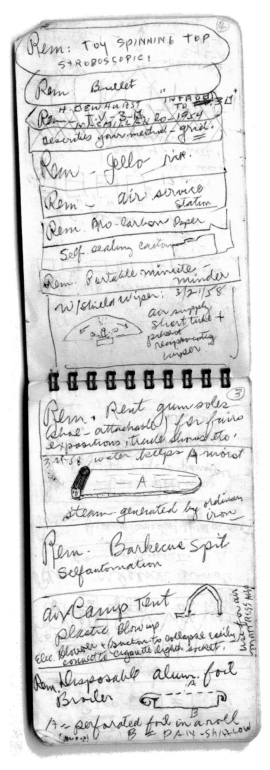

Fig. 26: Notebook of Joseph B. Friedman. 1958. Joseph B. Friedman Papers, 1915–2000, Archives Center, National Museum of American History, Smithsonian Institution.

period in between waking and sleep (#27). Julia Cameron's bestselling book *The Artist's Way* ups the ante to about 750 words in her famous Morning Pages dictate. Complement routinized brain dumps throughout the day with other modes of writing or drawing, be they long-form, spontaneous scribbling, sketching, mind mapping, journaling, or quick captures of brain bursts.

BONUS COMMENT

Did you know that the earliest known straws date from around 3000 BCE? And that for centuries they'd been fashioned by hand in various materials, from gold to grass reeds, until a fellow named Marvin Chester Stone patented the first industrially produced paper version in 1888?

Neither did I, until I began wading through the history of the drinking tube while researching this book.

My point? That real-life creativity is far more likely to take the form of a tweak than a leap, to be evolutionary rather than revolutionary, like Friedman's Flex-Straw. But that's okay, because it means that it lies within the power of nearly everyone to make the world a little better one small step at a time.

for locations in the home where pockets are commonly in short supply.

Fixed surfaces, whether wall-mounted drawing boards or walls treated with special paints or adhesive panels (#8), are better suited for places where collaboration, instruction, information sharing, and large-scale diagramming or picture making occur (think kitchens (#32), playrooms (#43), music rooms (#18), studios, and makerspaces (#41).

Make it a habit. Author and design hacker David Kadavy writes 100 words every day immediately on waking up, exploiting the fertile creative

RELATED TACTICS

#8. Put your walls to work.

#18. Make music.

#25. Sleep.

#27. Exploit the groggies.

#32. Cook.

#41. Make stuff.

#42. Pursue a hobby.

#43. Play.

TACTIC #41
MAKE STUFF

WHAT TO DO
Fabricate things by hand.

WHY DO IT?
Ideas travel from hand to mind as much as from mind to hand.

WHY DOES IT WORK?
Ever since the seventeenth-century French mathematician and philosopher René Descartes penned the immortal words "I think, therefore I am" (in his native tongue, *naturellement*), humans have grappled with a series of interrelated questions: what is the relationship between mind and body? Are they distinct or continuous substances? If distinct, what is the nature of pure consciousness? If linked, what are the mechanisms that bind them?

Frankly, I'm unequipped to address these ponderous lines of inquiry with genuine authority. What I do know, or observe, is that when it comes to formulating ideas, a popular attitude holds that creative insight is a quintessentially mental phenomenon originating in the unseen workings of the mind.

A consummate symbol of this perception is the idea bulb (#22). Much about the bulb's graphic representation reinforces the premise that ideas are immaterial. Depicting the "aha" moment as a flash of light, for instance. Showing the bulb floating in space as if impervious to gravity. Placing it in proximity to the head of the figure experiencing the creative insight, thereby suggesting that ideas are rooted in cognitive rather than somatic functions.

And yet, it should be evident from the contents of this book that imaginative world-building is by no means a purely disembodied act of mental will. Rather, it is a complex interplay of mind, body, and external conditions. Witness the number of tactics where our physical state influences idea production, whether related to posture (#s 13, 28), body temperature (#23), or activities such as walking (#38), exercising (#33), showering (#35), and cooking (#32).

One piece of our anatomy, however, deserves to be singled out for its synergistic connection to our mental faculties: the hand. Frank Wilson, author of *The Hand: How Its Use Shapes the Brain, Language, and Human Culture,* minces few words in tracing this symbiotic relationship to our evolutionary beginnings. "Any theory of human intelligence which ignores the interdependence of hand and brain function, the historic origins of that relationship, or the impact of that history on developmental dynamics in modern humans, is grossly misleading and sterile," declares Wilson, in what passes for fighting words in academia.

Workshop. Emmitsburg, Maryland. Architecture and interior design by Jim Rill, AIA, and Rich Rossi for Rill Architects. Photography by James Ray Spahn.

Professor of education Keith Sawyer extends Wilson's sentiment to the creative realm, even going so far as to elevate the manual over the mental in a hybrid method of idea development termed *thinkering*:

The word "thinkering" was coined by writer Michael Ondaatje in his novel *The English Patient*. It describes a powerful tool for creativity: when we tinker with our hands, we're more likely to have new ideas. We usually assume that creativity starts with a mental idea, and that once it's completely thought out, we start to make

it. But psychologists have recently shown that that's backward, just as Ondaatje observed. New studies show that our innermost thoughts are built on bodily action, not the other way around.

Actually, studies linking creativity to operations of the hand have been around a while; as far back as 1967, for instance, the British play theorist Brian Sutton-Smith found that subjects given a few minutes to fiddle around with a common household product at the beginning of an alternative use test outperformed those compelled to perform the same exercise without the touch

Kitchen. Mill Valley, California. Architecture by Michael Rex Architects. Interiors by Anamar. Photography by Michael Keeney.

experience. Conclusion? Descartes was mistaken in at least one sense: creativity was never all in our heads.

HOW TO DO IT

Set up a makerspace. A makerspace is a place in which to manually produce goods. Crafts, hobby, and sewing rooms, workshops, and studios are common room types expressly designed for maker activities. Dining rooms, laundry rooms, mud-rooms, and children's bedrooms can be pressed into service on an as-needed basis as well.

Kitchens are makerspaces by nature, and not solely for food (#32). With their deep counter-tops placed at stand-up height, durable finishes, generous storage, abundant task lighting, heating and refrigeration equipment, a ready water supply, and a newfound status as the social focal point

of the modern home, they're ideal for bringing non-culinary things into the world too.

And then there's the garage. A fabled space in the mythology of American inventiveness, the garage has midwifed a slew of innovative ventures, from mega-companies like Apple, Amazon, Hewlett-Packard, the Walt Disney Company, Mattel, and Harley-Davidson, to major music acts like Creedence Clearwater Revival (known in their garage band days as the Golliwogs) and Nirvana. Not to mention all the lesser known inventions, handiworks, and personal creative projects to flow out of these quarters, both quirky and consequential.

What is it about the space that has made it such a powerful incubator of innovation? Let's start with the fact that the garage is typically an appendage of the main dwelling. That puts all the comforts and conveniences of home close by for when they're needed, while still providing the physical, psychological, and social separation between living and idea space so vital for getting creative work done.

Logistically, they're a dream. Operating costs hover around zero. The commute is short, leaving more time for productive work. They're open 24/7.

Size is another contributing factor. Garages tend to be big, often the biggest room in a residence. They have to be to perform their nominal function, which is storing cars (the word garage derives from the French verb *garer*, to shelter). It also explains why garages are almost always wide open inside, with few if any intervening columns or interior partitions divvying up the interior. In architecture school we refer to this kind of interior as *universal space*, because you can do practically anything in the world in it.

With flexibility of space comes flexibility of use. Want to start a band? Drag some amps and recording equipment into your garage, pull a few musicians off the street, and you've got yourself a music studio. Hoping to launch an online bookstore instead, as Jeff Bezos did in his Seattle house in 1996? Grab an unused door, lay it across a trestle in the garage, stack your books on top, then pack them into shipping cartons as orders roll in. Or maybe you need affordable factory space to set up a drill press for manufacturing an audio oscillator, your startup's inaugural product? That was the issue facing partners Bill Hewlett and David Packard in 1938. Their solution: rent the carriage house behind the Palo Alto apartment where Packard and his young bride lived. It was a wise choice. The structure's utilitarian interior finishes undoubtedly stood the wear and tear far

better than if they'd located the fledgling operation in the couple's living room.

Beyond their practical advantages, resilient finishes also reinforce the identity and functionality of the garage as a place for making a mess by making things (#44). Especially things that necessitate the kind of dirty work you'd never think to do inside the nicely furnished areas of the home, like banging, hammering, soldering, sculpting, drilling, heating, firing, gluing, inking, potting, or pouring, mixing, and applying indelible fluids, such as paint or oil. (All activities, it should be noted, involving the human hand.)

The configuration of the garage shell works to creative advantage too. Typically, three sides of the structure are bounded by straight, often unbroken walls—perfect for storing supplies and equipment and butting work surfaces up to. The fourth side is invariably taken up almost entirely by one or more large doorways, their breadth allowing bulk goods and groups of people to move in and out of the space easily, without having to trespass through the home proper.

Having a large, porous means of access between garage and outside is a boon to creativity insofar as it turns the garage into a semipublic space directly accessible from the street. As a result, people from outside the home are often invited to gather there to engage in the kinds of collaborative, social, and fun behavior from which fresh insights spring.

Put all these factors together, and it's hardly surprising that one of history's most famous episodes of communal creativity occurred in a residential garage. The location: Menlo Park, California; the date, March 5, 1975. The occasion: the launch of the Homebrew Computing Club. In attendance was Steve Wozniak, along with about thirty other proto-geeks.

"That night turned out to be one of the most important nights of my life," Wozniak recounted later. Surrounded by like-minded techies, stimulated by shoptalk, and treated to a demonstration of the landmark Altair computer, as well as his first look at a specification sheet for a microprocessor, Woz was primed to have an epiphany. And he did. A big one. "This whole vision of a personal computer just popped into my head," he recalled. "That night, I started to sketch out on paper what would later become known as the Apple I."

Needless to say, nothing has been quite the same since.

RELATED TACTICS AND EXPLAINERS

#8. Put your walls to work.
#32. Cook.
#40. Pick up a pencil.
#42. Pursue a hobby
#43. Play.
#44. Make a mess. Or not.
Explainer II: We Are Who We Have Always Been

TACTIC #42
PURSUE A HOBBY

WHAT TO DO
Take up a pastime with marginal relevance to your principal creative interest or professional expertise.

WHY DO IT?
A 2014 study found that people who invested in a hobby improved creative task performance in their vocations as well.

WHY DOES IT WORK?
Gandhi had his *charka*, a hand-cranked wooden wheel used for spinning cloth. Henry Ford restored old watches and old buildings (yay), Sylvia Plath kept bees. Among the currently living, Angelina Jolie collects daggers (don't ask),

Google cofounder Sergey Brin enjoys high-flying trapeze, and Warren Buffett apparently plays a mean ukulele.

I know—we mortals can barely find the time to feed ourselves, yet these high achievers somehow manage to sink untold hours into hobbies largely unrelated to their core competencies.

But maybe that explains why they're high achievers.

Consider this: a lot of creative professionals today invest the bulk of their mental energy to becoming experts in their fields. They figure that the more adept and knowledgeable they are in their domain, the greater their aptitude for generating novel and useful ideas.

Garage, workshop, and office. Cape Elizabeth, Maine. Architecture by Caleb Johnson Studio. Interior design by Krista Stokes. Photography by Trent Bell.

The dogged pursuit of excellence comes at a price, however—what creativity academics call *the cost of expertise*. Among these costs is a possible loss of ideational skepticism, a disinclination to question the assumptions underlying one's field for fear of destabilizing the scaffolding of one's own reputation. Imaginal complacency and a proclivity to defend the status quo set in instead.

How to combat such mental ossification? One strategy is to alter your area of focus. As the scholar Mark Runco has observed, some very eminent people became eminent only after shifting their attention to another field. Darwin, for instance, went from the study of geology to evolutionary biology, Jean Piaget from biology to cognitive developmental psychology, and Sigmund Freud from physiology to psychiatry.

A more radical transformation is to change careers altogether. Examples abound among the celebrated. The actor Harrison Ford started life as a carpenter, the musician Elvis Costello as a computer programmer. John Glenn traveled from weightless outer space to the US Senate (a body occasionally known for its gravity). Runco and others would argue that each owed at least a portion of their subsequent accomplishments to entering their new domains with fresh eyes and renewed inquisitiveness, along with some potentially serviceable skills acquired during their earlier employments.

Something else might have been at play. To first enter a field is necessarily to approach it from the outside, casting neophytes in a peripheral position relative to their field that Runco terms *professional marginality*. Marginality can benefit idea origination insofar as the novice generally has little turf to protect and therefore feels less handcuffed by old ways of doing things. It also gives the newcomer a detached perspective on the nature of the problems to be solved, a degree of objectivity sometimes absent among those who have long been close to the subject.

Obviously, jettisoning your career can be tumultuous. But putting all your cognitive eggs in one basket has its own downsides, as I pointed out above. The antidote? Follow the lead of Jolie, Brin, and Buffett, and get yourself a hobby.

Much good could come of it. Among other things, researchers have found that channeling energy into a creative pastime can relieve stress, afford pleasure, enhance self-esteem, expand social networks, raise productivity, improve health, and attain life-work balance. That should be convincing enough by itself. But they've also discovered that gaining fluency in a variety of subjects can make you better at almost everything, including your creativity-demanding day job. The reason is that with each new skill you develop, you're forging new neural pathways in regions of the brain that might otherwise have remained fallow, thereby strengthening the brain's processing power overall.

That's a pretty good return on investment for the price of a ukulele.

HOW TO DO IT

Home is the natural habitat of the hobbyist, or at least its common jumping-off point. Consider these pointers before incorporating a new pastime into your home.

Assess your needs. Is your avocation an indoor or outdoor activity? Outdoor activities generally

Potting area and mudroom. Minneapolis, Minnesota. Architecture and interior design by Meriwether Felt, AIA. Photography by Susan Gilmore.

taking over your neighbor's apartment to accommodate it. Instead, use your imagination to uncover hidden assets. Popping up a roof dormer over a low-ceilinged space, reclaiming an apartment balcony that previously afforded views for a couple of mops and a bucket, removing closet doors, or incorporating your tools and supplies into the decor are the sort of moves that can transform underused space into gold.

Plan well. "Measure twice, cut once," goes the old saw among carpenters intent on avoiding wastage by taking the time up front to do things right. The same applies to fitting out a hobby space; a bit of forethought can pay big dividends later, especially when serious money is to be spent. And don't be shy about applying inherited wisdom to your project. Laying out a workshop, for instance, should follow the same principle as a kitchen, in which the three most important elements in the space—refrigerator, sink, and stove in the kitchen, worktable, tools, and machinery in the workshop—stand in a triangular relationship to each other in plan. Other types of hobbies will tender their own norms. Research them first, or consult a professional who already has.

Mudroom. Cape Elizabeth, Maine. Architecture by Caleb Johnson Studio. Interior design by Krista Stokes. Photography by Trent Bell.

call for a transitional space or depository in which to stow the required gear. A closet, a freestanding or built-in storage unit, mudroom, garage, or shed will often do the trick.

Indoor pursuits are a hobbyhorse of a different color. Much will depend on whether you're engaged in clean or dirty work. In the latter case, your priorities should be work surface, material durability, storage and organization, lighting, ventilation, and access to utilities. Clean hobbies, like dagger collecting (I said not to ask), impose fewer demands and offer greater leeway as to location.

Exploit underutilized space. Adopting a hobby shouldn't require a new wing on your house or

RELATED TACTICS

#5. Display art.

#14. Bring nature in.

#18. Make music.

#19. Let in natural light.

#32. Cook.

#33. Exercise.

#34. Do yoga. Or meditate.

#37. Take a break.

#40. Pick up a pencil.

#41. Make stuff.

#43. Play.

#46. Read.

#47. Get out of the house.

#48. Really get out of the house.

TACTIC #43
PLAY

WHAT TO DO
Design areas of your home for play.

WHY DO IT?
Play is the essence of creativity.

WHY DOES IT WORK?
"Every child is an artist," Pablo Picasso is often quoted as saying. "The problem is how to remain an artist once he grows up."

But is Picasso right? Is every child an artist, meaning, are people born genetically predisposed to be creative? Positive psychologist Abraham Maslow clearly thought so. "Creativity is a characteristic given to all human beings at birth," he sunnily declared, reminding us once again why he's celebrated as the father of the upbeat school of thought. As to why play is so integral to human inventiveness, let's hear first from Stuart Brown, who literally wrote the book on the subject, called *Play: How It Shapes the Brain, Opens the Imagination, and Invigorates the Soul*:

> I don't think it is too much to say that play can save your life. It certainly has salvaged mine. Life without play is a grinding, mechanical existence organized around doing the things necessary for survival. Play is the stick that stirs the drink. It is the basis of all art, games, books, sports, movies, fashion, fun, and wonder—in short, the basis of what we think of as civilization. Play is the vital essence of life. It is what makes life lively.

Wow! That's certainly taking play to an even higher plane than expected. Still, the kernel of Brown's statement is that play lies at the heart of creativity in all its cultural and emotional manifestations.

Let's turn next to author Jordan Ayan, who further dissects the relationship between play and creativity:

> Play is a vital component of the creative process. Play eases you into a state of mind that contains many of the elements you

Child's bedroom. Brooklyn, New York. Architecture and interior design by Gaby and Donald M. Rattner. Photography by Raimondo di Egidio.

Tree house. Philadelphia, Pennsylvania. Architecture by Verner Architects. Photography by Todd Mason for Halkin Mason Photography.

need to be creative—curiosity, imagination, experimentation, fantasy, speculation or what if, role playing, and wonder. Through play you open up your creative spirit to the fanciful mental processes that allow you to make new connections, see new images, and get new insights. In their book *Wake Up Your Creative Genius*, Kurt Hanks and Jay Parry sum it up nicely: "A person might be able to play without being creative, but sure can't be creative without playing."

Let's give the last word to Swiss developmental psychologist Jean Piaget, who puts it even more succinctly: "Play is the answer to how anything new comes about."

HOW TO DO IT

Design play spaces for flexibility. Flexibility is a hallmark of creative thinking, rigidity its antithesis. This holds true for the inside of a room as much as it does for the inside of the mind. The last thing you want to do in an area designed for play, therefore, is to bog it down with scads of sedentary, single-purpose furniture. I suggest stocking it instead with movable, multifunctional, and rearrangeable pieces (#9).

Furnish tools, materials, and surfaces for handiwork. We discover a lot about our creativity by making stuff (#41). Keep play areas well stocked with tools and materials that can be used to construct a variety of objects forged by hand.

Get physical. Provide equipment and space for physical activities and movement, indoors and out.

TIPS FOR CHILDREN

As the experts I cite attest, our proclivity to play is intrinsic to creative behavior at all ages. But it takes on special importance during childhood, when our brains are developing most rapidly, and before we're exposed to the various educational, social, and professional pressures that threaten to suppress our urge to create later in life. To nurture creativity from the start, consider these additional recommendations when fitting out homes with growing children:

Let the youngsters decorate. Studies show time and again that workers are happier in their surroundings when they're permitted to personalize their workspace with their own decorative touches. Children react much the same when given a say in shaping their rooms. As creativity scholar Mihaly Csikszentmihalyi observes, this is doubly important when it comes to children's bedrooms,

Entry front. South Portland, Maine. Architecture by Caleb Johnson Studio. Photography by Trent Bell.

which is where young people store their most prized possessions, and where they feel most empowered to cultivate a sense of autonomy and self.

Encourage kids to be show-offs. Children can be very prolific in the production of handiwork. Reinforce the urge to create by providing them with sufficient shelving, stands, easels, picture frames, and furnishings on which to display their proudest moments.

Toys "r" good. Interactive, hands-on, reconfigurable, and open-ended free-play toys are even better. Same goes for grown-up playthings, by the way!

You can't be serious. It's a common tale. Architect and spouse have child. Architect and spouse go to store to shop for said child. Architect feels slightly queasy at sight of miles and miles of overdecorated and garishly colored toys made of plastics and other icky inorganic materials. Architect and spouse wander into furniture department, where architect doubles over in pain at sight of equally repellent cribs, changing tables, and rockers.

Architect goes home, insists on populating said room with products brought to market by fellow architects or designers who have endured similar experience.

Problem? You bet. Those rooms look smashing in shelter magazines, but they're utterly devoid of *humor*, which is coincident with creative thinking. Absolutely, keep it tasteful, but keep it light.

Study. Melbourne, Victoria, Australia. Architecture by Austin Maynard Architects. Photography by Peter Bennetts.

*Dolls' house of Petronella Dunois. Artisan unknown. Dutch.
c.1676. Rijksmuseum, Amsterdam.*

RELATED TACTICS

#2. Look at something blue.

#3. Work under a lofty ceiling.

#4. Take in a view.

#5. Display art.

#8. Put your walls to work.

#9. Be flexible.

#12. Choose curved over straight.

#14. Bring nature in.

#16. Make it beautiful.

#18. Make music.

#19. Let in natural light.

#20. Be smart with your lighting.

#40. Pick up a pencil.

#41. Make stuff.

#44. Make a mess. Or not.

#46. Read.

TACTIC #44
MAKE A MESS. OR NOT.

WHAT TO DO
Let yourself be messy. But not too messy.

WHY DO IT?
A 2013 study revealed that an untidy work environment is favorable to creative risk-taking.

WHY DOES IT WORK?
A raging debate runs through the creative community that to this day has yet to be settled. So divisive is the issue that otherwise friendly parties united by a common interest in nurturing the human imagination have been known to come nearly to blows.

The question is this:

Messy desk or a neat desk?

Let's review the evidence.

For a cluttered desk:

Albert Einstein, Mark Twain, Mark Zuckerberg, Steve Jobs, Susan Sontag, Sigmund Freud, Abraham Lincoln, Oscar de la Renta, Al Gore, Zappos founder Tony Hsieh, filmmaker Tim Burton, food writer Nigella Lawson, Martin Luther King Jr.

Now, the evidence for a neat desk:

Eleanor Roosevelt, Jane Austen, Yves St. Laurent, chairman of Sequoia Capital Michael Moritz, founder of Craigslist Craig Newmark, Anna Wintour, author of the best-selling *The Life-Changing Magic of Tidying Up: The Japanese Art of Decluttering and Organizing* Marie Kondo, me (I just wanted to see myself mentioned in the same paragraph as these other people).

So who wins?

Hard to say solely from the lists above, although admittedly the first group is tough to beat for total brain cell count. Rather than polling, however, we might be better served by examining the scientific evidence.

In 2013 psychologist Kathleen Vohs and several colleagues at the Carlson School of Management, University of Minnesota, looked at how orderliness impacts human behavior and creativity. Among their discoveries was that people brainstorming around an unkempt table turned out a greater quantity of original ideas than people seated at a tidy one, and quicker too. Vohs attributed this behavior to the influence of cultural norms that reinforce a connection between neatness and virtue—witness the old adage that cleanliness is next to godliness. Since creativity by definition subverts convention, she reasoned, it follows that

Mark Twain (Samuel Clemens), possibly at his residence in New York City. 1901. Photograph by Theodore C. Marceau. Library of Congress.

a disheveled environment primes seditious and unorthodox thinking.

So it appears Professor Einstein and his coterie of mess-ianic geniuses fall on the right side of the brain, so to speak.

Score one for the slobs.

But don't change from filer to piler just yet. The researchers also observed that people in orderly settings make more rational decisions than people in slovenly surroundings.

Score one for the neatniks.

So where does that leave us? With this advice from Vohs: "If you have a big assignment for work that involves following the rules and not taking any chances—accounting, for example—then having a clean or tidy environment would be really conducive to reaching that goal. But if your assignment is being creative and coming up with something bold and new, then messing up your environment would help you with that."

In sum, muss for divergency, fuss for convergency.

Beware of extremes in either direction, though. Radical congestion can easily devolve into debilitating dysfunction. Severely spartan surroundings, by contrast, might deny you the raw materials with which to effect at least the semblance of disorder observed to spur problem solving. Worse, it could trigger outright idea deprivation. Einstein himself alluded to the connection in a quip commonly attributed to him.

"If a cluttered desk is a sign of a cluttered mind," he once asked, "then what are we to think of an empty desk?"

Score another for the slobs.

HOW TO DO IT

Follow the formula or follow your instinct. In a perfect world, you'd have two separate yet seamlessly integrated micro-environments in which to operate: one outfitted for analytic tasks and the other for synthetic tasks. This being the real world, few people enjoy such a luxury. Besides, some of us would have a difficult time stepping out of character in maintaining one or the other as prescribed above even if we did. Forcing ourselves to be contrary to our natures could raise stress levels and undermine the quest for optimal creativity.

On the other hand, quite a sizable population feels stressed out from their own disarray. If that describes your situation, you'll be happy to hear that there are numerous techniques for reining in uncontrolled clutter. These are roughly divided between physical storage solutions and mental adjustments. Augmenting messiness, on the other hand, requires no special talent beyond finding a way to remain relaxed while letting go.

Ultimately, the best course of action might be to follow your instinct in maintaining workspace order. Be mindful, though, of what the state of your stuff can do to your head.

BONUS SECTION: USEFUL FIGURES

According to a 2005 survey by Pendaflex, a company best known for its paper management system, people fall into three categories when it comes to organizing work surfaces:

- 48 percent: People who are "pilers." They organize paper by stacking it on their countertops.
- 38 percent: People who are "filers." They file rather than pile, and often carry management titles.
- 14 percent: People classified as "tossers." They discard frequently in order to keep their work surfaces spare and uncluttered.

TACTIC #45
BE ALONE

The best thinking has been done in solitude. The worst has been done in turmoil.
—*Thomas Edison*

WHAT TO DO
Spend a portion of your idea time by yourself.

WHY DO IT?
Ideas are the product of the individual.

WHY DOES IT WORK?
They were among the most consequential creative duos of the twentieth century, yet they couldn't have been more different in personality. Steve Jobs was an ambitious, arrogant, high-energy extrovert who relished collaborating with (or sometimes pilfering from) other creative people, mastered audiences with aplomb, and wallowed in media attention. Steve Wozniak remains a self-effacing, soft-spoken, publicity-shy technological wiz and certified introvert whose most daring act of public display so far has been to do a few whirls on *Dancing with the Stars*.

Of the two profiles, it's the extrovert who's been adopted as the model for today's creative professional. Quite logically too, since creative industries operate under the mantra that innovation is by definition a collaborative and social undertaking. You can't be a shrinking violet and expect to succeed in an environment built on teamwork and human interaction, the thinking goes.

If you want to see the concrete manifestation of the ascendancy of the extrovert in the creative

Breakfast room. Bluffton, South Carolina. Architecture by Frederick + Frederick Architects. Photography by Helen Norman.

economy, pay a visit sometime to offices belonging to Apple, Google, or any of the other forward-looking enterprises that have built out their physical plant around this idea. Almost everything you'll see represents the desire for human interaction. Gone are the separate offices, screened off cubicles, partitions, and other barriers to the flow of information typifying the workplace of yesterday. Now workers sit side by side at open tables with not much between them other than air—that is, if they're seated at all. At some companies, people work standing up or go without assigned desks, a practice called *hot-desking*. Not only is it thought that unmooring employees from fixed stations accelerates workflow, it's also believed to bring about the kind of serendipitous collisions of people and ideas that lead to innovative breakthroughs (#32). Gaming areas (#43), social hubs, meeting spots, the placement of food (#31) and restroom facilities, and circulation patterns are deliberately planned to do the same.

It's enough to drive introverts crazy. Introverts like Susan Cain, a successful attorney who went on to write a best-selling book titled *QUIET: The Power of Introverts in a World That Can't Stop Talking*, and deliver an accompanying TED Talk watched by millions. Cain's message is that introverts could give a lot more to the world creatively if only work and learning environments weren't so crushingly hostile to them.

Home is a different story for Cain. Nearly every mention of home in her book is positive—as a refuge, a safe harbor, a welcoming place for

Living area. Tel Aviv—Yafo, Israel. Architecture by Pitsou Kedem Architects. Photography by Amit Geron.

introverts to live their lives and, if they're truly fortunate, to carry out their careers.

And why wouldn't she? Homes are uncrowded and placid compared to hyperactive workplaces crammed with staffers. Consider these statistics: about a quarter of the households in the United States today are occupied by a single person, another thirty percent by couples with no children. Overall, the average household numbers 2.6 occupants, a figure that's been shrinking for four decades. And it's not as if those 2.6 individuals stay indoors all day long; many are away for lengthy periods for work, school, or leisure. It's more a question as to whether someone at home will run into another person at all rather than how often it will happen in a day.

Even at full occupancy, people generally have more breathing room where they live versus where they work or study. Again, the numbers are revealing. The average footprint per office employee in the United States currently stands at about two hundred square feet. The standard minimum square footage per grade school student is a paltry thirty-five. Do the math for yourself to calculate your allotment of space at home. I'll wager you're doing well on that score.

So home can indeed serve as your creative haven. But is seclusion really best for creativity, as Cain maintains?

Not everyone thinks so. Creativity scholar Keith Sawyer takes issue with Cain's main assertion—as should be expected, given that Sawyer is the author of *Group Think: The Creative Power of Collaboration*, a tome whose central thesis is that "breakthrough ideas are largely due to exchange and interaction, and that's because breakthrough ideas always involve combinations of very different ideas," to cite Sawyer's own words. There being a natural limit to how many "different ideas" individuals can generate privately, the cocooning of the imagination that can result from an excess of solitude could be detrimental to the development of fresh insights, in Sawyer's view.

To be sure, the professor readily acknowledges the human need for periods of undisturbed contemplation and study during the creative process—what poet Emily Dickinson called "the appetite for silence." Where he differs with Cain is in his assessment of the value of groups. For Sawyer, they're the principal conduit to original thinking. For Cain, they're an impediment.

Or at least, they are for her, which I believe is ultimately the point to be made about her book. The fact is, most people are neither extreme extroverts, like Jobs, nor consummate introverts, like Cain and Wozniak. Rather, they fall somewhere in between. For the great majority of individuals, quietude is vital to maintaining productivity, but so is tossing one's thoughts into the giant idea blender that is the world. The issue for an individual such as yourself is therefore less about whether aloneness or engagement is more vital

Kitchen. Leura, Blue Mountains, New South Wales, Australia. Architecture and interior design by Danny Broe Architect. Photography by Karina Illovska.

to creativity, but how to find the balance between them that best works for you.

HOW TO DO IT

Find a way. Close a door. Steal into a basement or attic. Venture onto a porch, balcony, roof deck, or into a yard. Build a work shed, writer's hut, lab, or other accessory structure attached to or apart from the main dwelling. Take a shower or bath. Go for a walk. Cut off the phone, lock down the Internet. Do your creative work when others are asleep or out. Live alone.

RELATED TACTICS

#34. Do yoga. Or meditate.
#35. Take a shower or bath.
#38. Go for a walk.
#39. Daydream.
#46. Read.

TACTIC #46
READ

All that mankind has done, thought, gained or been: it is lying as in magic preservation in the pages of books.
—Thomas Carlyle

WHAT TO DO
Read a lot.

WHY DO IT?
Reading amplifies creativity.

WHY DOES IT WORK?
A recent survey by a major research organization asked people why they read. Back came a range of responses: for information, edification, relaxation, pleasure, entertainment, escape.

These are all valid and valuable reasons to read. But books do more than passively feed us facts, tickle our funny bone, or release us from the everyday; they also actively cultivate our creative personas. Author Jordan Ayan eloquently expresses the value of reading's reciprocal effect in a passage worth quoting at length:

Throughout most of our education, we are taught to read primarily for information rather than to discover how reading can influence our creativity. We were largely taught "power reading" instead of "reading power." In my view, one of the most important purposes of reading is to fuel your own ideas and creative work. The best reading is actually a life cycle with an author's ideas flowing into you, and your ideas then flowing back to the world in the form of things you create, works you do, and the people you affect.

The best kind of reading takes you out of your comfort zone. It engages your curiosity by letting you venture into the diversity of human life; it enhances your openness to new ideas and views of the truth; it teaches you to take risks by enabling you to try on new ideas or explore provocative topics in the safety of your home; and it fires up your energy and passion when you delve into causes or ideas that are profoundly meaningful to you.

In 1851, the German philosopher Arthur Schopenhauer wrote, "Reading is equivalent to thinking with someone else's head instead of with one's own." By reading, you're able to enter the minds of other people and add their thoughts and experiences to your own. By assimilating their visions, values, motivations, and perspectives, you supplement the storehouse of ideas from which you fuel your creative work.

Others second Ayan's sentiments, particularly his linking reading to breadth of knowledge and experience, traits long associated with superlative achievers. Psychologist Ron Friedman, for instance, notes that "creative geniuses tend to hold a broader array of interests than their average contemporary. While working to find a solution in one domain, they'll dabble

Window seat. Thornbury, Victoria, Australia. Building and interior design by Matthew Duignan for Mesh Design Projects. Photography by Peter Clarke.

in unrelated fields . . . it might look as if they are slacking off, but it's often these extraneous experiences that fuel their ability to find unexpected connections." Graphic designer and author Clement Mok believes the economy of the future will demand the same of everyone. "The next ten years will require people to think and work across boundaries into new zones that are totally different from their areas of expertise," he predicts. "They will not only have to cross those boundaries, but they will also have to identify opportunities and make connections between them."

Got it. Reading is good for creativity. It fills our idea cache, promotes diverse perspectives, encourages adventurousness, and inspires us to give back to the pool of human invention by creating things of our own.

HOW TO DO IT

Design spaces for reading. Reading is an activity best performed in comfortable solitude. Avoid heavily trafficked areas or locations susceptible to noise and distractions.

Opt for furniture that can accommodate lengthy periods of sitting; discomfort discourages duration. Ergonomically designed recliners, easy chairs, and sofas are well suited to protracted reading stints.

Nooks are an appealing alternative to freestanding pieces. A nook is a small-scale space within or adjacent to a larger space. Some nooks project outside the structure of the home, while others are contained within its perimeter. A bay window is an example of the first. Inglenooks and alcoves framed by built-in cabinetry or flanking interior partitions fall in the second category.

Dining area. London, United Kingdom. Architecture and interior design by Camilla Leech for Element Studios. "Bookworm" bookshelf designed by Ron Arad for Kartell, 1993. Photography by Paul Craig.

Windowed nooks are ideal for daytime reading. Install electric lighting for proper illumination after sunset in both windowed and blind nooks. A swing-arm sconce mounted on a side wall or mullion is optimal, though an overhead fixture or an adjustable floor lamp adjacent to the recess could suffice as well.

Make room for books. Even with the advent of electronic media, physical books remain an irreplaceable medium for transmitting written and pictorial content.

The means by which you store your books can have a major impact on the character of a space. Freestanding and wall-mounted units have the advantage of relative affordability and come in a great many configurations, some of them literally "bending" the traditional notion of what a bookshelf

should be. Built-in bookcases, by comparison, often entail costly construction, but they produce a highly pleasing effect through the seamless integration of printed matter and architecture.

Books historically have been placed in rooms associated with mindful pursuits, such as studies, libraries, and offices (Fig. 1). We're less rigid about that connection today. In addition to traditional locations, you'll now find bookcases in bathrooms, staircases, foyers, corridors, dormers, and even dining rooms, where they serve occupants with food for thought (see #11 for an impressive example).

Adopt a multi-tactical approach. Exploit the opportunity for cumulative effect by combining reading with other tactics. For instance, you could enjoy your book while lying down (#28) or walking (#38), though the second can cause trouble if you

Home office, kitchen, and entry. Philip Island, Victoria, Australia. Architecture by Andrew Simpson, Charles Anderson, and Emma Parkinson for Andrew Simpson Architects. Photography by Peter Bennetts.

Screened porch. Bluffton, South Carolina. Architecture by Frederick + Frederick Architects. Photography by Helen Norman.

Reading room. Marblemount, Washington. Architecture by David Coleman Architecture. Photography by Ben Benschneider.

aren't careful. A less risky strategy is to sit by a fire (#29) with a glass of wine or distilled spirit in hand (#30)—preferably the kind that warms your insides going down (#23). The ultimate sensorial synthesis? Design your bath or outdoor tub to be in view of a blazing fireplace, then add beverage, scent (#24), a bit of background music (#18), elements of Nature (#14) and, lest you forget the reason you're there, a book.

RELATED TACTICS

#14. Bring nature in.
#18. Make music.
#24. Pick up the scent.
#28. Lie down or recline.
#29. Make a fire. Or look at a picture of one.
#30. Have a drink.
#35. Take a shower or bath.
#38. Go for a walk.
#42. Pursue a hobby.

TACTIC #47
GET OUT OF THE HOUSE

WHAT TO DO
Periodically pursue or renew your creativity outside the home.

WHY DO IT?
Leaving home can stimulate the imagination, break mental impasses, and enliven mood.

WHY DOES IT WORK?
If there's a central message in this book, it's that there's no place like home for cultivating and exercising the creative impulse. Don't get me wrong, though: I don't claim that you'll never attain the same level of creative task performance enjoyed at home anywhere else. In fact, I can point to several situations where traveling outside your domestic safe space for periods longer than normally spent on a walk (#38) or other relatively brief interregnums could do wonders for idea production.

Take mental blocks. You've probably had them—the feeling that your insights lack insight, that your storehouse of ideas is emptier than a beach in a snowstorm, that you're mired in a mental gully. Sure, you could chain yourself to your standing desk, keyboard, or easel with a vow to stay with it until the idea spigot turns back on, but deep down you sense you're at a dead end. Something has to change, and it might well be your location.

Another sign that it's time to shift venues is that you talk to yourself a lot. Or maybe to your cat, dog, fish, plants, walls, or portrait of your Aunt Jenny. If so, it's hardly a laughing matter; isolation is a real affliction among stay-at-home creatives, particularly full-time professionals. That became starkly evident in a 2018 survey by the software company Buffer, which found that the number one struggle among remote workers—three quarters of whom are home-based—is loneliness.

Minerals Gallery, Natural History Museum. London, United Kingdom. Architecture by Alfred Waterhouse. 1864–1873. Photography by Mavis CW.

Coffee shop. Warsaw, Poland. Photography by Jacek Dylag.

Residence. Gallatin County, Montana. Architecture by John E. Sather for Swaback Architects + Planners.

A cloistered life can be extremely debilitating for your creativity. Among other things, it can cut you off from the very stuff ideas are made of—namely, the world at large. It can also deprive you of the opportunity to bounce your thoughts off of others for the purpose of getting vital real-time feedback. Left unaddressed, mental languor and creative stagnation could soon set in.

Unless you take steps to ameliorate the situation, that is. One remedy is to periodically remove yourself to unfamiliar or less frequented spaces to either practice or rejuvenate your creativity. After all, the fundamental tenet of environmental psychology—that you are *where* you are—cuts both ways. The routine occupation of a particular space can lead to routinized thinking. Change your space, change your mind.

The question is how.

HOW TO DO IT

Find a surrogate creative space. Seek out a location outside the home where you can set up creative shop on a regular or as-needed basis. Use the guidelines laid out in this book to identify viable candidates.

Your personality will play into your choices as well. You extroverts who relish human interaction will naturally gravitate to coffee shops, co-working facilities, bookstore cafés, hotel lobbies, transit hubs, and pedestrian-friendly public spaces.

Introverts and those with low sensory filtering should limit themselves to quieter environs, such as libraries, museums, parks and greens, and predominantly natural environments.

Go on vacation. A handful of studies have looked into whether vacations strengthen creative task performance among returning workers. So far the results are inconclusive. Subjects recorded a post-getaway spike in creativity assessment scores in two of the experiments, only to have the bump fade soon afterward. Another group cranked out a greater number of ideas after their time away, though judges failed to see any increase in originality. All three studies, however, have been criticized on technical grounds, making definitive

conclusions about the connection premature from a scientific standpoint.

This much does seem evident from other investigations into holiday effects: where you go and what you do matters. Sojourns into exotic cultures, immersion in natural landscapes, rigorous physical activity, travel, or intensely unusual and unexpected encounters—what scientists term *diversifying experiences*—are more likely to invigorate divergent thinking both during and after the period than passive and unchallenging itineraries.

Of course, your time away from home needn't be frenetic to be fruitful. Exhibit A: Bill Gates, known to go on "reading vacations" during which he spends his day plowing through a tote bag worth

Column of Pedro IV. Rossio Square, Lisbon, Portugal. Erected 1870. Photography by Vita Marija Murenaite.

Kaafu Atoll, Maldives. Photography by Ishan.

*Teardrop trailer. Designed and built by Rick Brewster for Camp Weathered. Woodacre, California.
Base model by Big Woody Campers. Photography by Kyawt Thiri Nyunt.*

of books (#46). Come to think of it, reading is a pretty good fallback strategy for getting away when you can't actually get away. For what do books do, if not dissolve the perceived boundaries of time and space that tether us to our material surroundings?

Take up temporary residence elsewhere. A second home is often an ideal creative retreat, provided you have the means to acquire one. Fortunately, thanks to rental services like Airbnb, decamping occasionally to alternative digs to resuscitate a stalled project or revive the urge to invent now lies in reach of the many. Ditto for doing a bit of mind-body wandering in stylishly designed mobile living quarters.

Then again, if you're really serious about improving yourself creatively, consider taking up residence for a few years *in another country*. The cognitive windfall could be enormous. You'll learn why in the next and final tactic of the book.

RELATED TACTICS

#1. Designate a creative space.
#37. Take a break.
#38. Go for a walk.
#46. Read.
#48. Really get out of the house.

Rome, Italy. Photography by Ludwig Thalheimer.

Dubai, United Arab Emirates. Photography by Nick Fewings.

Havana, Cuba. Photography by Eva Blue.

TACTIC #48
REALLY GET OUT
OF THE HOUSE

I haven't been everywhere, but it's on my list.
—Susan Sontag

WHAT TO DO
Live or study in a different country or region for a period of time.

WHY DO IT?
Relocation grows the mind.

WHY DOES IT WORK?
Sometimes the best way to catalyze creativity at home is to leave it for a long time.

Adam Galinsky should know. Currently the Vikram S. Pandit Professor of Business at Columbia University, his biographical description on the school's website runs for nearly four hundred words and overflows with accolades and accomplishments. He's written or coauthored over 150 scholarly articles on leadership, power, negotiations, decision-making, diversity, ethics, and creativity. He's gotten grants from the National Science Foundation and the American Psychological Association, serves as an associate editor of the *Journal of Experimental Social Psychology*, was selected as one of the World's Fifty Best B-School Professors by Poets and Quants, has won multiple awards for writing, teaching, and research excellence at Northwestern and Princeton Universities, is frequently cited in the media, and has consulted with and conducted executive workshops for hundreds of clients across the globe, including Fortune 100 firms, nonprofits, and local and national governments.

So when a fellow like Galinsky speaks about the impact leaving home to work or travel in another part of the world has on creative development, you're prone to sit up and listen.

"Foreign experiences increase both cognitive flexibility and depth and integrativeness of thought, the ability to make deep connections between disparate forms," he states. "The key, critical process is multicultural engagement, immersion, and adaptation. Someone who lives abroad and doesn't engage with the local culture will likely get less of a creative boost than someone who travels abroad and really engages in the local environment."

I'm unsure as to whether "integrativeness" is officially a word, but let's take Professor Galinsky at his. What he's asserting is that departing from the geography of everyday life for extended periods of time can stimulate fresh patterns of thought, further our ability to uncover previously unrecognized relationships among things and ideas, and deepen our knowledge base—all essential developments for cultivating the creative mind.

To arrive at his thesis, Galinsky and several colleagues analyzed the careers of 270 design directors from the world's leading fashion houses. Several were household names, at least

Kyoto, Japan. Photography by Sorasak.

Istanbul, Turkey. Photography by Luke Michael.

Guilin, China. Photography by Arthur Fellig.

in households with nice clothes: Karl Lagerfeld, Marc Jacobs, Giorgio Armani, Tom Ford, and Miuccia Prada, to mention a few of the bolder-faced figures. Less well-known professionals were scrutinized as well. Some subjects had substantial overseas stints under their belts by the start of the study, others not.

The apparel business is a good place to learn whether time spent in a distant locale will factor in a person's creative trajectory. For one thing, it's a global industry, so there's plenty of call for transplanting personnel to distant locations. For another, the business is notoriously reliant on relentless innovation and novelty to get customers to change their clothes season after season. Few fashionistas can afford the luxury of sitting on their well-manicured hands for long if they hope to survive, let alone flourish. Design shifts have to be rapid and deft enough to capture the hearts, minds, and wallets of the buying public. And since fashion is both a long-standing art form and a market, a designer's portfolio can be judged by the creative yardsticks of aesthetic invention (newness) and audience appeal (usefulness) relative to his or her peers.

Which is exactly what Galinsky did. Going back eleven years, the team plotted the sales and innovative quality of each designer's work relative to their base of operations before and during the study period. What they found was that designers with postings outside their native countries were more artistically progressive and engineered greater market success for their brands than those who stayed closer to home.

It doesn't take a doctorate in psychology or a flashy wardrobe to understand why. Moving to take a job elsewhere demands we leave our comfort zones, physically and emotionally. Old routines that we've unconsciously settled into no longer suffice to get us through our day. New ones have to be invented to take their place, putting our imaginations to work at finding fresh solutions to old problems.

Cultural differences add to the mental churn. Exposed to people with unfamiliar attitudes and practices, we become more self-aware of the ones we left behind, and are perhaps motivated to reconsider some of them. If little else, we're reminded that what might seem like the obvious answer to a practical or philosophical questions might in fact be merely one of several plausible responses. Realizing once again that there are multiple solutions to a problem helps jolt us out of the mental complacency that comes with formulaic behavior and cultural isolation.

Ironically, it's the very condition of unfamiliarity brought on by physical displacement that could account for the hike in creative output Galinsky discovered among fashion industry expats. Ironic, because familiarity is among those characteristics I tout as an essential quality in establishing the meaning and purpose of home. Familiarity turns out to be a double-edged sword. On the one hand, we crave a recognizable place in this world to call our own, to mitigate the tumult that lies beyond our front door. On the other, overabundant familiarity can undermine innovation by nudging us toward the tried-and-true, the habitual, and the pat. Too much familiarity in our lives and we risk eroding our creative urge, our innate drive to go places others dare not go. Too little and we lack a stable platform from which to launch our flights of fancy.

Counteracting the ossifying effects of over-familiarity by temporarily working abroad is only possible because our brains turn out to be remarkably pliant in their susceptibility to change. Scientists did not always appreciate this. Until a few decades ago it was thought that the brain aged like a tub of concrete. Not entirely without reason, given what seemed to be striking parallels between the two. As we age our brain matter and

Edinburgh, Scotland. Photography by Tim Martin.

Tangier, Morocco. Photography by Raul Cacho Oses.

Amsterdam, the Netherlands. Photography by Ján Jakub Naništa.

personalities acquire greater definition, just as concrete is slowly brought to a state of hardness by the controlled evaporation of its water content. By our middle years we're thought to be more or less "set" in our ways; concrete is likewise considered "set" when the drying-out process is completed. The surface of aged concrete is liable to be marred by fissures and spalling, a condition where chunks of material break away from the main mass. Their faces lined with age, elderly people are sometimes labeled as "cracked" should they appear forgetful, unfocused, or eccentric.

The parts of the analogy about concrete are true. The chronology of brain development it outlines is not. The truth is that our brains are far more resilient later in life than the average sidewalk. Sidewalks don't repair themselves when they're damaged, and they don't learn from experience for the duration of their lifecycle. Brains do both.

Scientists have coined the term *neuroplasticity* to describe the persistent elasticity of the human mind. At the risk of simplifying what is, after all, brain science, neuroplasticity refers to the ability of our brain to change, adapt, and grow according to our experiences. It does so by activating internal neural pathways each time we perform an action or undergo a sensory input. The more an experience is repeated, the stronger and more defined the pathways inside our brain become. The more defined the pathways, the more adept we are at navigating them.

I like to use the model of a grassy lawn to visualize the formation of these neural connections. Imagine a public park in your hometown. Let's say a concession stand is located at the far end of a lawn adjacent to the park entry. Each nice summer day at lunch you come to the park from work or home and cross the lawn to the stand. By the end of the summer you and others have trod so heavily along the route that a narrow strip of dirt and scruffy growth has been incised into the landscape. Having taken the walk so many times you can now do it with your eyes closed. That strip is the metaphorical equivalent of a neural pathway that's been seared into your brain after a period of focused and repetitive activity. The process by which you came to be able to do it without looking is called learning.

The same thing happens when you strive to acquire a skill. Practicing the piano several times a week, kicking a soccer ball hours on end, or studying quantum physics out of a textbook until it hurts, are all forging and strengthening the kinds of neural networks that will empower you to become proficient in your chosen field or activity.

With proper physical and mental regimens, our brains can continue to form new networks well into old age—with a few caveats. Should we stop traversing the lawn for extended periods, the grass will start to grow back in and the visible grooves ground into the landscape will eventually disappear. Same with a neural network associated with a skill or body of knowledge—either use it or lose it. But beware of monomanias. Should you take the same route every day and decline to explore other areas in the park by going down paths less traveled, you could well suffer the ills of overfamiliarity and mental stagnation that inhibit fresh viewpoints.

The fashion designers stationed abroad in Galinsky's study would seem to have the best of both worlds. They were able to continue practicing their craft but in a wholly new environment, one that undoubtedly gave rise to all sorts of novel life experiences and learning opportunities.

HOW TO DO IT

Get transferred or relocate abroad. Fortunately, you don't have to be transferred to a glamorous global hotspot halfway around the world to fortify your own neural networks. Indeed, Galinsky found that the literal distance

Prague, Czechia. Photography by A.C. Almelor.

Barra da Tijuca, Brazil. Photography by Breno Assis.

traveled and the duration of stay were less critical in elevating his subjects' creativity than the depth to which the transplants immersed themselves in their newly adopted locales. That opens up plenty of possibilities for the rest of us. For youngsters in school, a semester- or year-long study program abroad could instill in them a wider understanding of the world. For adults, an extended sabbatical leave from work or temporarily setting up shop in a region far from home base could bring similar benefits. Empty nesters, retirees, and remote workers are in a particularly good position to live somewhere else for a spell. My advice to all is, do so while you can.

RELATED TACTICS
#46. Read.
#47. Get out of the house.

CASE STUDIES

Home office and library. New Vernon, New Jersey. Architecture by Dubinett Architects. Interior design by Jane Connell for Fun House Furnishings & Design. Photography by Laura Moss.

CASE STUDY ONE

This charming room manages to pack in so many of the tactical cues discussed in the book that I found it helpful to list them in bullet form. Hat tip to the designer for adroitly pulling together so many creativity-positive design elements in a single space.

#1. Designate a creative space.
- Dedicated purpose of room

#2. Look at something blue.
- Wall color[1]

#3. Work under a lofty ceiling.
- Ceiling height of ten feet
- Ceiling painted white
- Vertical proportions of panel divisions
- Vertical proportions of bookcase
- Vertical proportion of framed botanic print on back wall
- Vertical folds in window drapes[2]

#4. Take in a view.
- Orientation of desk to window
- Seating under window

#5. Display art.
- Framed botanic print on back wall
- Horsehead sculpture on desk

#7. Embrace detail and complexity.
- High level of surface and spatial articulation

#10. Face your space.
- Orientation of desk to room

#12. Choose curved over straight.
- Elliptical desk
- Louis XV chairs
- Arched window

#14. Bring nature in.
- Framed botanic print on back wall
- Horsehead sculpture on desk
- Flower bouquet on desk
- Magnifying glass with roughly carved wood handle on desk
- Stone surfacing on counter behind desk
- Zebra hide rug
- Wood flooring
- Stylized branch chandelier

#16. Make it beautiful.
- High level of aesthetic unity

#19. Let in natural light.
- Arched window

#24. Pick up the scent.
- Flower bouquet on desk
- Aromatic candle on counter behind desk

#40. Pick up a pencil
- Tortoiseshell fountain pens in silver cup on desk

#46. Read.
- Books on shelves

Notes:

1. The attractive Admiral Blue on the walls certainly satisfies the tactical criterion from the strict standpoint of color selection. The darkness of the shade, however, might cause the walls to appear to advance into the room, creating the optical perception of diminishing rather than expansive space.

2. A stickler for detail would have the pattern imprinted on the drapes contain only vertical elements. But there's so much else going for the space that the effect is likely to be de minimis.

CASE STUDY TWO

At first glance, this home studio for a small graphic design business seems pleasant enough. The artwork on the walls (#5), the stylish trestle tables, light fixtures, and window shade, the fall of light on the floor (#19), and the duffel bag placed casually below the window, suggest a laid-back atmosphere that's creative and fun.

On second pass, however, the shortcomings of the space from a design psychology standpoint become noticeable.

There's the low ceiling height (#3), for example, as well as the apparent absence of wall color (#2). Even more problematic is that the person in the chair sits with his back to the room; this runs counter to the tenets of prospect-refuge theory, which suggest that we become relaxed and open-minded when we feel protected from the rear and have a sweeping view of the space before us (#10). His orientation also deprives him of a view through the window (#4).

Making matters still worse is that he's staring at a wall less than two feet away. His sense of physical space, and by extension, his mental space, are greatly truncated as a result (Explainer II).

Now the good news. Many of these faults are easily corrected.

Step one: Rearrange the furnishings so that the fellow gets to face into the room and has a view through the window.

Further steps: Add blue or green to the room palette. Bring in plants, flowers, and other organic and scented elements (#14). Get more out of the walls—a pinup board, shelving, or pegboard will activate the surfaces and provide some useful functionality (#8). Finally, convert one of the tables to a standing desk by adding a sit-to-stand desktop adapter or similar apparatus (#13).

To summarize:

Tactics currently in effect

#1. Designate a creative space.

#5. Display art.

#19. Let in natural light.

#43. Play.

Additional tactics that could be implemented to address design shortcomings

#2. Look at something blue.

#4. Take in a view.

#8. Put your walls to work.

#10. Face your space.

#13. Stand up for yourself.

#14. Bring nature in.

#24. Pick up the scent.

ADDITIONAL RESOURCES

Visit donaldrattner.com/resources for my list of recommended books, learning opportunities, events, and videos about creativity and innovation.

BIBLIOGRAPHY
Introduction
The Creative Home. Bloom, Nicholas, and John Roberts. "A Working from Home Experiment Shows High Performers Like It Better." *Harvard Business Review* (website). Jan. 23, 2015. goo.gl/oDo93X; Ditkoff, Mitch, and Tim Moore. "Where and When Do People Get Their Best Ideas? An Inquiry into the Top Catalysts of Creativity." *Idea Champions* (website). June 18, 2008. goo.gl/EXT5V9; Friedman, Ron. *The Best Place to Work: The Art and Science of Creating an Extraordinary Workplace.* New York et al.: Penguin Publishing, 2014. Ch. 2, sec. "The Lessons of Telecommuting: Why Employees Are Often More Productive at Home"; Gallagher, Winifred. *House Thinking: A Room-by-Room Look at How We Live.* New York et al.: Harper Perennial, 2006; Hiss, Tony. "Why We Need Home." *New York Times* (website). Apr. 7, 1991. goo.gl/ztV3tz; Howkins, John. *The Creative Economy: How People Make Money from Ideas.* London et al.: Penguin Books, 2013. BT/Management Today survey, Ch. 5. goo.gl/cfCfoL; Israel, Toby. *Some Place Like Home: Using Design Psychology to Create Ideal Places.* Princeton: Design Psychology Press, 2003; Kron, Joan. *Home-Psych: The Social Psychology of Home and Decoration.* New York: Clarkson N. Potter, 1983; Mallett, Shelley. "Understanding Home: A Critical Review of the Literature." *Sociological Review.* 52 (2004): 62–89. goo.gl/ff4ehK; Marcus, Clare Cooper. *House as a Mirror of Self: Exploring the Deeper Meaning of Home.* Lake Worth, FL: Nicolas-Hays, 1995; Rybczynski, Witold. *Home: A Short History of an Idea.* New York et al.: Penguin Books, 1986.

Creativity Defined. Kaufman, James C., and Ronald A. Beghetto. "Beyond Big and Little: The Four C Model of Creativity." *Review of General Psychology.* 13.1 (2009): 1–12. goo.gl/KT2gNg; Runco Mark, and Garrett J. Jaeger. "The Standard Definition of Creativity." *Creativity Research Journal.* 24:1 (2012): 92–96. goo.gl/kf3esr; Sawyer, Keith. *Explaining Creativity: The Science of Human Innovation.* New York et al.: Oxford University Press, 2006. Ch. 1, "Why Explain Creativity?"

The Science of Creativity. Guilford, J.P. "Creativity." *American Psychologist.* 5, 9 (Sept. 1950): 444–454. goo.gl/JMxUcZ; Kaufman, Scott Barry, and Carolyn Gregoire. *Wired to Create: Unraveling the Mysteries of the Creative Mind.* New York: Perigee, 2015; Pappano, Laura. "Learning to Think Outside the Box: Creativity Becomes an Academic Discipline." *New York Times* (website). Feb. 5, 2014. goo.gl/g78vFx; Runco, Mark. *Creativity: Theories and Themes: Research, Development, and Practice.* London et al.: Academic Press, 2014; Sawyer, Keith. *Explaining Creativity: The Science of Human Innovation.* New York et al.: Oxford University Press, 2006; Sternberg, Robert J., ed. *Handbook of Creativity.* Cambridge (UK): Cambridge University Press, 2009.

The Creative Process. Guilford, J.P. "Creativity." *American Psychologist.* 5, 9 (Sept. 1950): 444–454. goo.gl/JMxUcZ; —. *The Nature of Human Intelligence.* New York et al.: McGraw-Hill Book Company, 1967.

Measuring Creativity. Amabile, Teresa M. *Creativity in Context.* Boulder: Westview Press, 1996. Ch. 2, "The Meaning and Measure of Creativity"; Anderson, Tod. "Test Your Creativity: 5 Classic Creative Challenges." *99U* (website). goo.gl/QMxz9; Nilsson, Peter. "Four Ways to Measure Creativity." *Sense and Sensation* (website). Mar. 24, 2012. goo.gl/GNr80T; "Test Developer Profiles: E. Paul Torrance, Ph.D." *Mhhe* [McGraw-Hill Higher Education] (website). goo.gl/k3oDV4; Torrance, E.P. "Testing and Creative Talent." *Educational Leadership.* (Oct. 1962): 7–10, 72. goo.gl/SCSyfY.

The Psychology of Space. Anthes, Emily. "Building Around the Mind." *Scientific American Mind* (April/May 2009): 52–59. goo.gl/2QfB7j; Augustin, Sally. *Place Advantage: Applied Psychology for Interior Architecture.* Hoboken: John Wiley & Sons, 2009; Ford, Madeline. "What Is Priming? A Psychological Look at Priming and Consumer Behavior." *Motive Metrics* (website). July 1, 2013. goo.gl/A3WNdb; Lidwell, William, Kritina Holden, and Jill Butler. *Universal Principles of Design: 125 Ways to Enhance Usability, Influence Perception, Increase Appeal, Make Better Design Decisions and Teach Through Design.* Beverly, MA: Rockport Publishers, 2010. "Priming"; Jacobs, Charlotte DeCroes. *Jonas Salk: A Life.* Oxford: Oxford University Press, 2015. Ch. 17–18; Spencer, Christopher, and Kate Gee. "The Roots and Branches of Environmental Psychology." *The Psychologist.* 22 (Feb. 2009): 180–183. goo.gl/Ce6LRC; Steg, Linda, Agnes E. van den Berg, and Judith I. de Groot. *Environmental Psychology: An Introduction.*

Hoboken: John Wiley & Sons, 2013; Stewart, Barbara Lyons. *Flooring Psych: How to Avoid (Literally) Slipping and Tripping Through Life.* San Anselmo, CA: Architectural Design Psychology Press, 2015; Ulrich, Robert S. "View Through a Window May Influence Recovery from Surgery." *Science.* 224.4647 (Apr. 27, 1984): 420–421. goo.gl/yYJWkh; Vithayathawornwong, Supaporn, Sheila Danko, and Pamela Tolbert. "The Role of the Physical Environment in Supporting Organizational Creativity." *Journal of Interior Design.* 1, 22 (2003): 1–16. goo.gl/MtwRDz.

Brains and Bodies. Jacobs, Tom. "Debunking Myths About Creativity and the Brain." *Pacific Standard* (website). Feb. 23, 2017. goo.gl/5h-Cofk; Klinge, Kylah Goodfellow. "Mapping Creativity in the Brain." *The Atlantic* (website). Mar. 21, 2016. goo.gl/mo6kNK; Runco, Mark. *Creativity: Theories and Themes: Research, Development, and Practice.* London et al.: Academic Press, 2014. Ch. 3, "Biological Perspectives on Creativity."

Creativity Tactics. Nickerson, Raymond S. "Enhancing Creativity." *Handbook of Creativity.* Robert J. Sternberg, ed. Cambridge et al.: Cambridge University Press, 1999.

The Tactics

Creativity Tactics Group One: Appearance and Appurtenance

#1. Make a creative space. Currey, Mason. *Daily Rituals: How Artists Work.* New York: Alfred A. Knopf, 2013; Doorley, Scott, and Scott Witthoft. *Make Space: How to Set the Stage for Creative Collaboration.* Hoboken: John Wiley & Sons, Inc., 2012; Friedman, Ron. *The Best Place to Work: The Art and Science of Creating an Extraordinary Workplace.* New York et al.: Penguin Publishing, 2014. Ch. 2, "The Power of Place"; Lloyd, Peter. "Creative

Space." *Catalyst Ranch* (website). Retrieved Apr. 2, 2018. goo.gl/8rYmgM; Groves, Kursty, and Oliver Marlow. *Spaces for Innovation: The Design and Science of Inspiring Environments.* Amsterdam: Frame Publishers, 2016; Miller, Rex, Mabel Casey, and Mark Konchar. *Change Your Space, Change Your Culture: How Engaging Workspaces Lead to Transformation and Growth.* Hoboken: John Wiley & Sons, Inc., 2014; Rao, Srinivas. "The Profound Power of Consistency." *Medium* (website). July 24, 2017. goo.gl/mEZrBh; Williams, Alison. "A Grammar of Creative Workplaces." PhD diss. University of East London, 2013. Retrieved Nov. 5, 2016. goo.gl/1VqyYU; Weidlinger, Tom. "Working for God." *The Restless Hungarian* (website). July 3, 2015. goo.gl/1VqyYU; Wright, David W. "Eight Questions: Interview With Austin Kleon." *Sterling & Stone* (website). goo.gl/1Yhmh7.

#2. Look at something blue. Belluck, Pam. "Accurate Red, Creative Blue: Color Counts, Study Says." *New York Times* (website). Feb. 5, 2009. goo.gl/CKZyAc; Caan, Shashi. "Spatial Color: Experiencing Color in the Third Dimension." *SC Collective* (website). Feb. 26, 2006. goo.gl/FKFzrD and goo.gl/CMq6rd; Elliot, Andrew J., and Markus A. Maier. "Color and Psychological Functioning." *Current Directions in Psychological Science.* 16, 5 (2007): 250–254. goo.gl/zPJDHg; Elliot, Andrew J., and Martin V. Covington. "Approach and Avoidance Motivation." *Educational Psychology Review.* 13.2 (June 2001): 73–92. goo.gl/e8fTwS; Fields, R. Douglas. "Why We Prefer Certain Colors." *Psychology Today* (website). Apr. 1, 2011. goo.gl/1rKQQ; Guilford, J. P. "Cognitive Styles: What Are They?" *Educational and Psychological Measurement.* 40.3 (Oct. 1980): 715–735; Hering-Shepherd, Renate. "Color Psychology in Interior Design: Can the Psychology of Color Help You Decorate Your Home?" *Dream Home Decorating* (website). This is the lead article for an impressive series of blog posts on the psychology of color. goo.gl/suYahq; Mahnke, Frank H., and Rudolf H. Mahnke. *Color and Light in Man-made Environments.* New York et al.: John Wiley & Sons, 1993. An in-depth study of color psychology; Martin, G. Neil. "Seeing Red." *The Psychologist.* 30 (Aug. 2017): 48–53. goo.gl/Jpxxhb; Steele, Kenneth M. "Failure to Replicate the Mehta and Zhu (2009) Color-priming Effect on Anagram Solution Times." *Psychonomic Bulletin & Review.* 21 (2014):771–776. goo.gl/rNM54x; Zhu, Rui (Juliet), and Ravi Mehta. "Blue or Red? Exploring the Effect of Color on Cognitive Task Performances." *Science.* 32.5918 (Feb. 27, 2009): 1226–1229. goo.gl/vQBgGn.

#3. Work under a lofty ceiling. Jaffe, Eric. "Why Our Brains Love High Ceilings." *Co.Design* (website). May 5, 2015. goo.gl/6xoPjP; Lidwell, William, Kritina Holden, and Jill Butler. *Universal Principles of Design: 125 Ways to Enhance Usability, Influence Perception, Increase Appeal, Make Better Design Decisions and Teach Through Design.* Beverly, MA: Rockport Publishers, 2010. "Cathedral Effect": 38–39; Meyers-Levy, Joan, and Rui (Juliet) Zhu. "The Influence of Ceiling Height: The Effect of Priming on the Type of Processing That People Use." *Journal of Consumer Research.* 34.2 (Aug. 2007): 174–186. bit.ly/2WOhCAC; Oberfeld, Daniel, Heiko Hecht, and Matthias Gamer. "Surface Lightness Influences Perceived Room Height." *The Quarterly Journal of Experimental Psychology.* 63, 10 (Oct. 1, 2010): 1999–2011. goo.gl/gKuJcB; Vartanian, Oshin, et al. "Architectural Design and the Brain: Effects of Ceiling Height and Perceived Enclosure on Beauty Judgments and Approach-avoidance Decisions." *Journal of Environmental Psychology.* 41 (Mar. 2015): 10–18. goo.gl/Fp79Eq.

#4. Take in a view. Bogaard, Kela. "Interior Habitats: The Theory of Prospect and Refuge."

Contract Design (website). May 17, 2017. goo.gl/Ebc55Z; Boubekri, Mohamed, et al. "Impact of Windows and Daylight Exposure on Overall Health and Sleep Quality of Office Workers: A Case-Control Pilot Study." *Journal of Clinical Sleep Medicine.* 10, 6 (June 2014): 603–611. goo.gl/TP5zh2; Heerwagen, Judith H. "The Psychological Aspects of Windows and Window Design." *Proceedings of EDRA 21* (1990): 269–280; Jaffe, Eric. "Workers in Windowless Offices Lose 46 Minutes of Sleep a Night." *Co.Design* (website). Aug. 5, 2014. goo.gl/GzluBu; Kaplan, Rachel. "The Nature of the View from Home: Psychological Benefits." *Environment and Behavior.* 33 (2001): 507–542. goo.gl/RuUqc3; Liberman, Nina, et al. "Priming of Spatial Distance Enhances Children's Creative Performance." *Journal of Experimental Child Psychology.* 111 (2012): 663–670. goo.gl/ktzcaJ; McCoy, Janetta Mitchell, and Gary W. Evans. "The Potential Role of the Physical Environment in Fostering Creativity." *Creativity Research Journal.* 14 (2002): 3–4, 409–426. goo.gl/jqmkQ2; Shapira, Oren, and Nira Liberman. "An Easy Way to Increase Creativity: Why Thinking About Distant Things Can Make Us More Creative." *Scientific American* (website). July 21, 2009. goo.gl/bKP3Ri; Verderber, Stephen. "Dimensions of Person-window Transactions in the Hospital Environment." *Environment and Behavior.* 18 (1986): 450–466. goo.gl/g2zXa5.

#5. Display art. "8 Reasons Why Art Improves Your Thinking." *Care2* (website). February 27, 2015. goo.gl/zBWKHX; Briggs, Saga. "The Number One Predictor of Creativity? Openness to Experience." *InformED* (website). Nov. 8, 2016. goo.gl/yUJors; Chamorro-Premuzic, Tomas. "The Scientific Benefits of Mind-Wandering." *Fast Company* (website). Aug. 17, 2015. goo.gl/GXTBbo; Christensen, Julia, Guido Giglioni, and Manis Tsakiris. "'Let the Soul Dangle': How Mind-Wandering Spurs Creativity." *Medium* (website). Jan. 7, 2018. goo.gl/hG1Gk9; Hopper, Elizabeth. "The Link Between Creativity and Happiness." *Healthy Psych* (website). Sept. 30, 2015. goo.gl/PLtujg; Isen, Alice M. "An Influence of Positive Affect on Decision Making in Complex Situations: Theoretical Issues with Practical Implications." *Journal of Consumer Psychology.* 11, 2 (2001): 75–85. goo.gl/T9sbyM. Kaufman, Scott Barry, and Carolyn Gregoire. *Wired to Create: Unraveling the Mysteries of the Creative Mind.* New York: Perigee, 2015. Ch. 6, "Openness to Experience"; Kweon, Byoung-Suk, et al. "Anger and Stress: The Role of Landscape Posters in an Office Setting." *Environment and Behavior.* 40, 3 (May 2008): 355–381. goo.gl/qWAHLU; Lacey, Simon, et al. "Art for Reward's Sake: Visual Art Recruits the Ventral Striatum." *NeuroImage.* 55 (2011): 420–433. goo.gl/VDncX9; Liberman, Nira, et al. "Priming of Spatial Distance Enhances Children's Creative Performance." *Journal of Experimental Child Psychology.* 111 (2012): 663–670. goo.gl/ktzcaJ; McCrae, Robert R. "Creativity, Divergent Thinking, and Openness to Experience." *Journal of Personality and Social Psychology.* 52 6 (1987): 1258–1265. goo.gl/yVAqXe; Vartanian, Oshin, and Martin Skov. "Neural Correlates of Viewing Paintings: Evidence from a Quantitative Meta-analysis of Functional Magnetic Resonance Imaging Data." *Brain and Cognition.* 87 (2014): 52–56. goo.gl/ogWRrR.

#6. Think back. Sneed, Annie. "How Nostalgia Fuels Creativity." *Co.Design* (website). May 27, 2015. goo.gl/JRM36e; Shapira, Oren, and Nira Liberman. "An Easy Way to Increase Creativity." *Scientific American* (website). July 21, 2009. goo.gl/sh8V22; Van Tilburg, Wijnand A. P., Constantine Sedikides, and Tim Wildschut. "The Mnemonic

Muse: Nostalgia Fosters Creativity Through Openness to Experience." *Journal of Experimental Social Psychology.* 59 (2015): 1–7.

Explainer I: Space, Time, and Creativity. Shapira, Oren, and Nira Liberman. "An Easy Way to Increase Creativity." *Scientific American* (website). July 21, 2009. goo.gl/sh8V22; Trope, Yaacov, and Nira Liberman. "Construal-Level Theory of Psychological Distance." *Psychological Review.* 117, 2 (2010): 440–463. goo.gl/zt5Njn.

#7. Embrace detail and complexity. Amabile, Teresa. "How to Kill Creativity." *Harvard Business Review* (website). Sept.–Oct. 1998. goo.gl/mWhI32; Begley, Sharon. "How to Make Yourself More Creative." *Newsweek* (website). Nov. 17, 2009. goo.gl/EHdHhI; Csikszentmihalyi, Mihaly. *Creativity: Flow and the Psychology of Discovery and Invention.* New York et al.: HarperCollins, 2007; Mahnke, Frank H., and Rudolf H. Mahnke. *Color and Light in Man-made Environments.* New York et al.: John Wiley & Sons, 1993; McCoy, Janetta Mitchell, and Gary W. Evans. "The Potential Role of the Physical Environment in Fostering Creativity." *Creativity Research Journal.* 14 (2002): 3–4, 409–426. goo.gl/jqmkQ2; Otis, Laura. "A New Look at Visual Thinking." *Psychology Today* (website). Feb. 16, 2016. goo.gl/L777uR; Salingaros, Nikos A., and Kenneth G. Masden II. "Neuroscience, the Natural Environment, and Building Design" in *Biophilic Design: The Theory, Science, and Practice of Bringing Buildings to Life.* Stephen R. Kellert, Judith Heerwagen, and Martin Mador, eds. Hoboken: John Wiley & Sons, 2008; Shapira, Oren, and Nira Liberman. "An Easy Way to Increase Creativity." *Scientific American* (website). July 21, 2009. goo.gl/sh8V22.

#8. Put your walls to work. Busche, Laura. "How Working Walls Unlock Creative Insight." *Smashing Magazine* (website). Jan. 2, 2014. goo.gl/w9XIGv; Isaacson, Walter. *Einstein: His Life and Universe.* New York et al.: Simon & Schuster, 2007: Mastin, Luke. "Short-Term Memory and Working Memory." *The Human Memory* (website). goo.gl/ANhKHW; Tarr, Patricia. "Consider the Walls." *Young Children.* 59, 3 (May 2004): 88–92. goo.gl/HNCBnL; Vyas, Dhaval, and Anton Nijholt. "Artful Surfaces: An Ethnographic Study Exploring the Use of Space in Design Studios." *Digital Creativity.* 23, 3–4 (2012): 176–195. goo.gl/FQPSiL.

#9. Be flexible. Cook, Gareth. "The Power of Flexible Thinking." *Scientific American* (website). Mar. 21, 2018. goo.gl/3LSQrV; Guilford, J.P. "Creativity." *American Psychologist.* 5, 9 (Sept. 1950): 444–454. goo.gl/JMxUcZ; —. *The Nature of Human Intelligence.* New York et al.: McGraw-Hill Book Company, 1967; Lawrence, Robyn. "Meet the Next Generation of Incredibly Adaptable Homes." *Houzz* (website). July 2, 2013. goo.gl/ALyx6v; Seelig, Tina. *InGenius: A Crash Course on Creativity.* New York: HarperOne, 2012. Ch. Five, "The Table Kingdom."

#10. Face your space. Appleton, Jay. *The Experience of Landscape.* Hoboken: John Wiley & Sons, 1975; Augustin, Sally. *Place Advantage: Applied Psychology for Interior Architecture.* Hoboken: John Wiley & Sons, 2009. "Seat Placement"; Bogaard, Kela. "Interior Habitats: The Theory of Prospect and Refuge." *Contract* (website). May 17, 2017. goo.gl/Ebc55Z; Hildebrand, Grant. *The Wright Space: Pattern and Meaning in Frank Lloyd Wright's Houses.* Seattle: University of Washington Press, 1991; Pollan, Michael. *A Place of My Own: The Education of an Amateur Builder.* New York: Random House, 1997. Ch. 2, "The Site"; Waxman, Lisa. "The Coffee Shop: Social and Physical factors Influencing

Place Attachment." *Journal of Interior Design*. 31, 3 (2006): 35–53. goo.gl/MygAmB.

#11. Gather in a circle. Burkus, David. *The Myths of Creativity: The Truth About How Innovative Companies and People Generate Great Ideas*. San Francisco: Jossey-Bass, 2014. Ch. 7, "The Lone Creator Myth"; Catmull, Ed, and Amy Wallace. *Creativity, Inc.: Overcoming the Unseen Forces That Stand in the Way of True Inspiration*. New York: Random House, 2014. Ch. 1, "Animated"; Elmer, Vickie. "How to Boost Collaboration at Work: Sit at Round Tables." *Quartz* (website). July 10, 2013. goo.gl/oVIjO; Osmond, Humphry. "Function as the Basis of Psychiatric Ward Design." *Mental Hospitals: American Psychiatric Association*. 8, 4 (Apr. 1957): 23–29. goo.gl/7V56Kc; Sommer, Robert. "Sociofugal Space." *American Journal of Sociology*. 72, 6 (May 1967): 654–660. goo.gl/1MZdCX; Sommer, Robert, and Hugo Ross. "Social Interaction on a Geriatrics Ward." *International Journal of Social Psychiatry*. 4 (1958): 128–133. goo.gl/txDjAP; Tanne, Janice Hopkins. "Humphry Osmond." *BMJ*. 328, 7441 (Mar. 20, 2004): 713. goo.gl/jzTFSf; Zhu, Rui (Juliet), and Jennifer J. Argo. "Exploring the Impact of Various Shaped Seating Arrangements on Persuasion." *Journal of Consumer Research*. 40.2 (Aug. 2013): 336–349. goo.gl/m6KjnB.

#12. Choose curved over straight. Bar, Moshe, and Maital Neta. "Visual Elements of Subjective Preference Modulate Amygdala Activation." *Neuropsychologia*. 45 (2007): 2191–2200. goo.gl/a5KNde; Dazkir, Sibel S., and Marilyn A. Read. "Furniture Forms and Their Influence on Our Emotional Responses Toward Interior Environments." *Environment and Behavior*. 44.5 (Sept. 2012): 722–732. goo.gl/iKg8Lh; Howell, Kelly. "Stop Trying! Creativity's Ultimate Partner Is Relaxation." *Brain Sync* (website). N.d. goo.gl/m93QUm; Jaffe, Eric. "Why Our Brains Love Curvy Architecture." *Co.Design* (website).

Oct. 17, 2013. goo.gl/xV4BWb; Krampen, Günter. "Promotion of Creativity (divergent productions) and Convergent Productions by Systematic-relaxation Exercises: Empirical Evidence from Five Experimental Studies with Children, Young Adults, and Elderly." *European Journal of Personality*. 11 (1997): 83–99. goo.gl/sN8SiE; Vartanian, Oshin, et al. "Impact of Contour on Aesthetic Judgments and Approach-avoidance Decisions in Architecture." *Proceedings of the National Academy of Science*. 110 (June 18, 2013): 10446–10453. goo.gl/cJBuic.

#13. Stand up for yourself. Finch, Laura E., A. Janet Tomiyama, and Andrew Ward. "Taking a Stand: The Effects of Standing Desks on Task Performance and Engagement." *International Journal of Environmental Research and Public Health*. 14, 8 (Aug. 2017): 939. goo.gl/rsgs9J; Friedman, Uri. "A Global History of Sitting Down." *The Atlantic* (website). Aug. 30, 2016. goo.gl/X9X4bI; Knight, Andrew P., and Markus Baer. "Get Up, Stand Up: The Effects of a Non-Sedentary Workspace on Information Elaboration and Group Performance." *Social Psychological and Personality Science*. 5, 8 (2014): 910–917. goo.gl/VtwSpw; Levine, James A. *Get Up!: Why Your Chair Is Killing You and What You Can Do About It*. New York: St. Martin's Press, 2014; McKay, Brett & Kate. "Become a Stand-Up Guy: The History, Benefits, and Use of Standing Desks. *Art of Manliness* (website). July 5, 2011. goo.gl/zcRvHo; Wilmot, E. G. et al. "Sedentary Time in Adults and the Association with Diabetes, Cardiovascular Disease and Death: Systematic Review and Meta-analysis." *Diabetologia*. 55, 11 (Nov. 2012): 2895–2905. goo.gl/puHL99.

Explainer II: We Are Who We Have Always Been. Friedman, Ron. *The Best Place to Work: The Art and Science of Creating an Extraordinary Workplace*. New

York et al.: Penguin Publishing, 2014. Ch. 2, sec. "The Caveman's Guide to Building Better Offices"; Gallagher, Winifred. *New: Understanding Our Need for Novelty and Change.* New York: Penguin Books, 2011; Simonton, Dean Keith. *Origins of Genius: Darwinian Perspectives on Creativity.* New York et al.: Oxford University Press, 1999.

#14. Bring nature in. Begley, Sharon. "How to Make Yourself More Creative." *Newsweek* (website). Nov. 17, 2009. Effects of saccadic eye movement on divergent thinking. goo.gl/EHdHh1; Cooper, Cary, and Bill Browning. *Human Spaces: The Global Impact of Biophilic Design in the Workplace.* N.p.: 2015. Ch. 3, "Creativity." The authors cite a 15 percent increase in worker creativity in biophilic environments. goo.gl/GGEX3p; "Einstein's Corpus Callosum Reveals Clues to His Brilliance." *Sci Tech Daily* (website). Oct. 17, 2013. goo.gl/dHLLZ4; Jaffe, Eric. "Want to Be More Productive? Buy Some Desk Plants." *Co.Design* (website). Nov. 19, 2013. goo.gl/wIuLPc; Kaplan, Rachel. "The Role of Nature in the Context of the Workplace." *Landscape and Urban Planning.* 26 (1993): 193–201. goo.gl/udnM1D; —. "The Nature of the View from Home: Psychological Benefits." *Environment and Behavior.* 33 (2001): 507–542. goo.gl/BQVEbH; Kaplan, Stephen. "The Restorative Benefits of Nature: Toward an Integrative Framework." *Journal of Environmental Psychology.* 16 (1995): 169–182. goo.gl/4xrSZE; Kellert, Stephen R., Judith Heerwagen, and Martin Mador, eds. *Biophilic Design: The Theory, Science, and Practice of Bringing Buildings to Life.* Hoboken: John Wiley & Sons, 2008; Lichtenfeld, Stephanie, et al. "Fertile Green: Green Facilitates Creative Performance." *Personality and Social Psychology Bulletin.* 38, 6 (2012): 784–797. goo.gl/agLJ6Z; McCoy, Janetta Mitchell, and Gary W. Evans. "The Potential Role of the Physical Environment in Fostering Creativity." *Creativity Research Journal.* 14 (2002): 3–4, 409–426. goo.gl/jqmkQ2; Men, Weiwei, et al. "The Corpus Callosum of Albert Einstein's Brain: Another Clue to His High Intelligence?" *Brain: A Journal of Neurology* (Sept. 14, 2013). goo.gl/qVxYzQ; "Quantifiable Benefits of Access to Nature in Buildings." *Perkins+Will Research Journal.* 01, 01 (2009). goo.gl/Y2bD4w; Shibata, Seiji, and N. Suzuki. "Effects of an Indoor Plant on Creative Task Performance and Mood." *Scandinavian Journal of Psychology.* 45 (2004): 373–381. goo.gl/kTPQMJ; Williams, Florence. *The Nature Fix: Why Nature Makes Us Happier, Healthier, and More Creative.* New York: W.W. Norton & Company, 2017; Wilson, Edward O. *Biophilia: The Human Bond with Other Species.* Cambridge (MA) and London: Harvard University Press, 2003; Wiseman, Richard. *59 Seconds: Think a Little, Change a Lot.* New York: Alfred A. Knopf, 2009. "Nature Calls," 120–124.

#15. Get with your pet. Augustin, Sally. "6 Design Ideas for Happy Pets." *Houzz* (website). Nov. 18, 2013. goo.gl/udpdZz; Barker, Randolph T., et al. "Preliminary Investigation of Employee's Dog Presence on Stress and Organizational Perceptions." *International Journal of Workplace Health Management.* 5, 1 (2012): 15–30. goo.gl/MZBPzS; Borchard, Therese J. "6 Ways Pets Relieve Depression." *Psych Central* (website). May 19, 2013. goo.gl/sm2FJp; Evans, Lisa. "Your Definitive Argument for a Pet Friendly Office." *Fast Company* (website). Oct. 14, 2014. goo.gl/nvYDFU; "Pet Dog or Cat Controls Blood Pressure Better than ACE Inhibitor." *Newswise* (website). Nov. 8, 1999. goo.gl/wjz1Pb; Scott, Elizabeth. "How Owning a Dog or Cat Can Reduce Stress." *Very Well Mind* (website). September 27, 2017. goo.gl/F6Kp1c; Walden, Stephanie. "Home Design with Pets in Mind." *Mashable* (website). Nov. 28, 2014. goo.gl/8n3xyv.

#16. Make it beautiful. Hartnett, Kevin. "Beyond the 10,000-hour-rule: Experts Disagree About the Value of Practice." *Boston Globe* (website). Mar. 27, 2016. goo.gl/J9a7Dh; Ishizu, Tomohiro, and Semir Zeki. "Toward a Brain-based Theory of Beauty." *PLoS ONE.* 6, 7 (July 6, 2011): e21852. goo.gl/4kcLst; Kron, Joan. *Home-Psych: The Social Psychology of Home and Decoration.* New York: Clarkson N. Potter, 1983. On Maslow's 1956 experiment, 162ff.; Maslow, Abraham, and N. L. Mintz. "Effects of Esthetic Surroundings: Initial Effects of Three Esthetic Condition upon Perceiving 'Energy' and 'Well-being' in Faces." *Journal of Psychology.* 41 (1956): 247–254. goo.gl/iS8hqG; Rattner, Donald M. "How a Beautiful Room Can Change Your Mind." *Medium* (website). Feb. 5, 2018. goo.gl/p29LEv; Senior, Carl. "Beauty in the Brain of the Beholder." *Neuron.* 38, 4, (May 22, 2003): 525–528. goo.gl/gVyFQc; Vartanian, Oshin, and Martin Skov. "Neural Correlates of Viewing Paintings: Evidence from a Quantitative Meta-analysis of Functional Magnetic Resonance Imaging Data." *Brain and Cognition.* 87 (2014): 52–56. goo.gl/ogWRrR.

Creativity Tactics Group Two: Ambience
#17. Make noise. Cain, Susan. *Quiet: The Power of Introverts in a World That Can't Stop Talking.* New York: Broadway Books, 2013; "Chambre de Marcel Proust." *Carnavalet Paris* (website). Retrieved June 27, 2018. goo.gl/EkxDQo; Mehta, Ravi, Rui (Juliet) Zhu, and Amar Cheema. "Is Noise Always Bad? Exploring the Effects of Ambient Noise on Creative Cognition." *Journal of Consumer Research.* 39, 4 (Dec. 2012): 784–799. goo.gl/z50I9; Zabelina, Darya L. "Creativity and Sensory Gating." *Psychology Today* (website). Jan. 23, 2015. goo.gl/KByRTx.

#18. Make music. Gibson, Crystal, Bradley S. Folley, and Sohee Park. "Enhanced Divergent Thinking and Creativity in Musicians: A Behavioral and Near-infrared Spectroscopy Study." *Brain and Cognition.* 69 (2009): 162–169. goo.gl/iTJ7bo; Kaufman, Scott Barry. "What's the Size of the Mozart Effect? The Jury Is In." *Psychology Today* (website). Apr. 25, 2010. goo.gl/8HNviu; Medina, John. *Brain Rules: 12 Principles for Surviving and Thriving at Work, Home, and School.* Seattle: Pear Press, 2014. "Brain Rule #10: Music"; Rauscher, Frances, Gordon Shaw, and Katherine Ky. "Music and Spatial Task Performance." *Nature.* 365 (Oct. 14, 1993): 611. The original study proposing a Mozart Effect. goo.gl/bhWJ5y; Ritter, Simon, and Sam Ferguson. "Happy Creativity: Listening to Happy Music Facilitates Divergent Thinking." *PLoS ONE.* 12, 9 (2017): e0182210. goo.gl/tM49WS; Shiha, Yi-Nuo, Rong-Hwa Huangc, and Hsin-Yu Chianga. "Background Music: Effects on Attention Performance." *Work: A Journal of Prevention, Assessment & Rehabilitation.* 42, 4 (2012): 573–578. goo.gl/CTVyyx; Stewart, Dave, and Mark Simmons. *The Business Playground: Where Creativity and Commerce Collide.* Berkeley: New Riders, 2010. Ch. 5, "Tuning Up to Be Creative . . . Music Please, Maestro" describes several experiments linking creativity with music instruction.

#19. Let in natural light. Boubekri, M., et al. "Impact of Windows and Daylight Exposure on Overall Health and Sleep Quality of Office Workers: A Case-control Pilot Study." *Journal of Clinical Sleep Medicine.* 10, 6 (June 15, 2014): 603–11. goo.gl/AuqHMj; Heerwagen, Judith H. "The Psychological Aspects of Windows and Window Design." *Proceedings of EDRA 21.* (1990): 269–280; Jaffe, Eric. "Workers in Windowless Offices Lose 46 Minutes of Sleep a Night." *Co.Design* (website). Aug. 5, 2014. goo.gl/GzluBu; Riha, John. "Save Energy and Feel Better with Daylighting."

House Logic (website). Retrieved June 29, 2018. A thorough summary of techniques for optimizing daylight. goo.gl/cVkZ8L; Van Den Wymelenberg, Kevin. "The Benefits of Natural Light." *Architectural Lighting* (website). Mar. 19, 2014. goo.gl/rR37d0.

#20. Be smart with your lighting. Marshall, Gary. "What Is Smart Lighting? Everything You Need to Know for Your Connected Home." *Techradar* (website). July 9, 2017. goo.gl/GNgdMa; Van Den Wymelenberg, Kevin. "The Benefits of Natural Light." *Architectural Lighting* (website). Mar. 19, 2014. goo.gl/rR37d0.

#21. Dim the lights. Jacobs, Tom. "Dim Lighting Sparks Creativity." *Pacific Standard* (website). June 18, 2013. goo.gl/QCJ6zz; Steidle, Anna, and Lioba Werth. "Freedom From Constraints: Darkness and Dim Illumination Promote Creativity." *Journal of Environmental Psychology.* 35 (2013): 67–80. goo.gl/EZ4QbW.

#22. Switch on a filament bulb. Choi, Charles Q. "Light Bulbs Actually Spur Bright Ideas, Study Reveals." *Life Science* (website). May 4, 2010. goo.gl/J5NKAu; "How Many Visual Thinkers Does It Take to Change the Light Bulb? *Cognitive* (website). Sept. 12, 2016. goo.gl/3SvM8F; Leung, Angela K., et al. "Embodied Metaphors and Creative 'Acts'." *Psychological Science.* 23, 5 (2012): 502–509. goo.gl/sXcyVR; Marin, Alex, Martin Reimann, and Raquel Castaño. "Metaphors and Creativity: Direct, Moderating, and Mediating Effects." *Journal of Consumer Psychology.* 24, 2 (2013): 290–297. goo.gl/QJIWPU; Pink, Daniel H. *A Whole New Mind: Why Right-Brainers Will Rule the Future.* New York: Riverhead Books, 2006; Slepian, Michael, et al. "Shedding Light on Insight: Priming Bright Ideas." *Journal of Experimental Social Psychology.* 46 (2010): 696–700. goo.gl/kCPECt;

Tharp, Twyla. *The Creative Habit: Learn It and Use It For Life.* New York: Simon & Schuster, 2003.

#23. Adjust the thermostat. Belluck, Pam. "Chilly at Work? Office Formula Was Devised for Men." *New York Times* (website). Aug. 3, 2015. goo.gl/otfqbZ; Enander, A. E., and S. Hygge. "Thermal Stress and Human Performance." *Scandinavian Journal of Work Environment & Health.* 16, 1 (1990):44–50. goo.gl/29N1Bg; Hedge, Alan. "Linking Environmental Conditions to Productivity." *A Presentation at the Eastern Ergonomics Conference and Exposition, New York* (June, 2004). goo.gl/KHTu2A; Mahnke, Frank H., and Rudolf H. Mahnke. *Color and Light in Man-made Environments.* New York et al.: John Wiley & Sons, 1993. Ch. Two, "Perception of Temperature"; Ward, Adrian F. "Winter Wakes Up Your Mind—and Warm Weather Makes It Harder to Think Straight." *Scientific American* (website). Feb. 12, 2013. goo.gl/FjrEH2.

#24. Pick up the scent. Aarts, Henk, Rob Holland, and Merel Hendriks. "Smells Like Clean Spirit: Nonconscious Effects of Scent on Cognition and Behavior." *Psychological Science.* 16, 9 (2005): 689–693. goo.gl/xMJxUH; Augustin, Sally. *Place Advantage: Applied Psychology for Interior Architecture.* Hoboken: John Wiley & Sons, 2009. "Smelling: Magical, Mysterious, and Powerful"; Evans, Lisa. "6 Scents That Can Transform Your Mood and Productivity." *Entrepreneur* (website). (Oct. 8, 2012). goo.gl/V4h4Qv; Herz, Rachel S. "Do Scents Affect People's Moods or Work Performance?" *Scientific American* (website). Nov. 11, 2002. goo.gl/TFuWSE; Ritter, Simone M., et al. "Good Morning Creativity: Task Reactivation During Sleep Enhances Beneficial Effect of Sleep on Creative Performance." *Journal of Sleep Research.* 21 (2012): 643–647. goo.gl/W2RYyk.

Creativity Tactics Group Three: Action

#25. Sleep. Cantor, Joanne. "Sleep for Success: Creativity and the Neuroscience of Slumber." *Psychology Today* (website). May 15, 2010. goo.gl/VE6WKp; Jacobs, Tom. "Dream Recall Helps Boost Creativity." *Pacific Standard* (website). Jan. 4, 2017. goo.gl/mvRdyA; Ji, Daoyun, and Matthew A. Wilson. "Coordinated Memory Replay in the Visual Cortex and Hippocampus During Sleep." *Nature Neuroscience.* 10 (2007): 100–107. goo.gl/dft4nM; Medina, John. *Brain Rules: 12 Principles for Surviving and Thriving at Work, Home, and School.* Seattle: Pear Press, 2014; "The Secret to a Good Night's Slumber Is to Sleep in a Blue Bedroom." *Travel Lodge* (website). May 17, 2013. goo.gl/VHr9qJ; Yong, Ed. "A New Theory Linking Sleep and Creativity." *The Atlantic* (website). May 15, 2018. goo.gl/kmAoUC.

#26. Nap. Gaskill, Laura. "Carve Out a Neat Little Nook." *Houzz* (website). Oct. 6, 2014. goo.gl/59cpVJ; Mednick, Sara, and Mark Ehrman. *Take a Nap! Change Your Life.* New York: Workman Publishing Company, 2006; Mednick, Sarah, et al. "REM, Not Incubation, Improves Creativity by Priming Associative Networks." *Proceedings of the National Academy of Sciences.* 106, 25 (June 23, 2009): 10130–10134. goo.gl/vGRQfU; Story, Colleen M. "The Best Time to Nap for Optimal Creativity." *Writing and Wellness* (website). May 12, 2015. goo.gl/NWYUdo.

#27. Exploit the groggies. Bellis, Rich. "How to Design Your Ideal Workday Based on Your Sleep Habits." *Fast Company* (website). Nov. 26, 2017. goo.gl/RdXiYZ; Breus, Michael. *The Power of When: Discover Your Chronotype.* New York et al.: Little, Brown and Company, 2016. Ch. 9, "Sleep" and Ch. 12, "Creativity"; Charles, David. "Hypnagogia: How to Dream like Thomas Edison." *David Charles* (website). November 21, 2010. goo.gl/3KCFDz; Christensen, Tanner. "Why You're More Creative at Night and How to Reproduce the Effect." *Creative Something* (website). July 9, 2013. goo.gl/kxsKjb; Khazan, Olga. "When Fatigue Boosts Creativity." *The Atlantic* (website). Mar. 20, 2015. goo.gl/V9Vndn; Raz, Guy. "How Do You Get Over Writer's Block?" *Ted Radio Hour* (website). Oct. 3, 2014. goo.gl/xQzD9U; Wieth, Mareike B., and Rose T. Zacks. "Time of Day Effects on Problem Solving: When the Non-optimal Is Optimal." *Thinking & Reasoning.* 17, 4 (2011): 387–401. goo.gl/14N9qt.

#28. Lie down or recline. Brunner, Bernd. "7 Famous Authors Who Wrote Lying Down." *Huffington Post* (website). Jan. 7, 2014. goo.gl/Fu4Xeh; Gaskill, Laura. "How to Dress Your Daybed." *Houzz* (website). Oct. 31, 2014. goo.gl/uyrhKp; Lipnicki, Darren M., and Don G. Byrne. "Thinking on Your Back: Solving Anagrams Faster When Supine than When Standing." *Cognitive Brain Research.* 24 (2005): 718–722. goo.gl/PKSV9t; Wiseman, Richard. *59 Seconds: Think a Little, Change a Lot.* New York: Alfred A. Knopf, 2009. Ch. 4, "The Power of Creativity."

#29. Make a fire. Or look at a picture of one. "Creativity and Sleep." *Tuck Sleep* (website). Mar. 19, 2018. goo.gl/Z2YWhQ; Gregoire, Carolyn. "The Evolutionary Reason Why We Love Sitting By a Crackling Fire." *Huffington Post* (website). Nov. 18, 2014. goo.gl/yOvUwq; Lynn, Christopher Dana. "Hearth and Campfire Influences on Arterial Blood Pressure: Defraying the Costs of the Social Brain through Fireside Relaxation." *Journal of Evolutionary Psychology.* 12.5 (Nov. 2014): 983–1003. goo.gl/hsFP6r; Williams, Lawrence E., and John A. Bargh. "Experiencing Physical Warmth Promotes Interpersonal Warmth." *Science.* 322.5901 (Oct. 24, 2008): 606–607.

goo.gl/fQkV5Z; Wynn, Thomas. "Fire Good. Make Human Inspiration Happen." *Smithsonian* (website). Dec. 2012. goo.gl/tsdcjX.

#30. Have a drink. Hamblin, James. "Caffeine: For the More Creative Mind." *Atlantic Monthly* (website). Jun 24, 2013. goo.gl/Z2YWhQ; Hsu, Christine. "Drinking Alcohol May Significantly Enhance Problem Solving Skills." *Medical Daily* (website). Apr. 11, 2012. goo.gl/fCjCFi; Jarosz, Andrew F., Gregory J. H Colflesh, and Jennifer Wiley. "Uncorking the Muse: Alcohol Intoxication Facilitates Creative Problem Solving." *Consciousness and Cognition*. 21 (2012): 487–493. goo.gl/A2r3gW; Konnikova, Maria. "How Caffeine Can Cramp Creativity." *The New Yorker* (website). June 17, 2013. goo.gl/CzHBsD; Tanner, Christensen. "How Caffeine Affects Your Creativity." *Creative Something* (website). Sept. 5, 2012. goo.gl/qmTGmj.

#31. Eat brain food. Colzato, Lorenza S., Annelies M. de Haan, and Bernhard Hommel. "Food for Creativity: Tyrosine Promotes Deep Thinking." *Psychological Research*. 79 (2015): 709–714. goo.gl/HBWZVT; Conner, Tamlin S. et al. "On Carrots and Curiosity: Eating Fruit and Vegetables Is Associated with Greater Flourishing in Daily Life." *British Journal of Health Psychology*. 20, 2 (July 30, 2014): 413–427. goo.gl/HBWZVT.

#32. Cook.
The Commonalities of Cooking and Creativity: Kamozawa, Aki, and H. Alexander Talbot. "5 Factors Shaping Creativity in the Kitchen." *Ideas in Food* (website). Nov. 24, 2010. goo.gl/HTSkFc.

Combinatorial Creativity: Isaacson, Walter. *Einstein: His Life and Universe*. New York: Simon & Schuster, 2007; Isaacson, Walter. *Steve Jobs*. New York: Simon & Schuster, 2011; Popova, Maria. *Brain Pickings* (website). Numerous posts on combinatorial creativity: "Allergy to Originality: Mark Twain and the Remix Nature of All Creative Work, Animated." (Aug. 7, 2014). goo.gl/kS3ytc; "How Einstein Thought: Why 'Combinatory Play' Is the Secret of Genius." (Apr. 14, 2013). goo.gl/vTVGes; "How Remix Culture Fuels Creativity & Invention: Kirby Ferguson at TED." (Aug. 14, 2012). goo.gl/Qub3mw; "How the Gutenberg Press Embodies Combinatorial Creativity." (Nov. 2, 2012). goo.gl/VWw806; Sawyer, Keith. *Zig Zag: The Surprising Path to Greater Creativity*. San Francisco: Jossey-Bass, 2013. Achieving innovation through fusion, 153–172; Shirky, Clay. *Cognitive Surplus: Creativity and Generosity in a Connected Age*. New York: Penguin Books, 2010. Ch. 2, "Gutenberg Economics" positions the landmark invention within the evolution of the media industry; Wolf, Gary. "Steve Jobs: The Next Insanely Great Thing." *Wired*. 4.02 (Feb. 1996). goo.gl/Dvxcqt.

Social and Collaborative Creativity: Burkus, David. *The Myths of Creativity: The Truth About How Innovative Companies and People Generate Great Ideas*. San Francisco: Jossey-Bass, 2014. Ch. 7, "Lone Creator Myth." Edison and his light bulb, 106–110; Sawyer, Keith. *Group Genius: The Creative Power of Collaboration*. New York: Basic Books, 2007; Shenk, Joshua Wolf. *Powers of Two: Finding the Essence of Innovation in Creative Pairs*. New York: Houghton Mifflin Harcourt, 2014; "Who Invented the Light Bulb?" *Unmuseum* (website). goo.gl/MhjAp.

Fun Creativity: O'Toole, Garson. "Creativity Is Intelligence Having Fun." *Quote Investigator* (website). Mar. 2, 2017. goo.gl/LSkiBk.

Serendipitous Creativity: Johnson, Steven. *Where Good Ideas Come From: The Natural History of*

Innovation. New York: Riverhead Books, 2010. Serendipity, 107–109; Muller, Thor, and Lane Becker. *Get Lucky: How to Put Planned Serendipity to Work for You and Your Business*. San Francisco: Jossey-Bass, 2012; Paley, Steven J. *The Art of Invention: The Creative Process of Discovery and Design*. Amherst, NY: Prometheus Books, 2010. Ch. 4, "Accidental and Chance Observations." Invention of microwave, 84–85. Invention of Velcro, 35–36 et al.

Heuristic Creativity: Danner, John, and Mark Coopersmith. *The Other "F" Word: How Smart Leaders, Teams, and Entrepreneurs Put Failure to Work*. Hoboken: John Wiley & Sons, 2015; Friedman, Ron. *The Best Place to Work: The Art and Science of Creating an Extraordinary Workplace*. New York et al.: Penguin Publishing, 2014. Part One, Ch. One, "Why Great Workplaces Reward Failure"; Seelig, Tina. *InGenius: A Crash Course on Creativity*. New York: HarperOne, 2012; Shiv, Baba. "Why Failure Drives Innovation." *Stanford Graduate School of Business News* (website). Mar. 1, 2011. goo.gl/BoICMy; Simonton, Dean Keith. *Origins of Genius: Darwinian Perspectives on Creativity*. New York et al.: Oxford University Press, 1999.

Destructive Creativity: Christiansen, Clay. *The Innovator's Dilemma: The Revolutionary Book That Will Change the Way You Do Business*. Boston: Harvard Business Review Press, 1997; Cox, W. Michael, and Richard Alm, "Creative Destruction." *The Concise Encyclopedia of Economics, Library of Economics and Liberty* (website). goo.gl/j2BpyY; Ward, James. *The Perfection of the Paper Clip: Curious Tales of Invention, Accidental Genius, and Stationery Obsession*. New York: Touchstone, 2014.

Teachable Creativity: Pappano, Laura. "Learning to Think Outside the Box: Creativity Becomes an Academic Discipline." *New York Times* (website). Feb. 5, 2014. goo.gl/BbpUYp; Seelig,

Tina. *InGenius: A Crash Course on Creativity*. New York: HarperOne, 2012; Smith, Ned. "Who Says Creativity Can't Be Learned?" *Business News Daily* (website). May 7, 2012. goo.gl/8Hf8fN.

#33. Exercise. Blanchette, David M., et al. "Aerobic Exercise and Cognitive Creativity: Immediate and Residual Effects." *Creativity Research Journal*. 17, 2–3 (2005): 257–264. goo.gl/cRkFUz; Csikszentmihalyi, Mihaly. *Creativity: Flow and the Psychology of Discovery and Invention*. New York et al: HarperCollins, 2007; Davis, Jeffrey. "Science of Creativity Digest: Exercise Works." *The Creativity Post* (website). June 5, 2015. goo.gl/8hysvL; Heerwagen, Judith H., and Gordon H. Orians. "Adaptations to Windowlessness: A Study of the Use of Visual Decor in Windowed and Windowless Offices." *Environment and Behavior*. 18, 5 (Sept. 1, 1986): 623–639. goo.gl/QGVKb9; Medina, John. *Brain Rules: 12 Principles for Surviving and Thriving at Work, Home, and School*. Seattle: Pear Press, 2014. "Brain Rule #2: Exercise"; Steinberg, Hannah, et al. "Exercise Enhances Creativity Independently of Mood." *British Journal of Sports Medicine*. 31, 3 (Sept. 1997): 240–245. goo.gl/e657SU.

#34. Do yoga. Or meditate. Broad, William. *The Science of Yoga: The Risks and the Rewards*. New York: Simon & Schuster, 2012. Ch. VII, "Muse"; Colzato, Lorenza S., et al. "Prior Meditation Practice Modulates Performance and Strategy Use in Convergent- and Divergent-Thinking Problems." *Mindfulness*. 8, 1 (Feb. 2017): 10–16. goo.gl/CGg5dw; Davis, Jeffrey. "The Science of Creative Insight & Yoga." *Psychology Today* (website). Nov. 21, 2012. goo.gl/xFwcYK; Gorny, Eugene. "Creativity as a Cultural Construction." *Dictionary of Creativity: Terms, Concepts, Theories & Findings in Creativity Research* (website). 2007. goo.gl/H9j3x9; Herrmann, Ned. "What Is the

Function of the Various Brainwaves?" *Scientific American* (website). goo.gl/QzKcns.

#35. Take a shower or bath. Baird, Benjamin et al. "Inspired by Distraction: Mind Wandering Facilitates Creative Incubation." *Psychological Science.* 23, 10 (Oct. 2012): 1117–1122. goo.gl/C3y5VM; Ditkoff, Mitch. "20 Reasons Why People Get Their Best Ideas in the Shower." *The Heart of Innovation* (website). Sept. 24, 2014. goo.gl/448gvI; Duhigg, Charles. *The Power of Habit: Why We Do What We Do in Life and Business.* New York: Random House, 2014; "Bathtime Brainwaves." *Harvey Water Softeners Ltd* (website). Retrieved June 19, 2018. goo.gl/54evj9; Hansgrohe SE. "Shower for the Freshest Thinking." (Press release). Apr. 2014; Kaufman, Scott Barry, and Carolyn Gregoire. *Wired to Create: Unraveling the Mysteries of the Creative Mind.* New York: Perigee, 2015; Lax, Eric. *Conversations with Woody Allen: His Films, the Movies, and Moviemaking.* New York: Alfred A. Knopf, 2007. Allen on showering, 78; Widrich, Leo. "Why We Have Our Best Ideas in the Shower." *Buffer* (website). Feb. 28, 2013. goo.gl/858X6a.

#36. Dress nicely. Adam, Hajo, and Adam D. Galinsky. "Enclothed Cognition." *Journal of Experimental Social Psychology.* 48 (2012): 918–925. goo.gl/oUDjM; Jarrett, Christian. "The Smart Creative's Guide to Dressing for Work." *99U* (website). goo.gl/9ELyH; Peluchette, Joy V., and Katherine Karl. "The Impact of Workplace Attire on Employee Self-Perceptions." *Human Resource Development Quarterly.* 18, 3 (2007): 345–360. goo.gl/CnIisu; Shapira, Oren, and Nira Liberman. "An Easy Way to Increase Creativity: Why Thinking About Distant Things Can Make Us More Creative." *Scientific American* (website). July 21, 2009). goo.gl/bKP3Ri; Slepian, Michael L,. et al. "The Cognitive Consequences of Formal Clothing." *Social Psychological and Personality Science.*

6, 6 (2015): 661–668. goo.gl/CGxzNk; Trope, Yaacov, and Nira Liberman. "Construal-Level Theory of Psychological Distance." *Psychological Review.* 117, 2 (2010): 440–463. goo.gl/zt5Njn.

#37. Take a break. Baird, Benjamin, et al. "Inspired by Distraction: Mind Wandering Facilitates Creative Incubation." *Psychological Science.* 23, 10 (Oct. 2012): 1117–1122. goo.gl/C3y5VM; Beeftink, Flora, Wendelien van Eerde, and Christel G. Rutte. "The Effect of Interruptions and Breaks on Insight and Impasses: Do You Need a Break Right Now?" *Creativity Research Journal.* 20, 4 (2008): 358–364. goo.gl/CEkVqE; Jabr, Ferris. "Why Your Brain Needs More Downtime." *Scientific American* (website). Oct. 15, 2013. goo.gl/eTqiq4; Richtel, Matt. "Digital Devices Deprive Brain of Needed Downtime." *New York Times* (website). Aug. 24, 2010. goo.gl/pcZyAG.

#38. Go for a walk. Bartolome, Gerardo. "Darwin's Sandwalk at Down House." *YouTube* (website). Mar. 16, 2014. goo.gl/vLBEJQ; Jabr, Ferris. "Why Walking Helps Us Think." *The New Yorker* (website). Sept. 3, 2014. goo.gl/8P8NEq; Oppezzo, Marily, and Daniel L. Schwartz. "Give Your Ideas Some Legs: The Positive Effect of Walking on Creative Thinking." *Journal of Experimental Psychology: Learning, Memory, and Cognition.* 40, 4 (2014): 1142–1152. goo.gl/GDxd7e.

#39. Daydream. Ayan, Jordan. *Aha!: 10 Ways to Free Your Creative Spirit and Find Your Great Ideas.* New York: Three Rivers Press, 1997. "Strategy 9: Release Your Alterconscious"; Bachelard, Gaston. *The Poetics of Space.* New York: Penguin Books, 1964; Dorsch, Fabian. "Focused Daydreaming and Mind-Wandering." *Review of Philosophy and Psychology.* 6, (2015): 791–813. goo.gl/hP6mx4; McMillan, Rebecca L., Scott

Barry Kaufman, and Jerome L. Singer. "Ode to Positive Constructive Daydreaming." *Frontiers in Psychology*. 23 (Sept. 2013). goo.gl/JRVg3F.

#40. Pick up a pencil. Broda-Bahm, Chris. "The Straight Truth About the Flexible Drinking Straw." *Smithsonian National Museum of American History* (website). June 1, 2002. goo.gl/rsMzf3; Didion, Joan. "On Keeping a Notebook." *Slouching Towards Bethlehem*. New York: Farrar, Straus & Giroux, 1968; Thompson, Derek. "The Amazing History and the Strange Invention of the Bendy Straw." *The Atlantic* (website). Nov. 22, 2011. goo.gl/brN RAi; Wilson, Frank R. *The Hand: How Its Use Shapes the Brain, Language, and Human Culture*. New York: Vintage Books, 1999.

#41. Make stuff. Audia, Pino G., and Christopher I. Rider. "A Garage and an Idea: What More Does an Entrepreneur Need?" *California Management Review*. 48, 1 (Fall 2005): 6–27. goo.gl/dowGpt; Isaacson, Walter. *Steve Jobs*. New York: Simon & Schuster, 2013. Ch. 5, "The Homebrew Computer Club"; McNerney, Samuel. "A Brief Guide to Embodied Cognition: Why You Are Not Your Brain." *Scientific American* (website). Nov. 4, 2011. goo.gl/Gf5Tw4; Rendina, Diana. "Defining Makerspaces: What the Research Says." *Renovated Learning* (website). Apr. 2, 2015. goo.gl/NeE4Hz; Sawyer, Keith. *Explaining Creativity: The Science of Human Innovation*. New York et al.: Oxford University Press, 2006. "The Eighth Step: MAKE. How Getting Your Ideas Out into the World Drives Creativity Forward"; Wilson, Frank R. *The Hand: How Its Use Shapes the Brain, Language, and Human Culture*. New York: Vintage Books, 1999.

#42. Pursue a hobby. Eschleman, K., et al. "Benefiting from Creative Activity: The Positive Relationships Between Creative Activity, Recovery Experiences, and Performance-related Outcomes." *Journal of Occupational and Organizational Psychology*. 87, 3 (2014): 579–598. goo.gl/p6TTRX; Runco, Mark. *Creativity: Theories and Themes: Research, Development, and Practice*. London et al.: Academic Press, 2014; Yang, Jia Lynn, and Jerry Useem. "Secrets of Greatness: Multiple Hobbies Improve Performance." *Fortune Magazine* (website). Oct. 26, 2006. goo.gl/qGS2mw.

#43. Play. Ayan, Jordan. *Aha!: 10 Ways to Free Your Creative Spirit and Find Your Great Ideas*. New York: Three Rivers Press, 1997. "Strategy 4: Be Sparked by Play and Humor"; Brown, Stuart, and Christopher Vaughan. *Play: How It Shapes the Brain, Opens the Imagination, and Invigorates the Soul*. New York: Avery, 2009; Csikszentmihalyi, Mihaly, and Eugene Rochberg-Halton. *The Meaning of Things: Domestic Symbols and the Self*. Cambridge (UK): Cambridge University Press, 1981; Ogata, Amy F. *Designing the Creative Child: Playthings and Places in Midcentury America*. Minneapolis: University of Minnesota Press, 2013.

#44. Make a mess. Or not. Dovey, Dana. "A Messy Desk May Spark Creativity, But at a Price: What Science Has to Say About Being Organized vs. Being Messy." *Medical Daily* (website). Nov. 12, 2015. goo.gl/W7nGSJ; Kondo, Marie. *The Life-Changing Magic of Tidying Up: The Japanese Art of Decluttering and Organizing*. New York: Ten Speed Press, 2014; Tate, Andrew. "5 Reasons Creative Geniuses Like Einstein, Twain and Zuckerberg Had Messy Desks—And Why You Should Too." *Canva* (website). May 29, 2015. goo.gl/Rr4CiT; Vohs, Kathleen D., Joseph P. Redden, and Ryan Rahinel. "Physical Order Produces Healthy Choices, Generosity, and Conventionality, Whereas Disorder Produces Creativity." *Psychological Science*. 24, 9 (2013): 1860–1867. goo.gl/PtXEit.

#45. Be alone. Cain, Susan. *Quiet: The Power of Introverts in a World That Can't Stop Talking.* New York: Broadway Books, 2013; Hunter, Jennifer. "Design Tips for Introverts & Extroverts (and How to Tell Which One You Are)." *Apartment Therapy* (website). June 17, 2014. goo.gl/PRGKwM; Sawyer, Keith. "Does Solitude Enhance Creativity? A Critique of Susan Cain's Attack on Collaboration." *The Creativity Guru* (website). Jan. 16, 2012. goo.gl/EkILc2; —. *Group Genius: The Creative Power of Collaboration.* New York: Basic Books, 2007.

#46. Read. Ayan, Jordan. *Aha!: 10 Ways to Free Your Creative Spirit and Find Your Great Ideas.* New York: Three Rivers Press, 1997. "Strategy 5: Expand Your Mind Through Reading"; Friedman, Ron. *The Best Place to Work: The Art and Science of Creating an Extraordinary Workplace.* New York et al.: Penguin Publishing, 2014; Pink, Daniel H. *A Whole New Mind: Why Right-Brainers Will Rule the Future.* New York: Riverhead Books, 2006. Ch. 6: "The Boundary Crosser"; "Why People Like to Read." *Pew Research Center* (website). Apr. 5, 2012. goo.gl/CbcixB.

#47. Get out of the house. Griffis, Hailley. "State of Remote Work 2018 Report: What It's Like to Be a Remote Worker in 2018." *Buffer* (website). Feb. 27, 2018. goo.gl/KJRG38; Kaplan, Isaac. "Want to Be More Creative at Work? Stop Working." *Artsy* (website). Mar. 22, 2018. goo.gl/d9FcWb; Ritter, Simone M., et al. "Diversifying Experiences Enhance Cognitive Flexibility." *Journal of Experimental Social Psychology.* 48, 4 (July 2012): 961–964. goo.gl/Q5ZpfU.

#48. Really get out of the house. Crane, Brent. "For a More Creative Brain, Travel." *The Atlantic* (website). Mar. 31, 2015. goo.gl/toZyOd; Galinsky, Adam, et al. "Fashion with a Foreign Flair: Professional Experiences Abroad Facilitate the Creative Innovations of Organizations." *Academy of Management Journal.* 58 (Feb. 2015): 195–220. goo.gl/sgpBKI; Maddux, William W., and Adam D. Galinsky. "Cultural Borders and Mental Barriers: The Relationship Between Living Abroad and Creativity." *Journal of Personality and Social Psychology.* 96, 5 (2009): 1047–1061. goo.gl/PNRMCR.

FIRM DIRECTORY

22 Interiors. 22interiors.com

Alan Williams Photography.
alanwilliamsphotography.com

Alec Hemer Photography. alechemer.com

Alicia Taylor Photography.
aliciataylorphotography.com

Alison Damonte Design. alisondamonte.com

alsoCAN Architects. alsocan.com.au

Alvhem. alvhem.com

Amit Geron Photography. amitgeron.com

Amy Bartlam Photography. amybartlam.com

Analogue Design Studio.
analoguedesignstudio.com

Andrew Simpson Architects. asimpson.com.au

Angie Seckinger. angieseckinger.com

Apartment Apothecary. apartmentapothecary.com

Au fil des Couleurs. aufildescouleurs.com

Austin Maynard Architects.
maynardarchitects.com

Beatrice Pediconi. beatricepediconi.com

Ben Benschneider Photography.
benschneiderphoto.com

Bergen School of Architecture. bas.org

Black Oak Builders. blackoakbuilders.co.uk

Blackstone Edge Studios. blackstoneedge.com

Blaine Harrington Photography.
blaineharrington.com

Blondino Design. blondinodesign.com

Brantley Photography. brantleyphotography.com

Brian Flaherty Photography.
brianflahertyphoto.com

Bruce Damonte Architectural Photographer.
brucedamonte.com

Caleb Johnson Studio. calebjohnsonstudio.com

Cameron R. Neilson Photographer.
cameronrneilson.com

Camp Weathered. campweathered.com

CHD Interiors. chdinteriors.com

Chris Snook Photography.
chrissnookphotography.co.uk

Cim EK. cimek.se

Dagliesh Gilpin Paxton Architects.
dgparchitects.com

Danny Broe Architect. dannybroearchitect.com

David Coleman Architecture. davidcoleman.com

Davignon Martin Architecture.
davignonmartin.ca

Dino Tonn Photographer. dinotonn.com

Donald M. Rattner, Architect. donaldrattner.com

Dressing Rooms. dressingroomsdesign.houzz.com

Dubinett Architects. dubinett.houzz.com

Durston Saylor Photography. durstonsaylor.com

Element Studios. elementstudios.co.uk

Epoch Solutions. epochcabinetryforthehome.com

Eric Figge Photography. ericfiggephoto.com

Eric Roth Photography. ericrothphoto.com

Eymeric Widling Photography.
eymericwidling.com

Feldman Architecture. feldmanarchitecture.com

Ferguson & Shamamian Architects.
fergusonshamamian.com

Francis Dzikowski/Otto. fdphoto.biz

Frederick + Frederick Architects.
f-farchitects.com

Fun House Furnishings & Design.
funhousefurnishings.com

Gamble + Design. gambleplusdesign.com

Garrison Foundry. garrisonfoundry.com

Garrison Hullinger Interior Design.
  garrisonhullinger.com
Gordon Beall Photography. gordonbeall.com
Halkin Mason Photography.
  halkinmasonphotography.com
Helen Norman Photographer.
  helennorman.com
Hoo. hoo-residence.com
ICOSA Design. icosadesign.com
IdeaPaint. ideapaint.com
IndigoJungle Interior Styling. indigojungle.com.au
Jakub Szczęsny.
  culture.pl/en/artist/jakub-szczesny
James French Photography. jfrench.co.uk
James Ray Spahn Photographer.
  jamesrayspahn.com
Jennifer Pacca Interiors.
  jenniferpaccainteriors.com
Jesús Granada Photography. jesusgranada.com
Jimmy White Photography. jimmywhitephoto.com
Joe Fletcher Photography. joefletcher.com
JMA Interior Design. jma-ids.com
John McManus Photographer.
  jmcmanusphoto.carbonmade.com
Jordan Rosenberg Architects. jrarchitect.com
Karina Illovska Photography.
  karinaillovska.com.au
Katharine Peachey Photography.
  katharinepeachey.co.uk
Ken Stabile Photography. kenstabile.com
Krista Stokes. kristastokes.com
Kyawt Thiri Nyunt. kyawtthiri.com
Laura Moss Photography. lauramoss.com
Linda Chase Associates. lindachaseassociates.com
Marc & Co. marcandco.com.au
Mark Davidson Photography.
  markdavidsonphotography.com
Mark Dziewulski Architect. dzarchitect.com
Matt Silk Photography. mattsilk.com
Matt Waclo Photography.
  mattwaclophotography.com

Matthew Millman Photography.
  matthewmillman.com
Meriwether Felt, AIA. meriwetherinc.com
Mesh Design Projects.
  meshdesignprojects.com.au
Michael J. Lee Photography.
  michaeljleephotography.com
Michael D. Beckwith Photography.
  michaeldbeckwith.com
Michael Rex Architects. michaelrexarchitects.com
Mick Hales Photography. mickhales.com
Molo. molodesign.com
Nest. nest.com
New Frontier Tiny Homes.
  newfrontiertinyhomes.com
Nicholas Yarsley Photography.
  nicholasyarsley.co.uk
Nico Marques Architectural Photography.
  nicomarques.com
Olson Photographic. olsonphotographic.com
Paul Craig Interior Photography. pcraig.co.uk
Paul Warchol Photography.
  warcholphotography.com
Peter Bennetts Photography. peterbennetts.com
Peter Clarke Photography. peterclarke.com.au
Peter Rymwid Photography. peterrymwid.com
Pfeiffer Lab. pfeifferlab.com
Phillip Ennis Productions. phillip-ennis.com
Pitsou Kedem Architects. pitsou.com
Platform 5 Architects. platform5architects.com
Polish Modern Art Foundation. fundacjapsn.pl
Post Architecture. postarchitecture.com
Revelateur Studio. rvltr.studio
Ric Kokotovich Photographer. rickokotovich.com
Richard Leo Johnson/Atlantic Archives.
  atlanticarchives.com
Rill Architects. rillarchitects.com
Robert A.M. Stern Architects. ramsa.com
Robert Harvey Oshatz, Architect. oshatz.com
Robin Baron Design. robinbarondesign.com
SC Collective. sccollective.com

South Coast Architects. southcoastarchitects.com
SpaceCraft Architecture. spacecraftarch.com
STACT. getstact.com
Stephen Clegg Design. stevencleggdesign.com.au
Stretch Design. elizabethstretch.com
Studio Bergtraun Architects.
    studiobergtraun.com
StudiObuell Photography. studiobuell.com
Studio V Interiors. studiovinteriors.com
Susan Gilmore Photography.
    susangilmorephoto.com
Swaback Architects + Planners. swaback.com
Tate Studio Architects. tate-studio.com
Thompson Photographic.
    thompsonphotographic.com

Tim Cuppett Architects. cuppettarchitects.com
TransFORM. transformhome.com
Trent Bell Photography. trentbell.com
Treve Johnson Photography. archive.treve.com
Urban Angles. urbanangles.com
Van Ellen + Sheryn Architects.
    vanellensheryn.com
Verner Architects. vernerarch.com
Victoria Hagan Interiors. victoriahagan.com
Whit Preston Photography. whitpreston.com
YAMAMAR Design. yamamardesign.com
Zest Architecture. zestarchitecture.com

ACKNOWLEDGMENTS

I first wish to thank all the design and building professionals, firms, and photographers who graciously assented to providing images of their beautiful work for this book. My words would have far less value without them.

Thanks as well to literary agent Giles Anderson, editor Abigail Gehring, and the entire team at Skyhorse Publishing for bringing the project into their respective folds. The volume you readers now hold in your hands is a product of their efforts to a degree that is difficult to appreciate until one has experienced the publication process in its entirety.

Finally, my eternal gratitude to wife Gaby, who read through the manuscript as it developed and offered invaluable feedback. To both her and son Remy I owe further thanks for their patience and encouragement during the many, many months it took me to travel from idea to realization.

ABOUT THE AUTHOR

Donald M. Rattner is the founder and principal of Donald M. Rattner, Architect (donaldrattner.com), an award-winning consultancy advising designers and users in the development of creative space for workplace, residential, wellness, hospitality, and retail environments.

Educator and author as well as practitioner, Rattner's publications include *The Creativity Catalog: Parallel of the Classical Orders of Architecture*; entries in professional reference books, and numerous contributions to print and online channels. He has taught at the University of Illinois, New York Academy of Art, New York University Division of Real Estate Studies, Parsons School of Design, and online. Workshop and lecture venues include NeoCon, Creative Problem Solving Institute, Creative Mornings, AIA chapter events, and many others in the United States and abroad.

His work has been featured on CNN and in such publications as the *New York Times, Town & Country, House & Garden, Robb Report, Residential Architect, Builder, Traditional Building Magazine, L-Magazine*, and *Design Milk*.

Rattner holds a Bachelor's degree in art history from Columbia and a Masters of Architecture from Princeton.